To Anne

Contents

Preface

PREFACE

This book has been written to give a clear and concise exposition of the principles of Irish business law. It is designed primarily for students sitting examinations in third level colleges and professional institutes, but it is also relevant to students taking an introductory law course.

The book is laid out in seven sections, and includes a total of thirty-two chapters. Each chapter contains:

(a) a list of the important topics covered by the chapter;
(b) a summary of the purpose of the chapter;
(c) a presentation of the related rules of law in a style and format which will help students to assimilate the necessary facts;
(d) a progress test based on, and cross-referenced with, the contents of the chapter; and
(e) a list of the important cases and/or statutes referred to in the chapter, where applicable.

Each section is completed with a series of examination questions from past papers of professional institutes.

Every effort has been made to illustrate the various principles of law by relevant cases, in a style of presentation which should enable students to read the text and obtain a thorough understanding of the subject matter in a relatively short period of time. I have attempted to state the law as at 1 January 1991.

I wish to thank my family for their constant support; Michael who started this endeavour with me, and Deirdre who helped me complete it; my colleagues at Senior College, Dun Laoghaire for their encouragement and assistance; and the Institute of Accounting Technicians in Ireland, the Institute of Chartered Secretaries and Administrators, the Chartered Institute of Management Accountants and the Chartered Association of Certified Accountants for permission to use selected examination questions.

November 1991   Niall Sheeran

INTRODUCTION TO THE
STUDY OF LAW

The functions and sources of law
The divisions of law—civil and criminal
Administration of law
Structure of the courts

chapter 1

THE FUNCTIONS AND SOURCES OF LAW

Topics covered in this chapter are:

- Functions of law
- Sources of Irish law
- Historical sources of law
- Legal sources of law

Summary of the chapter

This chapter examines the purpose and effect of Irish law and how that law has come into being.

• Functions of law

1. The law is the body of rules imposed by a State upon its members, designed to regulate human conduct within that State. The courts interpret these rules of conduct, decide whether they have been broken and pass sentence or make an award of compensation. A certain standard of behaviour is thereby maintained amongst the members of the State in the interest of the common good.

2. The law is not static. It changes and develops, reflecting the values and institutions of each era. Not alone does it define and safeguard rights of property and uphold public order, but it is also used to develop the national economy and to deal with social problems.

• Sources of Irish law

3. The term 'sources of law' is used in several different senses.
(a) Historical sources—generally regarded as common law and equity.
(b) Legal sources—the means by which the law is currently brought into existence.

There are five legal sources:

  (i)   legislation (statute law)
 (ii)   subordinate legislation (statutory instruments)
(iii)   the Irish Constitution 1937
 (iv) European Community Law
  (v) judicial precedent—interpretation of statutes

• Historical sources of law

4. Irish law is a common law system derived from English law. It was implemented after a conquest which replaced the highly developed

native Brehon laws. Since the foundation of the Irish Free State in 1922, however, Irish law has developed a character of its own with the coming into effect of a written Irish Constitution (Bunreacht na hÉireann) on 29 December 1937 and the enactment of different statutes.

5. Because of the similarities between the legal systems of Ireland and England, having in most areas of the law a common base, it is necessary to refer initially to the historical development of English law.

Common law

6. At the time of the Norman Conquest in 1066 there existed a primitive legal system based on local custom. Afterwards, these local customs were unified into one system of law with the King at its head. A judicial system was gradually established through the Justices who travelled to different parts of the realm to settle criminal and civil disputes. Although these Justices at first applied the customary law of the neighbourhood, often hearing their cases with the assistance of a local jury, they developed rules of law, selected from the differing local customs which they had encountered, applied uniformly in all trials throughout the kingdom. This ancient unwritten law was made common to the whole of England and Wales, and for this reason was known as 'common law' (*ius commune*). The Irish had generally become entitled to the benefits of the common law by 1331.

7. To commence an action before any of these courts a writ had to be obtained. This specified the ground of complaint and gave a brief summary of the facts on which the plaintiff required judgment. After a period of time it was decided that writs could only be issued in one of the established forms in order to bring a grievance before the royal courts. The fact that no new types of writ could be issued unless it was approved or developed by Parliament made the common law system very rigid and hence an inadequate way of providing justice.

8. Over the years, the common law grew into a rigid and harsh system. Rules of procedure were complex, and any minor breach of these could leave a plaintiff, who had a good case, without a remedy. A plaintiff could be frustrated in civil actions, where the only remedy which the common law courts could grant was an award of damages. He could even find himself unable to enforce a judgment given in his favour because there was no suitable common law remedy. The practice grew in such cases of dissatisfied litigants petitioning the King to exercise his prerogative power in their favour. The King, through his Chancellor, set up the Court of Chancery to deal with these petitions.

Equity

9. The body of law developed by the King's Court, and administered by the Court of Chancery was called Equity. Initially, in dealing with each petition the Chancellor's concern was to establish the truth of the situation and to impose a just solution without undue regard for technicalities or procedural points. Gradually, the court began to be guided by its previous decisions and formulated a number of general principles, known as the 'maxims of equity' upon which it would proceed. These are still applied today when equitable relief is claimed.

10. The following are some examples of the many maxims:

(a) *He who seeks equity must do equity.* A person who seeks equitable relief must be prepared to act fairly towards his opponent as a condition of obtaining relief.

(b) *Equity looks to the intent rather than the form.* Although a person may attempt to pretend that he is doing something in the correct form, equity will look to see what he is really trying to achieve.

(c) *He who comes to equity must come with clean hands.* To be fairly treated, the plaintiff must also have acted properly in his past dealing with the defendant.

(d) *Equality is equity.* What is available to one person must be available to another. This reflects the effort made by the law to play fair and redress the balance.

11. Equity was not a complete alternative to the common law. Instead, it provided a gloss on the law by adding to and improving the common law. The major changes produced by the interaction of equity and common law included:

(a) the recognition and protection of rights by equity for which the common law gave no safeguard;

(b) the more effective procedure of equity in bringing a disputed matter to a decision;

(c) the development under equity of discretionary remedies.

12. By its nature, the Court of Chancery was bound to come into conflict with the common law courts. This rivalry was resolved in 1615 by a decision of the King that where common law and equity conflicted, equity would prevail.

13. By the nineteenth century it became the rule for judges in the Court of Chancery and the common law courts to respect and follow previous decisions and precedents. In view of the fact that the separate existence of the Court of Chancery and the common law courts was not satisfactory, it was decided to merge the administration of equity and common law. Reforms were introduced in Ireland by the Judicature (Ireland) Act, 1877, which established a logical court structure, simplified procedures and fused the administration of common law and equity. The Act decreed that in cases of conflict, equity should still prevail over common law.

• Legal sources of law

Legislation or statute law

14. Legislation is the laying down of legal rules by an institution which is recognised as having the right to make law for the community. Such laws are known as statutes.

15. Our oldest statutes were ordinances made by English kings before parliaments existed, and which were applied to Ireland. The Parliament of Ireland made statutes for this country until the Act of Union, 1800 joined Ireland and Great Britain in the United Kingdom of Great Britain and Ireland. Between 1800 and 1922, statutes applying to Ireland were made in the Parliament at Westminster. Upon the establishment of the Irish Free State in 1922, legislative independence was restored. From 1922 to 1937, the legislative source was the Oireachtas of Saor Stát Éireann and, from 1937, under the Constitution, the Oireachtas. Legislation prior to 1922 continues in force, by virtue of Article 50 of the Constitution, to the extent that it is not inconsistent with the provisions of the 1937 Constitution.

16. Our current legislative body, therefore, is the Oireachtas which is empowered by our Constitution to legislate for the country. Article 15.2.1 states:

> The sole and exclusive power of making laws for the State is hereby vested in the Oireachtas: no other legislative authority has powers to make laws for the State.

The Oireachtas consists of two houses, being Dáil Éireann and Seanad Éireann, and the President.

17. Superior legislation, i.e. laws enacted by the legislature before they become law, are known as Bills. A Bill must go through five stages in each House of the Oireachtas. The first stage, which may take place in either the Dáil or the Seanad, consists of placing the title of the Bill before the House. After this the Bill is printed, but if it does not pass this stage then the Bill is defeated. Otherwise the printed Bill is circulated and given a second reading. The minister responsible for guiding the Bill through the Oireachtas normally explains the nature of his intended legislation and often goes through the Bill section by section. The third stage is the committee stage. The 'committee' is normally the entire House, except where the Bill is of a highly technical nature, in which case it is examined by a Standing Committee representing the main parties and including some members at least who specialise in the relevant subject. The Bill is examined section by section and may be amended. The fourth stage is the report stage. Further amendments may be made. If the government has undertaken in committee to reconsider certain points, it often puts forward its final amendments at this stage. The fifth stage is the final reading. The Bill is then referred to the other House where a similar process must be followed. The Taoiseach then presents to the President, for his signature, all Bills passed by both Houses of the Oireachtas. It is then promulgated by the President who publishes a notice in Iris Oifigiúl (the Official Gazette) stating that the Bill has become law, and is now called an Act.

18. If at a later date a statute, or part of a statute, is found to be repugnant to the Constitution, it can be declared invalid by the High Court or, on appeal, by the Supreme Court.

19. Judges have established certain guidelines—which are not rules of law—to assist themselves in interpreting statutes. The three recognised judicial approaches to statutory interpretation are:

(a) *The Literal Rule.* This is the basic rule of interpretation. A judge must give to words their literal or usual meaning unless the Act defines or restricts the meaning to be taken.

(b) *The Golden Rule.* Where a literal interpretation of the statute would lead to an absurd or inconsistent result, the courts will usually attempt to modify the strict grammatical meaning of words in order to avoid such a result. Where a statute permits two or more possible meanings, application of the golden rule is not inconsistent with the literal rule, since the literal rule cannot be applied in such cases.

(c) *The Mischief Rule.* Where an Act is passed to remedy a mischief, the court must adopt the interpretation which will have the effect of remedying the mischief in question. The judge must look at the law which existed prior to the statute and then the defect in the law which the statute purported to remedy. The statute should then be construed in such a way to suppress the defect and advance the remedy.

Subordinate legislation

20. Subordinate, or 'delegated', legislation arises from laws laid down by a body or individual to whom the Oireachtas, i.e. the superior legislature, has delegated power to make regulations for specified purposes. The Oireachtas has delegated such power to government ministers, local authorities and other bodies.

21. Delegated legislation saves the time of the Oireachtas, by allowing it to concentrate on debating matters of general policy. It enables the government to act quickly in emergency situations, since such legislation may be implemented swiftly. Finally, it provides greater flexibility, because subordinate legislation can be added to or modified easily and quickly when it becomes outdated or impractical.

22. Delegated legislation is implemented by statutory instruments, orders, regulations and bye-laws which have the same force of law as statutes passed by the Oireachtas.

23. Delegated legislation must be reasonable, must apply basic fairness of procedures and must be *intra vires*, i.e. within the confines of powers delegated under statute. If delegated legislation is beyond the powers of those exercising it, it may be challenged in the courts on the grounds that it is *ultra vires* and be declared by the court as void.

24. Subordinate legislation is reviewed by the Seanad Select Committee on Statutory Instruments.

The Irish Constitution 1937 (Bunreacht na hÉireann)

25. The Constitution, which came into effect on 29 December 1937, is the basis of our constitutional law. The law of the Constitution:

(a) regulates the structure and function of the principal organs of government;
(b) regulates the relationship of these organs to each other and to the citizen.

It deals with such topics as the nation, the state, the office and function of the President, the Oireachtas, the government and the courts. It also concerns itself with the Attorney General, the Council of State and the Comptroller and Auditor General. It contains a section which guarantees certain fundamental rights to every citizen. These include personal rights (Article 40) and rights relating to the family (Article 41), education (Article 42), private property (Article 43) and religion (Article 44).

26. The Constitution has a higher status than any other domestic law in that it may only be changed by a majority of voters in a referendum and in that any legislation which is held to be repugnant to the Constitution is invalid.

27. The President has power, after consulting the Council of State, to refer a Bill before it becomes law to the Supreme Court for a decision as to its constitutionality. Legislation enacted by the Oireachtas may be challenged under the Constitution in the High Court, and on appeal in the Supreme Court, by the President or by any party with an actionable interest.

Case: Murphy v Attorney General (1980)

Article 41 of the Constitution declares that the State pledges to guard with special care the institution of marriage on which the family is founded, and to protect it against attack. The plaintiff challenged parts of the income tax code which taxed a married couple living together more heavily than two single persons living together with similar incomes.

Held: The nature and potentially progressive extent of the burden was a breach of the pledge by the State to guard with special care the institution of marriage. The provisions in the Income Tax Act, 1967 were therefore held to be unconstitutional.

Case: Educational Company of Ireland v Fitzpatrick (1961)

Article 40.6.1 of the Constitution guarantees the right of freedom of association. Employees of the company, who were members of a union, in order to force their employer to employ only trade union labour, picketed the premises in an attempt to force all the employees to join the union.

Held: Employees who, when being employed, were not required to belong to a union had the constitutional right to dissociate. Thus, picketing for the purpose of forcing persons to join a union against their wishes was inconsistent with the right to freedom of association and, hence, unconstitutional.

European Community law

28. On the accession of Ireland to the European Community in January 1973, the Constitution has no longer been supreme in all respects. A constitutional amendment was necessary to allow laws of the Community made externally, and not by organs established under the Constitution, to be part of our domestic law. Such a modification was accepted by the People in a referendum on the third amendment to the

Constitution on 10 May 1972 and was enforced by special statutes, namely, the European Communities Act, 1972 and the European Communities (Amendment) Act, 1973.

29. The primary law of the Community, which is contained in the principal treaties, i.e. the Treaty of Paris, 1951 and the Treaty of Rome, 1957, takes precedence over domestic law. This primary law is self-executing in that ratification of the treaties means that the provisions of the treaties become automatically embraced in the law of the State.

30. The secondary law of the Community, made by the Council of Ministers or the Commission, consists of Regulations which apply to the Member States immediately without further legislation. Directives are made obligatory by special statutes or statutory instruments if necessary. Decisions, Recommendations and Opinions expressing the Council of Ministers' and Commission's views may also be issued. These, however, are only binding on the parties concerned, and are merely persuasive in other disputes.

31. While it is true that membership of the EC does restrict the supremacy of the Constitution, the community law to which Ireland must ultimately conform is made as a result of negotiation and often agreement between the Irish government and the other governments of the EC. The Irish government has the support of a majority of members of the Dáil. Therefore the Oireachtas through government action has indirect influence, to a certain extent, on the EC law-making process.

Judicial precedent

32. Common law and equity have been developed through the centuries by judges in giving their decisions in the courts. Judge-made law involved the application of customary law to new situations, thereby maintaining consistency. As the law became more sophisticated, the decisions of the judges were recorded and reports were made of law cases. It became possible to follow previous decisions of judges and this brought about a level of certainty and progressive development in judge-made law. The reform introduced by the Judicature Acts, 1873–75 led to the modern doctrine of precedent which depends for its operation on the fact that the courts are organised in a hierarchy.

33. Judicial precedent is the application of a principle of law, as laid down by a higher court, or a court of equal status, on a previous occasion in a similar case to the case before the court. This is known as the doctrine of *stare decisis*. A precedent (or previous decision) may be persuasive or binding.

34. A *persuasive precedent* is one which does not have to be followed by a court. The judge, however, may be influenced by it because it is worthy of the court's respect.

35. A *binding precedent* is a decision which the court must follow. This is based on the view that it is not the function of a judge to make law, but to decide cases in accordance with existing rules. Not all of the decision is binding on a later court, but only its authoritative element which is called the *ratio decidendi* (reason for the decision). This is the principle of the law upon which the judgment was based. The remainder, known as *obiter dicta* (by the way), are comments not directly related to the case and do not constitute binding precedent.

36. Not every decision made in a court is binding as a judicial precedent. The court's status has a significant effect on whether its decisions are persuasive, binding or disregarded. The higher the court, the more universally followed will be the decision. A superior court may overrule or replace a precedent set in a lower court. The old principle is then void of authority and is replaced by the new principle. Courts of equal seniority have no power to overrule each other, and decisions of such courts act as persuasive authority only. Finally, the court may decide that the *ratio decidendi* of the previous case is not relevant to the current action because of factual differences which justify the court in not following the earlier case. This is known as 'distinguishing' the case, and allows a different legal principle to be formulated.

37. The highest court of authority, the Irish Supreme Court, binds all the courts. Because it is the highest court it is not bound by decisions of any other court. Since 1965, however, it has broken with its tradition of always following its own previous decisions, and also the decisions of those courts which had preceded it as the court of ultimate jurisdiction.

38. In the State (Quinn) v Ryan (1965), the Supreme Court declared unconstitutional a statutory provision which it had previously declared constitutional in the earlier case of the State (Duggan) v Tapley (1952). This more liberal approach was extended beyond the confines of constitutional issues in the Attorney General v Ryan's Car Hire Ltd (1965). In this case, Justice Kingsmill Moore, while accepting the need to follow precedents in order to avoid uncertainty in the law, was of the opinion that 'the rigid rule of *stare decisis* must in a court of ultimate resort give place to a more elastic formula. Where such a court is clearly of the opinion that an earlier decision was erroneous, it should be at liberty to refuse to allow it, at all events, in exceptional cases.'

39. The Supreme Court will only overrule a previous decision where there is substantial agreement among the members of the court that there are compelling reasons for doing so. Hence, though not recognised in the Constitution, the doctrine of precedent is strongly adhered to in the courts.

IMPORTANT CASES

Numbers in brackets refer to paragraphs of this chapter

Murphy v Attorney General (1980)..(27)
Educational Company of Ireland v Fitzpatrick (1961).....................(27)

PROGRESS TEST

Numbers in brackets refer to paragraphs of this chapter

1. What are the functions of law? (2)
2. List (i) the historical, and (ii) the legal sources of law. (3)
3. Explain how common law and equity developed as part of Irish law. (4–13)
4. Describe the stages through which a Bill must pass before becoming law. (17, 18)
5. What is statutory interpretation? (19)
6. State the main advantages of delegated legislation. (21)
7. Describe how the Constitution has a higher status than any other domestic law. (26, 27)
8. How are the principles of European Community law incorporated into Irish law? (29, 30)
9. Explain the doctrine of stare decisis. (33–5)
10. On what grounds may a court avoid a binding precedent? (36–9)

chapter 2

THE DIVISIONS OF LAW—CIVIL AND CRIMINAL

Topics covered in this chapter are:

- Civil proceedings
- Criminal proceedings

- Distinction between civil and criminal wrongs

Summary of the chapter
In order to be able to understand fully the court system, it is first necessary to have an understanding of the classification of law.

Introduction

1. Law is the body of rules imposed by a state upon its members, designed to regulate human conduct within that state.

2. The most fundamental distinction in the classification of law is that drawn between civil law and criminal law. The objectives of both, though closely connected, are clearly different.

• Civil proceedings

3. Civil law exists to deal with civil, or private, wrongs. The object of civil law is the resolution of disputes over the rights and obligations of individuals dealing with each other. It is up to the injured party to commence a civil action to seek compensation for a loss which he has suffered.

4. In most civil cases, there will be a plaintiff (the aggrieved party) and a respondent or defendant (offending party). The plaintiff sues the defendant. A civil action must be proven on the balance of probabilities by the plaintiff in order to succeed.

5. Civil cases use the names of the parties, the plaintiff's name being placed first, for example, 'Noonan v Murphy (1987)'. In some civil cases, there will not be a plaintiff and a defendant. For example, if an application were made to the court to interpret Murphy's will, the case would be known as 'Re Murphy'.

6. Some of the many categories of civil law are:

(a) *Contract*. This determines whether agreements made by persons have given rise to obligations which are enforceable by law.

(b) *Tort*. This determines whether a civil wrong has been committed by one person against another, infringing a general duty imposed on him by law, e.g. the duty not to cause damage to a person's property, person or name.

(c) *Commercial law*. This covers contractual matters relating to negotiable instruments, agency, sale of goods and hire purchase.

(d) *Employment law*. This covers contractual relationships between the employer and the employee.

7. The general purpose of any judgment in civil proceedings is to impose a settlement on the matter, by ensuring that the injured party is compensated for any damage, if any, which the court finds suffered by him. The concept of punishment does not exist. The main remedies for civil wrongs are:

(a) an award of damages;

(b) an injunction to stop the defendant doing something (a prohibitory injunction) or to command the defendant to do something (a mandatory injunction);

(c) an order for specific performance, where the court compels the offending party to perform his obligations under a contract;

(d) a refusal of further performance, where there has been a breach of condition and the innocent party is relieved from further liability to perform his obligations.

• Criminal proceedings

8. Criminal law exists to deal with criminal, or public, wrongs. It is a set of standards imposed by a society on its individuals, breaches of which incur sanctions to punish the offender.

9. Criminal proceedings are started by the State against the offender through the office of the Director of Public Prosecutions. Although most crimes have specific victims, e.g. rape, the victim does not have a say in whether a prosecution is brought. Neither does the victim benefit from a conviction, since fines are payable to the State.

10. In a criminal trial, the accused is presumed to be innocent until he is proven to be guilty. The prosecution (i.e. the State) must prove the accused's guilt beyond reasonable doubt.

11. The general purpose of any judgment in criminal proceedings is to punish the guilty party. The main judicial remedies for criminal wrongs are:

(a) fines;

(b) imprisonment;

(c) binding of a party to keep the peace;

(d) community service orders, as an alternative to (b).

• Distinction between civil and criminal wrongs

12. The distinction between a civil and criminal wrong is not found in the nature of the act or event itself, but in the legal consequences of it.

13. For example, a broken arm caused to a passenger of a taxi which has crashed is a single event which may give rise to a civil case (the passenger sues for compensation for pain and suffering caused by the wrong), and a criminal case (prosecution by the State for the offence of dangerous driving).

14. In some cases, therefore, the facts will indicate both a civil action and a criminal offence. In such cases, the victim will have to start a civil action separate from any prosecution brought by the State. The two sorts of proceedings are usually easily identified, however, since the procedures and terminology are different.

PROGRESS TEST

Numbers in brackets refer to the paragraphs of this chapter

1. Explain the object of (i) civil, and (ii) criminal law. (3, 8)
2. What is the standard of proof of civil proceedings? (4)
3. List four categories of civil law. (6)
4. What are the main judicial remedies for (a) civil, and (b) criminal wrongs? (7, 11)
5. Who starts criminal proceedings? (9)
6. What is the standard of proof of criminal proceedings? (10)
7. What is the distinction between civil and criminal wrongs? (12–14)

chapter 3

ADMINISTRATION OF LAW

Topics covered in this chapter are:

- The courts
- Personnel of the law

Summary of the chapter

Having considered what law is and how it is created, it is now necessary to consider how it is enforced.

Introduction

1. The law is made effective by the courts and the legal profession, supported by the State.

• The courts

2. The courts conduct an investigation into the liability or non-liability of the defendant in civil litigation, or a fair trial into the guilt or innocence of the accused in a criminal case. The courts depend on the parties in dispute to do the bulk of the work—this saves the courts from having to make a full investigation into the facts in dispute and then drawing the appropriate conclusions.

3. In civil cases, the plaintiff makes a precise claim or claims against the defendant and the latter defends the action. The plaintiff must prove the action on the balance of probabilities. This is what is known as an adversarial procedure—the courts are only concerned with ruling on the relevant issues brought to them for decision.

4. In criminal cases, the prosecution (the State) prepares its case precisely against the accused, and the accused attempts to counter it. The prosecution must prove the accused's guilt beyond reasonable doubt.

• Personnel of the law

5. The personnel of the law include those people, other than individual litigants, who are responsible for carrying out the process of law in the courts, offices and in education.

Solicitors

6. The solicitor's profession has been regulated by the Incorporated Law Society since the nineteenth century. This controls entry to the profession, exercises disciplinary power over its members and protects the public against work by unqualified persons.

7. A solicitor often carries out routine legal work for the public where there is no dispute in hand. This includes the formation of companies and partnerships, the drafting of wills and contracts, and the conveyancing of property.

8. In addition, where there is a dispute, the solicitor carries out office work in contentious matters, such as the preparation and/or settlement of issues in dispute. If the dispute goes to trial, the solicitor will gather the evidence, brief a barrister if necessary, conduct correspondence and attend preliminary hearings prior to the trial.

9. Solicitors are not involved exclusively in office work. A solicitor may, since 1971, also appear as an advocate, without counsel's assistance. While s/he may appear before all the courts in Ireland, the solicitor tends to restrict appearance to lower courts where the special talents of the barrister may not be needed.

Barristers

10. The barrister's profession is regulated by the Honourable Society of the King's Inns. There are two types of barrister, senior and junior counsel. A junior counsel is 'called to the Bar' in the Supreme Court by the Chief Justice. After some years as an experienced and successful member of the profession, the barrister may be called to the 'Inner Bar' and become a senior counsel.

11. The barrister is first and foremost a specialist in the art of advocacy, who presents a case in court on behalf of a client in a logical and effective manner. In legal actions, s/he can be essential to success, or the cause of failure, because of the adversarial procedure applied in courts.

12. The barrister also drafts legal documents, such as pleadings, and is used as an expert on matters of legal opinion.

13. A lay client cannot engage a barrister directly. This must be done by a solicitor. This is known as a 'brief'—a formal document requesting the barrister's assistance. The barrister is expected, unless there is a good reason, to act on such a request.

14. In the event of an important court action, the solicitor will gather the evidence, but will engage a barrister to draft the pleadings, to advise on the evidence and to present the case in court.

Judges

15. The judges of all courts are formally appointed by the President on the recommendation of the government in power when a vacancy arises.

16. Minimum periods of experience are a prerequisite. For appointment to the District Court, this period is at least ten years as a practising solicitor or barrister. Judicial positions in the High Court or Supreme Court are open to barristers with at least twelve years' experience. Judicial positions in the Circuit Court require at least ten years' experience as a barrister.

17. Judges can only be removed from office for stated misbehaviour or incapacity, and then only by means of resolutions passed by the Oireachtas. The independence of judges is further maintained by the fact that their salaries cannot be reduced.

18. The function of the judge is to apply existing rules of law to the case before him. The judge does not have a responsibility to investigate the total circumstances of the case. Instead, he must act as a neutral decision-maker, hearing facts and arguments presented by the parties, judging their merits, and applying the law accordingly.

19. Judges are capable, to a certain extent, of 'making law' through the interpretation of statutes and the doctrine of precedent.

Director of Public Prosecutions

20. This office was established by the Prosecution of Offences Act, 1974. The Director of Public Prosecutions is a civil servant. He is assisted by a staff of professional solicitors and civil service administrators.

21. His role concerns the prosecution of serious crimes in the name of the People. He usually institutes proceedings when a case is referred to him by the Gardaí, a government department, and in other cases when he considers that his intervention is required.

22. He is fully independent in the carrying out of his functions.

The Attorney General

23. The office of Attorney General was created in 1924. It was preserved under Article 30 of the Constitution. The Attorney General is appointed by the President on the nomination of the Taoiseach. He may be requested to resign, and will do so when the Taoiseach resigns.

24. The Attorney General is the legal adviser to the government in matters of law and legal opinion. He institutes and defends proceedings to which the State is a party. His consent may be required by the Director of Public Prosecutions to bring proceedings in the criminal courts, if a case is sufficiently important or serious.

25. Additional responsibilities may be conferred upon the Attorney General by law. One such responsibility is that of enforcing charitable trusts.

PROGRESS TEST

Numbers in brackets refer to paragraphs of this chapter

1. How does the court conduct an investigation in (a) civil, and (b) criminal cases? (2–4)
2. Describe the non-contentious office work performed by a solicitor. (7)
3. When is a solicitor likely to appear as an advocate? (9)
4. What are the functions of a barrister? (11, 12)
5. Identify the minimum periods of experience required for judicial appointments. (16)
6. Describe the role of the Director of Public Prosecutions. (21)
7. How is the Attorney General appointed? (23)

chapter 4

STRUCTURE OF THE COURTS

Topics covered in this chapter are:

- Jurisdiction of the courts
- The District Court
- The Circuit Court
- The High Court
- The Court of Criminal Appeal
- The Supreme Court
- Additional courts

Summary of the chapter

This chapter examines and describes the structure and jurisdiction of the courts to be found in the Republic.

• Jurisdiction of the courts

1. Some courts deal only with civil cases and others only with criminal. Most, however, can deal with both. The jurisdiction of the courts can depend upon where the defendant lives, where the crime or offence was committed, the type of legal problem involved, the seriousness of the offence and the amount of the claim or nature of the remedy sought.

2. The present structure of the Irish courts was first established by the Courts of Justice Act, 1924. It now derives its authority from Article 34 of the Constitution, which states that:

> Justice shall be administered in courts established by law by judges appointed in the manner provided by this Constitution, and, save in such special and limited cases as may be prescribed by law, shall be administered in public.

The structure of courts that exists today was formally established by the Courts (Establishment and Constitution) Act, 1961.

3. The court structure is organised on a hierarchical basis. At the bottom are the District Courts. At the top is the Supreme Court, which is the final court of appeal. In the middle are the Circuit and High Courts and the Court of Criminal Appeal.

• The District Court

4. This, the lowest court within our legal system, is a unified court which consists of a President and thirty-nine District Justices. For the

346.415
LIBRARY
60056078

exercise of its duties and functions, the Republic of Ireland is divided into over 200 District Court areas. District Justices travel around the country hearing cases in the District Courts. Each Justice sits alone.

5. The civil jurisdiction of the District Court covers a wide range of matters. It provides a cheap and quick forum for dealing with disputes of a local or relatively minor nature. In matters of contract and tort, the court has jurisdiction provided the amount claimed does not exceed £2,500. It grants dance hall and liquor licences, and can order ejectment for non-payment of rent, provided the annual rent does not exceed £2,500.

6. The criminal jurisdiction of the District Court covers summary offences and certain indictable offences. In either case, the offence must be a minor one under the Constitution.

7. A summary offence does not entitle a defendant to a trial by jury. It carries a maximum punishment of six months' imprisonment and/or a fine.

8. An indictable offence entitles a defendant to trial by jury. Providing the court considers the offence to be minor, and if the accused agrees to summary trial, the District Court can usually hear the case. In such cases, the maximum punishment is twelve months' imprisonment and/or a fine, i.e. whether a prima facie case exists to be answered by the defendant.

9. In serious cases, such as murder, sexual offences and treason, the District Court may conduct a preliminary hearing to decide whether or not sufficient evidence exists to commit the accused for trial by jury before a higher court, i.e. whether a prima facie case exists to be answered by the defendant.

• The Circuit Court

10. This is a unified court which consists of a President and twelve judges. The country is divided into eight circuits. Five judges are permanently assigned to the Dublin circuit. One judge hears cases in different towns on a number of occasions each year in each of the other circuits.

11. The civil jurisdiction of the Circuit Court is limited to claims up to £15,000. A defendant has a right of appeal against the decision of a Circuit Court judge, who sits alone when hearing a civil case, to the High Court. A Circuit Court judge may consult the Supreme Court on points of law.

12. An unsuccessful party in a District Court civil case can appeal to the Circuit Court. This will rehear the case and substitute its own decision if different.

13. The criminal jurisdiction of the Circuit Court covers indictable offences. In such cases, the Circuit Court consists of a judge and jury. Where the accused is found guilty, the Circuit Court judge may impose a punishment up to the maximum amount permitted by statute or common law.

14. A person convicted and punished in the District Court may appeal to the Circuit Court. The judge may completely rehear the case and reach his own conclusions. He may then decrease, let stand or increase the original punishment. He can only increase the punishment to the maximum which the District Court could have imposed.

• The High Court

15. The jurisdiction of the High Court extends to all matters whether of law or fact, civil or criminal. Article 34 of the Constitution provides as follows:

> The Courts of First Instance shall include a High Court invested with full original jurisdiction in and power to determine all matters and questions whether of law or fact, civil or criminal.

16. The High Court consists of a President, who is, *ex officio*, a judge of the Supreme Court and a member of the Council of State, and up to fourteen ordinary judges. Normally, the High Court hears cases with the judge sitting alone, but in certain important or serious cases three judges sit together.

17. A jury may be used by the High Court in civil cases. In such cases, a vote of nine out of twelve jurors is sufficient to award a judgment. The High Court can award unlimited damages.

18. When the High Court is hearing a criminal case it is known as the Central Criminal Court. It tries only serious crimes such as murder, attempted murder or conspiracy to murder. It also tries cases which have been transferred from the Circuit Court to avoid trial before a local jury.

19. The Central Criminal Court must use a jury in criminal cases where a plea of 'not guilty' has been made by the accused. In such cases, a majority verdict of ten jurors to two will suffice to determine the guilt of the defendant.

20. The High Court has a jurisdiction to give a ruling on the law as it affects the facts as stated by the District Court. The District Court, on its own behalf or on the application of one of the parties to the dispute, can submit the facts of a dispute in a formal document to the High Court.

Having heard the arguments regarding the point of law, the High Court will decide upon the matter and will give an opinion and direction to the District Court, who must apply the decision accordingly. This is known as an appeal by way of 'case stated'.

21. Finally, the High Court also possesses supervisory jurisdiction over the inferior courts, state bodies and individuals. The High Court has the power to issue an order of:

(a) *prohibition,* to prevent a person or body from exercising a power it does not legally have;
(b) *mandamus,* to compel a person or body to carry out a legal duty;
(c) *certiorari,* to stop a person or body who has exceeded their legal powers;
(d) *habeas corpus,* to require the accused and his detainer to attend before the High Court to explain the circumstances of, and justification for, detention.

• The Court of Criminal Appeal

22. This court hears appeals from the Circuit Court, the Central Criminal Court or the Special Criminal Court. The latter is a non-jury court which may be set up under Part V of the Offences Against the State Act, 1939, and has, once again, been operational since 1972. The justification given for the use of such a court is that, in certain circumstances, the ordinary courts are inadequate to secure the proper administration of justice and preserve public peace and order.

23. The Court of Criminal Appeal consists of three judges, one from the Supreme Court and two from the High Court. The court's decision is by majority, and only one judgment is given.

24. Leave to appeal to the Court of Criminal Appeal will usually be given only where there is a dispute on a point of law. However, it may also be given in exceptional circumstances where new evidence becomes available which could not have been presented before the original court.

• The Supreme Court

25. This is at the top of the hierarchy of courts. It is the court of final resort for cases commenced in the High Court, as well as for those cases which have been directly appealed on a point of law to the Supreme Court.

26. There is no rehearing of the case in the Supreme Court as the record of the trial court is used.

27. The Supreme Court consists of the Chief Justice and five ordinary judges. Three judges will usually form a quorum but, in constitutional cases, five judges will constitute a court.

28. The Supreme Court also has a consultative, as well as an appellate, jurisdiction. The President may consult it as to the constitutionality of a Bill presented to him for signature. The High Court and Circuit Court may consult it by way of 'case stated'.

• Additional courts

29. Apart from the civil and criminal courts operating in the Republic of Ireland, there are also other courts and tribunals which are of importance.

30. The European Court of Justice (cf. Chapter 29) and the European Court of Human Rights are just two of the extra-territorial courts whose decisions are binding when Ireland is a party to a dispute.

31. Administrative tribunals in Ireland itself act as courts in relation to taxation, social welfare benefits, planning, discrimination in employment and other administrative issues. Such tribunals are established by statute to settle disputes between individuals or between government agencies and individuals.

32. Examples of administrative tribunals include the Appeals Commissioners, Social Welfare Tribunals, the Planning Board, the Labour Court and the Employment Appeals Tribunal.

33. The Employment Appeals Tribunal (EAT) hears claims of unfair dismissal or redundancy under the Unfair Dismissal Act, 1977. It consists of a legally qualified Chairman and Vice-Chairman, together with an equal number of members nominated by the employers' organisations and the Irish Congress of Trade Unions (ICTU). A claim may come before the EAT from the employee directly or arising from the appeal, within six weeks, of a recommendation made by a Rights Commissioner. The EAT usually sits in a division consisting of either the Chairman or Vice-Chairman and two members — one nominated by the employers' organisations and the other nominated by the ICTU. It hears the evidence from both parties to the dispute and issues a determination. If the EAT deems the dismissal to be unfair, it may specify one of the remedies listed in the Unfair Dismissal Act, 1977, namely, reinstatement, re-engagement or compensation, which must be carried out by the employer within six weeks. If the remedy is not carried out within that time, the Minister for Labour may, at his own expense, take the case to the Circuit Court on behalf of the employee. Either party may appeal a determination of EAT, at their own expense, to the Circuit Court, within six weeks of the date of the issuing of the determination.

34. The advantages of administrative tribunals are that:

(a) they specialise in a particular field, and are composed of persons such as solicitors, judges and lay persons who have a specialised knowledge and experience in the field in question;
(b) they use more informal procedures than those familiar to courts;
(c) they are a less expensive method of resolving a dispute than a court action;
(d) they act more quickly than the courts, since they are able to meet by appointment when required.

35. On the other hand, the disadvantages of administrative tribunals are that:

(a) they may not, in certain cases, give reasons for their decisions;
(b) they may hear cases in private;
(c) they may not permit legal representation (at the initial proceedings, at least);
(d) they may not convince a party that a just and equitable hearing has been given to the case.

PROGRESS TEST

Numbers in brackets refer to paragraphs of this chapter

1. How has the present structure of the Irish courts been established? (2)
2. Give examples of the kind of case tried in (i) a District Court, (ii) a Circuit Court, and (iii) the High Court. (5, 9, 11, 18)
3. What is a summary offence? (6)
4. Who staffs (i) a District Court, (ii) a Circuit Court, (iii) the High Court, and (iv) the Supreme Court? (4, 10, 16, 27)
5. Describe the jurisdiction of the High Court. (15)
6. When are cases heard in the Central Criminal Court? (18)
7. What is 'case stated'? (20)
8. Explain the supervisory jurisdiction of the High Court. (21)
9. When will leave be given to appeal to the Court of Criminal Appeal? (24)
10. What matters does the Supreme Court deal with? (25, 28)
11. List four (a) advantages, and (b) disadvantages of administrative tribunals. (34, 35)

EXAMINATION QUESTIONS

Section 1: Introduction to the study of law

1. Explain the sources of law which a judge may use when deciding a dispute?

CIMA (November 1988)

2. Explain what is meant by the Doctrine of *stare decisis*. Do you consider that this doctrine is strictly applied in Irish Courts?

ICSA (December 1990)

3. The structure and organisation of the courts system is designed to administer justice. Discuss.

IATI (Autumn 1990)

ELEMENTS OF THE LAW
OF TORT

Principles of liability
Remedies
Negligence
Defamation

chapter 5

PRINCIPLES OF LIABILITY

Topics covered in this chapter are:

• The nature of a tort   • General defences

Summary of the chapter

A tort is defined as a civil wrong, and its principal rules as well as some of the defences are set out.

• The nature of a tort

1. A tort is a civil, as opposed to a criminal, wrong for which the normal remedy is a common law action for unliquidated damages (i.e. damages determined by the court, and not previously agreed by the parties).

2. The wrongs dealt with by the law of tort include:

(a) causing physical injury to another intentionally or negligently (trespass to the person and negligence);
(b) interfering with another's land or goods (trespass to land, trespass to goods and nuisance);
(c) making a false statement about another (libel and slander).

3. While each individual tort has its own rules governing liability, in general, the plaintiff must prove that:

(a) the defendant has infringed a right of his which is recognised by law; and
(b) some loss or damage was caused to him by the tortious act.

4. Loss or damage is not always essential before a cause of action arises in tort. In certain instances the plaintiff need not prove that he suffered any damage. All that he must show is that his legal right has been infringed. Examples of torts which are actionable *per se* include trespass and libel. In such cases, where there is an infringement of a legal right without harm, or *injuria sine damno*, the defendant will be held liable.

5. It does not necessarily follow that all actions which result in damage are actionable. The party suffering the damage must prove that some right recognised by law has been infringed. In cases where there is harm without the infringement of a legal right, or *damnum sine injuria*, the sufferer has no remedy.

• General defences

6. A defendant may try to refute an allegation that he has committed a tort. He need only argue a defence once the plaintiff has established the basic requirements of the tort.

7. There are a number of general defences in tort. These include:

(a) *Inevitable accident*

Injury, which could not be avoided by taking ordinary and reasonable precautions, is not actionable. The defendant need only show that no reasonable precaution would have prevented the occurrence of an accident. The circumstances of the case will determine what is 'reasonable'.

Case: Stanley v Powell (1891)

The defendant fired his gun at a pheasant, but the bullet ricocheted off a tree and injured the plaintiff.

Held: Since the act could not have been avoided by reasonable precautions, the defendant was held to be completely blameless and not liable in negligence.

(b) *Consent of the plaintiff ('volenti non fit injuria')*

A person who undertakes to run the risk created by the defendant cannot subsequently complain if, while doing so, he is injured—'to the willing there can be no injury'. For example, a wrestler could not sue as a result of a broken leg suffered in the ring.

Mere knowledge of the risk does not necessarily imply consent. The defendant must show that the plaintiff appreciated the physical risk and consented to run that risk to the extent of surrendering his legal rights. There must be no pressure on an employee to take the risk (e.g. the threat of loss of his job).

Case: Bolt v William Moss & Sons Ltd (1966)

The plaintiff was injured when falling off a painter's movable scaffold which was moved while he remained on it. This was done despite his being expressly warned by his employer of the danger involved.

Held: *Volenti non fit injuria* was a good defence, because the task was undertaken entirely with full knowledge of the risk involved.

Baker v T.E. Hopkins & Son Ltd (1959)

The defendants had been employed to clean out a well. The pump being used created poisonous fumes and the pump stopped. Contrary to the express orders of the defendants' managing director, two employees went down the well. They were overcome by the fumes. The plaintiff's husband, a doctor, was called immediately and, although warned not to go down into the well because of the fumes, he insisted on being lowered down by rope. He too was overcome by fumes and died.

Held: The defendants were liable for damages, as they had been in breach of their duty to take reasonable care of the doctor.

Case: Smith v Charles Baker & Sons (1891)

The plaintiff, who was employed at a quarry, was injured when a stone fell from a crane which his employers negligently used to swing stones over his head.

Held: While it could be shown that the plaintiff knew of the risk, it could not be shown that he freely consented to run that risk. Since he may have continued to work under the crane through fear of losing his job, the plaintiff was entitled to recover damages.

(c) *Necessity*
A tortious act, performed in order to prevent some greater evil, there being no reasonable alternative, is not actionable.

Case: Esso Petroleum Co. Ltd v Southport Corp. (1956)

An oil tanker owned by the appellants ran aground due to a fault in the steering gear. The master of the oil tanker decided to discharge some of the oil in order to save the ship and crew. The respondents subsequently sued the oil tanker owners for damage caused to the shore by oil carried on to it by the tide.

Held: The appellants had acted because of an imminent danger to prevent a greater danger and, accordingly, the necessity of the situation provided an adequate defence to the action.

Case: Cope v Sharpe (1912)

A fire broke out on the plaintiff's land. The defendant, a gamekeeper on adjoining land, set fire to heather on the plaintiff's land in order to create a fire-break so as to prevent the fire spreading to his employer's land. He was sued for trespass.

Held: Necessity was a good defence, since there was a real threat of a fire, and the defendant had acted reasonably.

Case: Lynch v Fitzgerald (1938)

The plaintiff claimed damages for the death of his son, who was killed by the Gardaí when they opened fire on a demonstration which had evolved into a riot.

Held: Necessity was not a good defence, since such a course could only be considered necessary as a last resort to protect lives or property. Damages were awarded to the father of the youth.

(d) *Statutory authority*
Where a statute has expressly authorised the action, or the action is a necessary consequence of what is authorised, this is a complete defence, provided the defendant can prove that any damage caused by his action did not arise as a result of negligence on his behalf.

Case: Smith v Wexford County Council (1953)

The defendants, who had a statutory duty to keep rivers clear, deposited large amounts of soil and vegetable matter on the plaintiff's land. Some of his cattle ate the roots, which were poisonous, and died.

Held: The defendants could not reasonably have foreseen the poisonous nature of the roots. Statutory authority was, therefore, a good defence.

IMPORTANT CASES

Numbers in brackets refer to paragraphs of this chapter

Stanley v Powell (1891) ....(7)
Bolt v William Moss & Sons Ltd (1966)...(7)
Baker v T.E. Hopkins & Son (1959)...(7)
Smith v Charles Baker & Sons (1819) ....(7)
Esso Petroleum Co. Ltd v Southport Corp. (1956) ....(7)
Cope v Sharpe (1912)...(7)
Lynch v Fitzgerald (1938) ....(7)
Smith v Wexford County Council (1953) ....(7)

PROGRESS TEST

Numbers in brackets refer to paragraphs of this chapter

1. Define a tort. (1)
2. Give three examples of the wrongs dealt with by the law of tort. (2)
3. Explain, using examples, what is meant by (i) *injuria sine damno,* and (ii) *damnum sine injuria.* (4, 5)
4. What are the four general defences in tort? (7)
5. When is inevitable accident a good defence? (7)
6. Is it possible to use consent as a defence if:
   (i) it has been obtained by fraud or threat; or
   (ii) it has not been expressed? (7)

chapter 6

REMEDIES

Topics covered in this chapter are:

- Damages
- Injunction

Summary of the chapter

This chapter sets out the different judicial remedies for tortious behaviour which may be sought, and the circumstances in which each will be given.

Introduction

1. The most common judicial remedies for tortious behaviour available from the courts are damages or an injunction.

• Damages

2. The main remedy for the victim of a tort is an award of damages. The measure of damages is the amount of money which will compensate the plaintiff for the damage caused or restore him to his original position. Tort damages are always unliquidated—determined by the courts and not previously agreed by the parties.

3. There are three main types of damages which may be awarded by a court:

(a) *Real damages:* The purpose of real damages (also known as compensatory damages), is to compensate the plaintiff, so far as money can do, for the loss, injury or damage suffered. The award of damages must take future loss into account, since only one action can be brought.

(b) *Nominal damages:* Where a tort is actionable *per se*, and the plaintiff proves the elements of the tort without showing real damage, the court will award a small sum known as nominal damages. For example, a simple trespass on to another's property.

(c) *Exemplary damages*: Where the court wishes to punish the defendant in addition to compensating the plaintiff, an additional sum, known as exemplary damages, is awarded. For example, damages awarded against the publisher of defamatory material so as to ensure that such damages would exceed the profits of the publication.

Case: Kennedy & Arnold v State (1988)

The plaintiffs, political journalists, sued the State for damages arising from an invasion of their constitutional right to privacy by way of the monitoring and recording of their telephone conversations.

Held: The plaintiffs were entitled to exemplary damages because the injury caused to them was serious and was premeditated.

• Injunction

4. An injunction is an equitable remedy. It is an order of the court which commands a party to do (a 'mandatory injunction'), or to refrain from doing (a 'prohibitory injunction') some particular deed. For example, an injunction may be granted by a court to prevent unlawful picketing (i.e. a tort of trespass).

5. An 'interlocutory injunction' is frequently granted to preserve the *status quo* until the action can come for trial. The court may then, if the facts warrant it, grant a 'perpetual injunction' which may take either of the two aforementioned forms.

6. An injunction will not be given where damages would be an adequate remedy or where the court could not properly supervise the enforcement of its decree.

IMPORTANT CASE

Number in brackets refers to paragraph of this chapter

Kennedy and Arnold v State (1988) ....(3)

PROGRESS TEST

Numbers in brackets refer to paragraphs of this chapter

1. What are the most common remedies for tortious behaviour? (1)
2. Explain what is meant by unliquidated damages. (2)
3. When are (i) compensatory, (ii) exemplary and (iii) nominal damages awarded? (3)
4. What is a 'prohibitory' injunction? (4)
5. Why may an 'interlocutory injunction' be awarded? (5)
6. Identify two situations when an injunction would not be given as a remedy for tortious behaviour. (6)

chapter 7

NEGLIGENCE

Topics covered in this chapter are:

- Nature of negligence
- Legal duty of care
- Breach of duty
- Consequential harm
- Contributory negligence
- Occupier's liability
- Vicarious liability
- Strict liability

Summary of the chapter

This chapter examines the basic components which must be present for a negligence action to be proved. It also considers the liability of an occupier of premises for injuries caused to persons while on those premises.

• Nature of negligence

1. Negligence is the breach of a legal duty of care, which causes loss or injury to the person to whom the duty is owed.

2. The duty of care may arise in a number of ways. It is owed, for example, by a motorist to all other users of the road, by a manufacturer to the consumers of the product, by an employer to the employees and by a professional to the clients.

3. To succeed in a negligence action the plaintiff must prove that:

(a) the defendant owed him a legal duty of care; and
(b) the defendant has been guilty of a breach of that duty; and
(c) the plaintiff suffered injury, damage or loss as a result of that breach.

• Legal duty of care

4. Not everyone who is 'careless' will be liable in negligence. It is only in certain limited circumstances that the law imposes a duty of care. A duty of care is owed to any person who we can reasonably foresee will be injured by our acts or omissions. Such persons are known as 'neighbours'.

5. In Donoghue v Stevenson (1932) the court ruled that a person could owe a duty of care to another with whom he had no contractual relationship.

Case: Donoghue v Stevenson (1932)

The plaintiff's friend purchased a bottle of ginger beer from a retailer and gave it to the plaintiff to consume. The bottle was opaque. The plaintiff drank a portion of the contents of the bottle, and then poured the rest into her glass. The remains of a small snail emerged from the bottle. The plaintiff subsequently became seriously ill and sued the defendant, the manufacturer, in negligence. The defendant argued that he did not owe a duty of care to the plaintiff since there was no contract between the defendant and the plaintiff (the purchaser having been the plaintiff's friend).

Held: The defendant had prepared the product in such a way as to show that he intended it to reach the ultimate consumer in the form in which it left him. He could reasonably foresee that somebody other than the original purchaser might consume the product, and, therefore, he was held liable to the plaintiff.

6. The 'neighbour principle' has been applied in several other cases since, such as:

Case: King v Phillips (1952)

The defendant carelessly drove his car over a boy's bicycle. The boy, who was not on his bicycle at the time, screamed. The plaintiff, his mother, on hearing the scream, looked out the window and saw the mangled bicycle, but not her son. As a result, she suffered a severe shock and became ill. She sued the defendant for negligence.

Held: The defendant could only reasonably foresee that his carelessness would affect other road users, and not persons in houses. The defendant was held not liable to the plaintiff, since he did not owe her a duty of care.

Case: Dutton v Bognor Regis U.D.C. (1972)

A building inspector, employed by the defendant, the council, examined the foundations of a house being built and passed them as fit. Three years later after the plaintiff had purchased the house from its original owner, cracks began to appear and the internal walls started to subside. The plaintiff had the house surveyed independently and was told that his house was built on a rubbish tip, which was an unstable foundation. He sued the council for negligence.

Held: The professional person who provided an opinion as to the safety of the house owed a duty of care, not only to the owner at that time, but to all subsequent owners who might suffer injury or loss as a result of its use. The defendant council was held liable.

Kelly & Others v Haughey, Boland & Co. (1987)

The plaintiffs, directors of Cavan Crystal Ltd, contracted to buy another company, Royal Tara China Ltd, having examined the audited accounts for a number of years' trading, as certified by a partner of the defendant accountancy firm. They subsequently sued the defendants for negligence, claiming that the stock figure had been understated and had resulted in the plaintiffs purchasing a company which was worth less than they had originally thought.

Held: Although the defendants had not taken reasonable care in the certification of the figures, they did not owe a duty of care to the plaintiffs, since they could not have foreseen that the company would be sold.

• Breach of duty

7. Given the existence of a duty of care in any particular case, it is then necessary to establish whether the defendant took reasonable care in the circumstances. The question posed is whether the defendant exercised the care that a reasonable man would have exercised.

Case: S.E.E. Co. Ltd v Public Lighting Services Ltd. (1988)

The defendants sold eight floodlighting masts, which complied with British standards of safety, to the plaintiffs. The plaintiffs erected these masts on a sports ground, but one of them collapsed during the course of a storm. The plaintiffs sued for negligence.

Held: There was no evidence that there had been a lack of reasonable care taken by the defendants, since the masts complied with standards accepted and used in Ireland.

8. If the defendant is acting in a professional or skilled capacity, he must exercise the care, skill and knowledge which could be reasonably expected from an accountant, dentist, doctor, plumber, carpenter or electrician, as the case might be.

9. A duty to take reasonable care to avoid a particular risk may vary with the magnitude of the foreseeable risk and the ease or difficulty of guarding against the risk involved.

Case: Latimer v AEC (1953)

The defendants' factory was flooded by a thunderstorm. This had the effect of making the floor slippery. Despite the defendants' efforts to clear the water and make the factory floor safe by the use of sawdust, the plaintiff slipped on one of these areas and injured himself. The plaintiff sued for negligence, alleging that the factory should have been closed.

Held: Economic factors had to be taken into account. The risk of injury did not justify the closure of the factory. The defendants exercised the care that a reasonable man would have exercised. They were not held liable.

Case: Paris v Stepney Borough Council (1951)

The plaintiff, who had only one eye, a fact which was known to his employer, was employed by the defendant as a vehicle welder. He lost his other eye when a spark flew into it. The plaintiff sued his employers for negligence, claiming that goggles should have been provided.

Held: While goggles were not usually provided for two-eyed welders, the employer should have provided them in this situation because of the greater risk involved. The defendant, therefore, had not taken reasonable care and was held liable.

Res ipsa loquitur

10. The burden of proving the tort of negligence rests on the plaintiff, except where the *res ipsa loquitur* (the thing speaks for itself) rule applies. Under this rule, the facts of a particular case may be such as to raise a presumption of negligence where there is no other obvious cause of the incident. The defendant must prove that, despite the facts, he did show reasonable care.

11. There is prima facie evidence of negligence when:

(a) the defendant has sole control of the incident;
(b) the defendant has knowledge denied to the plaintiff; and
(c) the damage is such that it would not normally have happened without some element of negligence by the defendant.

Case: Byrne v Boadle (1863)

A barrel of flour fell from the defendant's warehouse on to a public place, injuring the plaintiff, a passer-by. The burden of proof was placed by the court on the defendant, who was obliged to show that he had not broken his duty of care.

Held: The defendant could not prove he had taken reasonable care to ensure that such an accident would not happen. He was held to be negligent.

Case: Macon v Osborne (1939)

The plaintiff had a swab left in his body after an operation. Although he was unable to prove a breach of duty, since he was under anaesthetic at the time, he sued the surgeon for negligence.

Held: The presence of the swab in the patient's body provided prima facie evidence of a breach of duty. The surgeon was unable to prove that he had taken reasonable care. He was held liable.

Case: O'Loughlin v Kearney (1939)

The defendant had a trailer coupled to his car. It became detached and injured the plaintiff, who sued for negligence. The court placed the burden of proof on the defendant, who had to show that he had not broken his duty of care.

Held: The cause of the detachment remained unknown. The defendant, however, successfully proved that there was no defect in the coupling, and was thereby held not to be negligent.

• Consequential harm
12. The plaintiff must show that as a result of the breach of duty he has suffered some damage, loss or injury. For the claim to be proved, the harm must be:

(a) caused by the conduct of the defendant;
(b) sufficiently closely related to the negligent act; and
(c) either physical injury to the plaintiff's property, or economic loss consequential upon physical injury.

13. The court will then look at whether the harm which occurred was reasonably foreseeable, i.e. the defendant is only liable for the consequences of the act that a reasonable person could have foreseen.

Case: Overseas Tankship (UK) Ltd v Morts Dock & Engineering Co. Ltd (The *Wagon Mound*) (1961)

An action was brought against the owners of the *Wagon Mound* (a ship). The defendant's employees had spilt a large quantity of fuel oil into Sydney harbour, which had spread to another part of the harbour where the plaintiff was engaged in welding on his wharf. He had ceased welding until he had received expert advice that oil would not burn on water. The oil was ignited, however, by welding sparks which fell on cotton waste. Much damage was caused to the wharf.

Held: Harm to the wharf by fouling was foreseeable, but harm by fire was unforeseeable, since oil on water does not usually ignite. Damages were not awarded for harm caused by the explosion and fire.

• Contributory negligence

14. At common law, if the plaintiff was guilty of any negligent actions which contributed to the cause of the harm, the defendant could escape liability for negligence.

15. Since 1961, by virtue of the Civil Liability Act, 1961, where a person suffers harm partly as a result of his own fault, and partly due to the fault of another, the damages recoverable will be reduced according to his share of the responsibility.

Case: O'Leary v O'Connell (1968)

The defendant, a motor-cyclist, knocked down the plaintiff who was walking across a road. As a result, the plaintiff's leg was broken.

Held: Both parties were negligent in not keeping a proper look-out. The degree of fault was apportioned eighty-five per cent to the defendant and fifteen per cent to the plaintiff, and damages were awarded accordingly.

16. A person can be guilty of contributory negligence if his conduct, while in no way contributing to the accident itself, contributed to the nature and extent of his injuries.

Case: Sinnott v Quinnsworth Ltd (1984)

The plaintiff, a passenger in a car owned by the defendant, was injured in a collision between the car and a bus. Evidence showed that the injuries would have been less serious if the plaintiff had been wearing his seat-belt.

Held: The plaintiff's damages would be reduced by fifteen per cent.

• Occupiers' liability

17. Occupiers have a duty to exercise care towards persons who enter their premises, regardless of any contractual relationship between them. This liability is governed by the ordinary principles of negligence. It varies, however, with the occupiers' relationship to the visitor, who may be:

(a) an 'invitee', who comes on to the premises for some purpose in which the occupier has some interest;
(b) a 'licensee', who is permitted on to the premises for his own purpose; or
(c) a 'trespasser', who enters the premises without permission and has no right to be there.

Liability to invitees

18. An invitee is a person who comes on to the premises with the express or implied invitation of the occupier so as to confer some material or pecuniary benefit on him.

19. Customers in a shop, delivery men while on the premises for delivery, paying patrons at a dance or cinema and parents attending a school function are all classed as invitees.

20. The occupier of the premises has a duty towards an invitee to take reasonable care to prevent injury to him from any 'unusual danger' of which he knows or ought to know.

21. The courts have held a defective flag-pole, torn linoleum on a dance floor, a darkened staircase without a handrail which led to a toilet in a public house, and a greasy floor in a hotel, to amount to unusual dangers. However, a heap of rubbish in a timber yard was held not to be an unusual danger.

22. Where an occupier of premises takes reasonable care to prevent injury to an invitee from an unusual danger, he will not be liable for negligence. A warning of the danger will usually be sufficient since such a warning enables the invitee to proceed without danger.

Liability to licensees

23. A licensee is a person who comes on to the premises with the express or implied consent of the occupier, but only does so for the licensee's benefit.

24. Visitors to hospitals, parks, forests, museums, art galleries and churches open to the public, as well as children attending a school or using waste ground as a playground without objection are all classed as licensees.

25. The occupier of the premises has a duty towards a licensee to prevent injury to him from 'concealed dangers' of which he knows. The licensee must generally take the premises as he finds them. He cannot complain of obvious dangers or those which could be reasonably expected.

Case: Kirwan v Representative Church Body (1959)

The plaintiff, an elderly lady, injured herself while in a church to pray. She had caught her foot against a wooden ledge which bordered the aisle, and had fallen.

Held: The plaintiff was a licensee, although she had claimed the status of invitee because she had put an offering in a box on entering the church.

The wooden ledge was held not to be a concealed danger, and, as a result, her action failed.

26. What may be an 'obvious' danger to an adult may be a 'concealed' danger to a child.

Case: Bohane v Driscoll (1929)

The defendant, a teacher of a senior class, permitted the children of a junior class to sit beside a fire in his class-room throughout lunch-time, as the weather outside was bad. One of the junior children was burned, however, after the defendant had removed the fire-guard.

Held: While the removal of a fire-guard constituted an obvious danger to an adult, it remained a concealed danger to children. The defendant was negligent.

Liability to trespassers

27. A trespasser is a person who comes on to the premises without the express or implied consent of the occupier.

28. The occupier's duty of care to trespassers depends to a large extent on the circumstances of the case, such as the seriousness of the danger, the type of trespasser likely to enter, and in some cases the resources of the occupier. In general, however, the occupier of the premises has a duty not to leave his premises in a state or condition which is intended to injure a trespasser, or is so reckless that it is likely to injure any trespasser whose presence is known or ought to be known to him.

29. Although an occupier does not owe the same duty of care to a trespasser as he owes to a visitor, he must act by standards of common sense and humanity and warn or exclude, within reasonable limits, those likely to be injured by a known danger. The occupier can set deterrents but not traps. He can, for example, erect a barbed-wire fence, keep a guard dog or spike walls with glass to keep out trespassers.

Case: Bird v Holbrook (1828)

The defendant set up a gun in his garden so as to protect his flowers from thieves. The plaintiff innocently entered the defendant's garden to recover a hen which had wandered in there, activated the gun and received serious injuries.

Held: Although the plaintiff was a trespasser, the occupier still owed him a duty of care not to leave his property in a condition likely to injure him. The plaintiff was therefore entitled to damages for the injuries suffered.

30. Trespassers who are known to come habitually on to the premises, especially if they are children, and are not prevented from doing so, may be treated as licensees to whom the occupier owes a greater duty of care. Similarly, if the premises, or something on the premises, contains some allurement to a child, in that it is so attractive to him and compels him to play with it, while at the same time being a concealed danger, the child is converted from a trespasser to a licensee and the duty of care is one to protect him from concealed dangers.

Case: McNamara v E.S.B. (1975)

The plaintiff, a boy of eleven, climbed into an electricity substation, touched against an uninsulated conductor and seriously electrocuted himself. The wire fence surrounding the substation was, at that time, in the process of being repaired.

Held: The defendants were liable for the injuries caused to the boy, as they had failed to take adequate steps to ensure that a child trespasser would not be injured from concealed dangers.

31. A trespasser may also include a person who enters a part of a premises to which his invitation does not extend, or a person who remains on a premises after his invitation has ceased.

Case: O'Keeffe v Irish Motor Inns Ltd (1978)

The plaintiff, a hotel patron, was shown out the front door by the manager in the early morning, long after activities in the hotel had finished. He ran in the darkness towards the kitchen at the back of the hotel and fell over some barrels injuring himself.

Held: The invitee had become a trespasser when the accident happened and had no case against the defendant.

• Vicarious liability

32. A person may be held liable by law if he authorises another, either expressly or implicitly, to commit an action which causes injury or damage to another person. Hence, the general rule is that a person is liable in tort for his own actions only, but in some exceptional cases he may also be answerable for the acts of others.

33. Vicarious, or indirect, liability arises most commonly in the relationship between employers, their agents and their employees. An employer is generally liable for torts committed by an agent acting within the scope of his authority, or for torts of his employees committed in the course of their employment. However, where an agent or employee has acted negligently or has committed some other tort, they will themselves be liable.

Case: Ilkiw v Samuels (1963)

The defendant expressly instructed an employee not to allow anybody else to drive his lorry in any circumstances. Some time later it became necessary to move the lorry away from a conveyor belt, and the afore-mentioned employee allowed another person to drive it. This person was unable to stop the lorry and, as a result, injured the plaintiff, who sued the defendant for negligence.

Held: Although the employee had been negligent in allowing some-body else to drive the lorry, this negligence arose in the course of the employment. Accordingly, the defendant (i.e. the employer) was held to be vicariously liable.

Case: Doyle v Fleming's Coal Mines Ltd (1953)

The plaintiff, a lorry driver, made a delivery on the instructions of his employer. Afterwards, he spent a considerable amount of time in a licensed premises. On his return, he was involved in an accident.

Held: The employee was not acting in the course of his employment when he committed the tort. His employer, therefore, was not liable.

Case: Quilligan v Long (1953)

The plaintiff, a taxi-driver, took his employer's taxi home without his permission. He left it unlocked outside his house with the key in the ignition. The car was stolen and was involved in an accident.

Held: The employee's negligence did not occur within the scope of his employment and his employer was not liable.

• Strict liability

34. Liability is strict, i.e. it may arise without fault, where a person collects or stores non-natural things on their property which are likely to do harm if they escape from the property. The defendant need not have acted either negligently or intentionally for strict liability to apply.

Case: Rylands v Fletcher (1868)

The defendant, a mill owner, employed independent contractors to con-struct a reservoir on his land for the purpose of supplying water for his mill. During the work, the contractors found disused mine shafts which, unknown to them, had an adjoining passageway with mine shafts on the plaintiff's neighbouring land. They did not fill in these shafts. When the reservoir was filled with water, the water escaped through the old mine shafts and flooded the plaintiff's land. The plaintiff sued for negligence.

Held: Although the defendant had not been negligent, since he had employed competent workmen and was himself unaware of the existence of the disused mine shafts, he was none the less personally liable, and not merely vicariously liable, for the contractors' negligence.

35. The rule in Rylands v Fletcher has been applied to the escape of many non-natural things beyond the boundaries of the defendant's land such as water, gas, chemicals, animals, vibrations and explosives.

Case: Berkery v Flynn (1982)

The defendant built a slurry pit on his own land. An overflow of slurry entered the general water system and subsequently contaminated the contents of a well on the plaintiff's land. The plaintiff was dependent on supplies from this well for both farming and domestic purposes.

Held: The plaintiff was able to recover damages under the rule in Rylands v Fletcher because he had an interest in the polluted well, and the loss was a sufficiently direct consequence of the escape of the slurry into the general water system.

36. Some defences to the rule are available. The defendant will have a defence if he can prove that:

(a) the escape was caused by:
    (i) the action of the plaintiff;
    (ii) an act of God; or
    (iii) a third party over whom he had no control.
(b) the accumulation was made:
    (i) with the express or implied consent of the plaintiff; or
    (ii) under statutory authority.

IMPORTANT CASES

Numbers in brackets refer to paragraphs of this chapter

PROGRESS TEST

Numbers in brackets refer to paragraphs of this chapter

1. Define negligence. (1)
2. List the basic components which must be present for a negligence action to be proven. (3)
3. To whom is a legal duty of care owed? (4, 5)
4. What is meant by *res ipsa loquitur*? (10, 11)
5. Identify the factors which must exist for a claim of consequential harm to be proven. (12)
6. When can a person be guilty of contributory negligence? (16)
7. Describe the duty of care which occupiers of premises have towards (i) invitees, (ii) licencees, and (iii) trespassers. (20, 25, 28, 29)
8. Distinguish between an unusual danger and a concealed danger. (21, 25, 26)
9. When may an invitee be treated as a trespasser? (31)
10. What is meant by vicarious liability? (32, 33)

chapter 8

DEFAMATION

Topics covered in this chapter are:

- Libel
- Slander
- Innuendo

- Defences
- Mitigation and aggravation of damages

Summary of the chapter

The law guards a person's good name, more specifically, his interest in his reputation. This chapter examines the different forms of defamation and the factors which must exist for a plaintiff to succeed in such an action.

Introduction

1. Defamation is the publication of a false statement which tends to injure the plaintiff's reputation, or causes him to be shunned by ordinary members of society. Publication is defined as being the communication of the defamatory matter to some person other than the person about whom it is made.

2. There are two forms of defamation recognised by the law, namely, libel and slander.

• Libel

3. Defamatory matter is classed as libellous if it is in permanent form, or if it is for general reception. For example, writing, pictures, films, records, television or radio.

4. Libel is actionable per se, i.e. without proof of actual damage suffered.

5. A libel which tends, or is likely, to cause a breach of the peace is a criminal offence as well as a tort. In such a case of criminal libel, however, publication to the defamed party alone is sufficient since such action may tend to cause a breach of the peace.

• Slander

6. Defamatory material is classified as slanderous if it is in a transient form, for example, words or gestures.

7. Slander is not a crime. In most cases slander is not actionable per se. The plaintiff must prove that he suffered special damage, i.e. actual material loss capable of monetary evaluation. Examples of this would include loss of employment or loss of a contractual business advantage, and not merely loss of friendship or reputation.

8. Slander, like libel, is actionable per se, however, where it imputes:

(a) that the plaintiff has committed a criminal offence punishable with imprisonment;
(b) that the plaintiff is suffering from certain existing diseases, such as venereal disease or Aids;
(c) unchastity, adultery or lesbianism in a woman;
(d) that the plaintiff is incompetent in any office, profession, trade or business held or carried on by him.

In each of these situations, the plaintiff need not establish any special damage in order to recover for slander.

Establishment of a case of defamation
9. If a plaintiff is to succeed in a defamation action he must show:

(a) that the statement is defamatory. This would be so where the words would tend to lower the plaintiff in the estimation of right-thinking members of society generally.

Case: Bennett v Quane (1948)

The plaintiff, a solicitor, brought a case against a doctor who had said of him, 'He brought an action to the Circuit Court instead of the District Court to get more costs for himself.'

Held: The words, which had suggested that the plaintiff had brought a case in a higher court merely to secure extra fees, were defamatory.
(b) that it refers to the plaintiff, expressly or by implication, in such a way as to be reasonably understood by others as referring to him.

Prior to the Defamation Act, 1961, even if a statement was true of someone else to whom it referred, the plaintiff could none the less recover if he showed that it also referred to him.

Case: Newstead v London Express Newspapers Ltd (1939)

The defendants published a statement in their newspaper that 'Harold Newstead, thirty-year-old Camberwell man' had been convicted of bigamy. There were, however, two Harold Newsteads living in the same area and of about the same age. So, while the statement was true in respect of a Camberwell barman of that name, it was untrue of the plaintiff.

Held: The plaintiff had been defamed because the words clearly, though innocently, referred to him, and he recovered damages.

(c) that it has been published by the defendant, i.e. communicated to at least one person other than himself.

Case: Coleman v Kearns Ltd (1946)

The plaintiff was accused by an employee of the defendant of having stolen goods from the defendant's shop. This accusation was made in a public street in the presence of others.

Held: The accusation of theft in these circumstances was publication of a false statement and thereby defamatory.

In addition, as outlined above, in most cases of slander, i.e. where it is not actionable per se, the plaintiff must prove that he suffered special damage.

• Innuendo

10. A plaintiff may succeed in an action for defamation even if the words used are not prima facie defamatory, i.e. defamatory in their ordinary meaning. To do so he must claim, and be able to prove an innuendo, i.e. by giving the words a certain meaning they are defamatory. An innuendo, therefore, is a statement by the plaintiff of the meaning that he attributes to the words.

Case: Tolley v J.S. Fry & Sons Ltd (1931)

The defendant, a chocolate manufacturer, published an advertisement showing a cartoon of the plaintiff, a well-known amateur golfer, and a limerick including both the plaintiff's and defendant's names. Neither the cartoon nor limerick were by themselves defamatory, but the plaintiff brought a libel action alleging an innuendo since he had not given consent for his name and picture to be used in this way.

Held: It was reasonable to infer that reasonable people would think that the plaintiff had received some financial reward for the use of his name, thereby compromising his amateur status. His libel action, therefore, succeeded.

• Defences

11. The common defences available in an action for defamation are:

(1) Consent

(2) Justification

(3) Fair comment
(4) Absolute privilege
(5) Qualified privilege

Consent

12. A person may consent to the publication of defamatory statements about themselves. This might, for example, be to enhance their career. The consent must be to the actual publication, however, in order to be effective as a defence to the tort of defamation.

Case: Green v Blake (1948)

The decision of a complaint made against the plaintiff, a racehorse owner, was published in the *Racing Calendar*. The plaintiff argued that the entry of a horse in a race did not amount to consent to the publication of such decisions.

Held: Such publication was defamatory. The mere submission to a set of rules was not sufficient consent for the publication of the decision.

Justification

13. If the statement is true in substance, the defence of justification is available. It is not necessary, therefore, to show that every detail of the statement is true.

Case: Alexander v N.E. Railway Company (1865)

The plaintiff, a train passenger, was convicted of failing to pay his train fare. Subsequently, the defendants published a poster stating that his sentence was a fine or 'three' weeks' imprisonment. The alternative, however, should have been 'two' weeks' imprisonment.

Held: This was but a small inaccuracy. The statement remained true in substance, and the defence of justification was not defeated.

14. The law does not allow a person to recover damages in an action for defamation for an apparent injury to a character he either does not have, or ought not, to possess. A person convicted of rape can be called a rapist.

15. The defence of justification is rarely used, because the onus of its establishment rests on the defendant. If this defence fails, the court may award exemplary damages to the plaintiff because the defendant has repeated, and continued to repeat, during the trial the defamatory statement.

Fair comment

16. Where a statement of opinion is a fair comment made in good faith on a matter of public interest, it is not actionable.

17. To be successful in this defence, it is necessary to prove:

(a) that the comment was based on facts which were true, or substantially true. No comment could be fair if it was based on false facts.

(b) that the comment was fair, and made in good faith, i.e. was an honest expression of the defendant's opinion. The comment, therefore, cannot be motivated by malice.

(c) that the subject matter commented upon was of public interest or concern. Examples of such matters are the conduct of politicians or the administration of justice.

Case: Cohen v Daily Telegraph Ltd (1968)

The plaintiff alleged defamation in an article published by the defendants. The defendants pleaded a defence of fair comment on the grounds that the subject matter commented upon was of public interest. Furthermore, the defendants provided additional information to the court of events which had happened after the article had been published in an attempt to refute the allegation of defamation.

Held: The defence of fair comment was not open to the defendants as the facts which were in existence at the time the article was published could not be relied upon.

Absolute privilege

18. No action lies for defamation, however false or malicious the statement, if it is made in either House of the Oireachtas or is contained in official reports or publications of the Oireachtas. Absolute privilege also covers statements made in the course of judicial proceedings by judges, counsel, juries or witnesses. This includes statements made in connection with a trial, such as communications between clients and solicitors.

Case: Macauley & Co. Ltd v Wyse-Power (1943)

An action for slander was taken against a Circuit Court judge because of remarks he had made during a case which seriously attacked the reputation and character of the plaintiff.

Held: The judge was protected by privilege, and the case was dismissed.

19. Absolute privilege is granted, therefore, in cases where complete freedom of expression is considered of paramount importance.

Qualified privilege

20. The defence of qualified privilege is available when a person makes a communication under some duty—legal, social or moral—to a person who has some corresponding interest to receive it. This privilege will apply provided the communication is not made more widely than necessary, and provided it is not motivated by malice.

Case: Watt v Longsdon (1930)

The plaintiff, a company employee, sued a director of the company for defamation because the director, on receipt of allegations of drunkenness, dishonesty and immorality by the plaintiff, had shown these allegations to the chairman of the company and to the plaintiff's wife. Although the allegations were completely unfounded, the defendant believed them to be true. The defendant pleaded the defence of qualified privilege.

Held: Qualified privilege was a valid defence for the communication to the chairman of the company, since both a duty to make the statement, and an interest in receiving it, were present. The defence of qualified privilege in respect of the communication to the plaintiff's wife failed, however, because the defendant had no legal, social or moral duty to communicate such allegations. The plaintiff, therefore, was entitled to damages.

• Mitigation and aggravation of damages

Mitigation

21. The defendant may mitigate his payment of damages by:

(a) making an apology and an offer of amends. An offer of amends means that he must offer to publish an appropriate correction of the words complained of, and a sufficient apology to the injured party; or
(b) producing evidence of the plaintiff's bad reputation prior to the publication of the defamation; or
(c) proving provocation by counter-defamation; or
(d) showing that the plaintiff had previously obtained compensation in respect of a similar defamation.

Aggravation

22. The defendant, however, may aggravate his payment of damages by:

(a) pleading the defence of justification for his defamation which the court subsequently finds to be unfounded; or
(b) the method he uses in communicating the defamatory material; or
(c) his conduct throughout the trial.

IMPORTANT CASES

Numbers in brackets refer to paragraphs of this chapter

PROGRESS TEST

Numbers in brackets refer to paragraphs of this chapter

1. What is defamation? (1)
2. Distinguish between libel and slander. (3–8)
3. Discuss the three things a plaintiff must show in order to succeed in an action for defamation. (9)
4. Can a plaintiff succeed in a defamation action even if the words used are not prima facie defamatory? (10)
5. When is consent a valid defence to the tort of defamation? (12)
6. Why is the defence of justification rarely used? (15)
7. Identify those factors which must be proven in a defence of fair comment. (17)
8. Distinguish between 'absolute' and 'qualified' privilege. (18, 19, 20)
9. How may a defendant mitigate his payment of damages? (21)

EXAMINATION QUESTIONS

Section 2: Elements of the Law of Torts

1. (a) What is a tort?
   (b) Identify and explain the general defences which can be raised to answer an action in tort.

I.A.T.I. (Autumn 1990)

2. Write a note on the main ingredient of the tort of negligence.

I.A.T.I. (Summer 1990)

3. (a) Explain the meaning and effect of the following defences which may be put forward to an action to tort:

   (i)   consent;
   (ii)   contributory negligence; and
   (iii) statutory authority.

(b) What remedies may follow a successful tort action?

C.I.M.A. (May 1988)

THE LAW OF CONTRACT

The nature of a contract
Offer and acceptance
Consideration
Intention to create legal relations
Terms of a contract
Form of a contract
Misrepresentation
Mistake in contract
Duress and undue influence
Contracts illegal or contrary to public policy
Capacity to contract
Discharge of contract
Remedies for breach of contract

chapter 9

THE NATURE OF A CONTRACT

Topics covered in this chapter are:

- The concept of a contract
- The essentials of a contract

- Void, voidable
  and unenforceable contracts

Summary of the chapter

The law of contract is based on enforcement of the freely negotiated agreement of the parties to a contract. This chapter sets out the essential characteristics of such a contract.

- **The concept of a contract** *executone, applicable*

1. A contract is an agreement enforceable at law between two or more persons whereby rights are acquired by one or more persons in return for certain acts or forbearances on the part of the other or others.

2. It has been described as the 'most important legal mechanism for business activity'. Indeed, almost all transactions made by, or on behalf of, a business will be governed by the principles of contract. These include the sale of goods and supply of services, the purchase of materials and the hiring of employees.

3. The factor which distinguishes contractual from other legal obligations is the agreement of the parties. The parties to a contract may, within well-defined limits, make 'law' binding on themselves. Common law and statute law, however, are used in certain circumstances to interfere directly with freedom of contract in order to redress the balance in favour of the weaker party. Common law, for example, attempts to protect minors from onerous contracts, while statute law achieves its objectives by implying terms, in favour of the weaker party, into certain contracts regardless of the wishes of the parties.

- **The essentials of a contract**

4. For a contract to be valid, and therefore binding on the parties, there are certain essential requirements:

(a) there must be an agreement made as a result of an offer and an unequivocal acceptance of that offer;

(b) the contract must be either under seal or there must be consideration;

(c) there must be an intention to create legal relations;

(d) the parties must have capacity to contract;

(e) there must be genuine consent to the terms by all parties to the contract;

(f) the terms of the contract must be legal and capable of performance.

• Void, voidable and unenforceable contracts

Void contracts

5. A void contract is not a contract at all, and is but an agreement without legal effect. The expression usually describes a situation where the parties have attempted to contract, but the law will not give effect to their agreement because, for example, there is a common mistake on some major term, or it has been entered into by a minor for the supply of goods other than necessities. The parties are not bound by such an agreement, and if they transfer property under it, they can sometimes recover such property from the person in possession.

Voidable contracts

6. A voidable contract is a contract in which the law allows one of the parties to withdraw from it if he wishes, thus making it void. It remains valid, however, unless and until the innocent party chooses to terminate it. A contract might be voidable if one of the parties to that contract had been a minor or had been induced by undue influence or misrepresentation to enter that contract. If the parties transfer property before the avoidance of the contract, then such property is usually irrecoverable from a third party.

Unenforceable contracts

7. An unenforceable contract is a valid contract which will not be enforced by the courts because of the lack of legal evidence, e.g. the written evidence for a contract for the sale of land. If a contract is deemed to be unenforceable, therefore, and either party refuses to perform or to complete his part of the performance of the contract, the other party cannot compel him to do so. Any property transferred under an unenforceable contract cannot be recovered — even from the other party to the contract.

PROGRESS TEST

Numbers in brackets refer to paragraphs of this chapter

1. Define a contract. (1)
2. Distinguish between contractual and other legal obligations. (3)
3. Give six essential elements of a binding agreement. (4)
4. Distinguish between a void and a voidable contract. (5, 6)
5. When can a party to an unenforceable contract bring a successful action in respect of that contract? (7)

chapter 10

OFFER AND ACCEPTANCE

Topics covered in this chapter are:

- Requirements of a valid offer
- Recognising an offer
- Termination of an offer
- Requirements of a valid acceptance

- Communication of acceptance
  —general rules
  —exceptions

Summary of the chapter

A contract is based on the agreement or mutual consent of the parties involved. This chapter examines both the offer and acceptance which lead to binding agreement.

---

1. The first essential of a valid contract is the agreement or mutual assent of the parties involved. In the event of a dispute about such agreement, the courts seek to discover whether there was *consensus ad idem* (agreement as to the essential point), i.e. whether the words and conduct of the parties are sufficient to lead a reasonable person to assume that they had reached agreement with respect to the same subject matter. The court may examine the negotiations surrounding the transactions to see if there was a definite *offer* made by one party which was clearly accepted without qualification by the other party.

• Requirements of a valid offer
2. An offer exists where the offeror undertakes to be contractually bound if the offeree makes an unconditional acceptance. It is a definite promise to be bound on certain specific terms. The essentials of a valid offer are as follows:

(a) 'The terms of an offer must be clear, certain and complete.' It cannot be vague. Otherwise the court may hold that there was a failure to make a complete agreement.

Case: Gunthing v Lynn (1831)

The offeror promised to pay a further sum for a horse if it was 'lucky'.
　　Held: The offer was too vague. The court was unable to give effect to the alleged agreement, because no clear meaning could be determined.

(b) 'The offer must be communicated to the other party.' An offer can be communicated to a particular person, a group of persons or to the public at large. It can be accepted by anybody who comes within the terms of the offer.

Case: Carlill v Carbolic Smoke Ball Co. (1893)

The defendants undertook, in various advertisements, to pay £100 reward to anyone who caught influenza after having sniffed a smoke ball three times daily for two weeks. The plaintiff used the smoke ball as prescribed, and caught influenza after more than two weeks' treatment, and while still using the smoke ball. She then claimed her £100 reward.

Held: It was an offer to the public at large which the plaintiff could accept, and had accepted, by performance of the conditions in the offer.

(c) 'The offer must be made by written or spoken words, or may be inferred by the conduct of the parties.' It can be communicated by letter, telephone, telex or any means of communication which is appropriate and reasonable in the circumstances.

(d) 'The offer must be intended as such before a contract can arise.' If it is not made with a view to a legal relationship, e.g. if the offer excludes recourse to the courts for its enforcement, then it will not constitute an offer.

• Recognising an offer

3. Only an offer in the proper sense, i.e. made with the intention that it shall become binding when accepted, will be recognised so as to form a binding contract. An offer must be distinguished from the following which are not offers:

(a) The answer to a question or the supplying of information;
(b) An invitation to treat;
(c) A statement of intention;
(d) An option.

The answer to a question or the supplying of information

4. An offer must not be confused with the answer to a question or the supplying of information.

Case: Harvey v Facey (1893)

The plaintiff telegraphed to the defendant: 'Will you sell us Bumper Hall Pen? Telegraph lowest cash price.' The defendant telegraphed in reply: 'Lowest price for Bumper Hall Pen £900.' The plaintiff regarded this as an offer and telegraphed: 'We agree to buy Bumper Hall Pen for £900 asked by you.' The defendant made no further reply.

Held: No contract had been made. The second telegram was merely a statement of the price which the defendant would sell for, if and when he chose to sell his property. It was not an offer which the plaintiff could accept, but the supply of information in response to a question.

5. If, however, in the course of negotiations for a sale, the seller states the price at which he will sell, that statement may be an offer which can be accepted.

An invitation to treat
6. An invitation to treat is an invitation to another person to make an offer. An 'offer' can be converted into a contract by acceptance, provided the other requirements of a valid contract are present, but an 'invitation to treat' cannot be 'accepted'.

7. To advertise goods or to exhibit goods for sale in a shop window or on the open shelves of a self-service shop is to invite customers to make offers to purchase, or an 'invitation to treat'.

Case: Fisher v Bell (1961)

A shopkeeper was prosecuted for 'offering for sale' offensive weapons by displaying flick-knives in his shop window.

Held: Although he had exhibited the flick-knives, accepted buyers' offers and sold the goods, he had not offered them for sale, because goods on display are not on offer for sale, but an invitation to treat.

Case: Pharmaceutical Society of Great Britain v Boots Chemists (1952)

By statute, certain drugs containing poisons could only be sold 'under the supervision of a qualified pharmacist'. Boots operated a self-service shop, with the drugs displayed on open shelves and with a qualified pharmacist located at the check-out. The Pharmaceutical Society brought an action against Boots Chemists for being in breach of their supervisory requirements.

Held: The display of goods was only an invitation to treat—the selection and presentation of the goods by the customer was the offer and the taking of money by the pharmacist at the cash-desk was the acceptance. Therefore, Boots Chemists did not commit an offence, because the sale took place at the check-out.

Case: Minister for Industry and Commerce v Pim Bros Ltd (1966)

A coat was displayed for sale in the defendants' shop window. It had a notice of the cash price and a weekly sum attached to it.

Held: This did not constitute an offer to sell which could be made a contract of sale by acceptance. It was simply an invitation to treat for the sale of the article with an indication that credit facilities were available.

8. The publication of a prospectus by a company in respect of the issue of shares is an invitation to the public to make offers. The company has only a limited number of shares and cannot intend to allot whatever number the public may apply for.

9. The advertisement of an auction, or the putting up of items for bids, is an invitation to treat and not an offer to sell to the highest bidder. The offers come from successive bidders, and the fall of the auctioneer's hammer is the acceptance. A bidder may retract his offer until the hammer falls. However, if the auction is advertised as being 'without reserve', this constitutes a firm offer to sell to the highest bidder.

10. A tender is an estimate submitted in response to a prior request. An invitation for tenders to supply goods or services is not an offer but an invitation to others to make offers. The tenders made, however, are normally recognised as legal offers which may lead to a binding contract if accepted. A tender must be accepted as tendered or there may be no agreement.

A statement of intention

11. If a person states that he intends to perform some act, and ultimately does not carry out his stated intention, no rights may be conveyed on another party who may suffer loss due to non-performance. For example, were a father to state that one of his sons or daughters would be a beneficiary of his estate, this alone would not confer any contractual rights on the respective party.

An option

12. An option is the right to buy or sell something at a specified price. It is, in effect, a conditional contract. The person who is offered the option is not bound to take it up, i.e. he can fail to exercise his option. The person offering the option, however, is legally bound by it in the event of the option being exercised.

• Termination of an offer

There must be some duration for which an offer or counter-offer stands and is open to acceptance by the offeree leading to a contract. This duration must be at least long enough to give the offeree an opportunity to reply to the offer. An offer, however, does not continue indefinitely and can be terminated without maturing into a contract in any of the following circumstances:

(a) if the offeror has revoked (withdrawn) it;
(b) if it has expired by lapse of time;
(c) if the offeree has rejected it or made a counter-offer;
(d) if there is a failure of an express or implied condition;
(e) if the offeree or offeror dies.

Revocation

14. The offeror may revoke (withdraw) his offer at any time before it has been accepted. This is true even when the offeror undertakes that his offer shall remain open for acceptance for a specified time, unless by a separate contract (an 'option') he is given consideration in return for keeping the offer open for the whole of the specified time.

Case: Routledge v Grant (1828)

The defendant, in an offer to buy the plaintiff's house, laid down a requirement of his offer being accepted within six weeks. Within that period, he withdrew his offer.

Held: The offeror was entitled to revoke his offer at any time prior to acceptance because no option agreement existed.

15. Revocation of an offer is only effective if it is communicated to the offeree, before acceptance, either by the offeror or by any third party who is a sufficiently reliable informant.

Case: Billings v Arnott & Co. Ltd (1945)

The defendants offered to pay employees who joined the Defence Forces half their salary up to £2 per week. The plaintiff informed his employers that he intended to avail of their offer, but was told that he could not do so as another employee from the same department had already done so and that he, the plaintiff, could not be spared.

Held: It was too late for the defendants to withdraw the offer once it had been accepted.

Case: Dickinson v Dodds (1876)

The defendant offered by letter to sell property to the plaintiff for £800, saying 'this offer to be left open until Friday 12 June, 9.00 a.m.'. On Thursday 11 June, the plaintiff delivered a letter of acceptance to an address at which the defendant was no longer residing so that the defendant did not receive it. The defendant sold the property on Thursday 11 June, to another buyer. A Mr Berry, who had been an intermediary between the plaintiff and the defendant, informed the plaintiff of this sale. Mr Berry, nevertheless, delivered a duplicate of the plaintiff's letter of acceptance to the defendant at 7.00 a.m. on Friday 12 June.

Held: There was no contract, the offer having been revoked before acceptance and communication by a third party being valid. An offer to sell a particular item is revoked by implication, therefore, if the item is sold to another person.

16. Revocation communicated by post only takes effect from the time of receipt and not from the time of posting.

Case: Byrne v Van Tienhoven (1880)

The defendant, who resided in Cardiff, offered by letter dated 1 October to sell goods to the plaintiff, who resided in New York. On 8 October, the defendant wrote to the plaintiff revoking his offer. The plaintiff received the letter of offer on 11 October and telegraphed his acceptance of the offer. He confirmed this acceptance by letter dated 15 October. The letter of revocation was received by the plaintiff on 20 October.

Held: The letter of revocation had no effect until received; it could not revoke the contract made by acceptance of the offer on 11 October.

Lapse of time

17. An offer will terminate at the end of the time specified in the offer, or if no time-limit is specified, it will terminate after a reasonable time. What is reasonable depends on the nature of the contract and the circumstances of a particular case (on what is usual and to be expected).

Case: Walker v Glass (1979)

The defendant offered to sell his house to the plaintiff, the offer to remain open until a specified date. The defendant wrote to the plaintiff before that date revoking the offer.

Held: The defendant was free to revoke his offer at any time before acceptance by the plaintiff.

Case: Ramsgate Victoria Hotel Co. v Montefiore (1866)

The defendant offered in June 1864 to take shares in the plaintiff's hotel, and paid a deposit to the company's bank. The plaintiff did not reply, but in November 1864 the company sent him an acceptance by issue of a letter of allotment. The defendant refused to take the allotted shares and to pay the balance due on them, contending that his offer had expired and could no longer be accepted.

Held: The defendant's offer was for a reasonable time only. The courts considered that five months was much more than that. The refusal to take the shares was justified, therefore, since the plaintiff's delay had caused the defendant's offer to lapse.

Rejection of the offer or a counter-offer

18. An offer may be terminated if outright rejection is communicated to the offeror or if a counter-offer is made by the offeree. An attempt to accept an offer on terms, other than those contained in the offer, is a rejection accompanied by a counter-offer. A rejected offer cannot subsequently be accepted.

Case: Hyde v Wrench (1840)

The defendant offered to sell his farm to the plaintiff for £1,000. The plaintiff made a counter-offer in writing of £950, which the defendant rejected. The plaintiff then wrote accepting the original offer of £1,000. The defendant refused to sell, and the plaintiff sued for breach of contract.

Held: The counter-offer of £950 terminated the original offer of £1,000. Therefore, when the plaintiff purported to accept at £1,000, there was no offer in existence to be accepted, and no contract could be formed.

19. A request as to whether or not additional terms would be acceptable does not constitute a counter-offer and, therefore, does not, by itself, terminate an offer.

Case: Stevenson v McLean (1880)

The defendant offered to sell iron to the plaintiff at £2 per ton cash. The plaintiff wrote and asked whether the defendant would agree to a contract providing for credit facilities. On receiving no reply, the plaintiff accepted the offer as made.

Held: There was a contract, since the inquiry was not a counter-offer but a request for information as to a variation of terms. It was not a rejection, and did not terminate the defendant's offer.

Failure of an express or implied condition

20. An offer cannot be validly accepted if it is made subject to an express or implied condition, and this condition fails.

✷Case: Financings Ltd v Stimson (1962) ✷

The defendant, who wished to purchase a car, signed a hire-purchase form on 16 March. The form stated that the agreement would only become binding when the plaintiffs signed the form. The car was stolen from the plaintiffs' premises on 24 March, and was recovered badly damaged. The plaintiffs signed the form on 25 March.

Held: The defendant was not bound contractually to take the car. There was an implied condition in the defendant's offer that the car would remain in the same condition until the moment of acceptance. The condition had failed.

Death of the offeree or offeror

21. Death of the offeree probably terminates an offer, because an acceptance can only be made by an offeree or his authorised agent.

22. Death of the offeror terminates the offer unless the offeree accepts it in ignorance of the offeror's death, and the offer is not of a personal nature requiring the skills of the deceased, e.g. singing in a concert. If the offer, therefore, can be completed equally well by the deceased's personal representatives, then they will probably be obliged to fulfil it upon acceptance by the offeree.

• Requirements of a valid acceptance

23. An acceptance takes place when an offeree unqualifiedly accepts an offer made by an offeror. In most cases there is little difficulty in deciding whether an offer is accepted. Where negotiations are complicated, however, the courts may be called upon to examine the correspondence and surrounding circumstances in order to establish whether, on a true construction, the parties agreed to the same terms.

The essentials of a valid acceptance are as follows:

(a) 'Acceptance may be oral, written or implied from conduct.' An example of acceptance being implied from conduct would be the dispatching of goods in response to an offer to buy.
(b) 'Acceptance must be clear and unqualified and must exactly match the offer.' A counter-offer or a conditional assent is insufficient and causes the original offer to lapse.

Case: Neale v Merrett (1930)

The defendant made an offer to sell land to the plaintiff for £280. The plaintiff replied accepting the offer, enclosing £80 and promising to pay the balance in four monthly instalments.

Held: The proposal for deferred payment was a variation of the terms implicit in the offer. Since the normal terms of a contract for the sale of land are that the entire price is payable as a single sum at completion, it was held that there had been no acceptance.

(c) 'Acceptance must be communicated to and received by the offeror.' Otherwise, no enforceable agreement will exist between the parties.

• Communication of acceptance—general rules

24. Acceptance must be communicated by the offeree, or by someone with his authority, to the offeror.

Case: Powell v Lee (1908)

The plaintiff applied for the post of headmaster of a school. After being interviewed, the management passed a resolution appointing him, but made no decision as to how the appointment was to be communicated. One of the managers, without authorisation, informed the plaintiff that he had been appointed. The management subsequently appointed another candidate. The plaintiff sued for breach of contract.

Held: Since acceptance had not been properly communicated to the plaintiff, there was no valid contract.

25. The offeror may expressly or impliedly stipulate the method of communicating acceptance, but unless he states that this is the only adequate method of acceptance, the offeree may accept by some other method, so long as the offeror suffers no disadvantage.

Case: Yates Building Co. v R.J. Pulleyn & Sons (York) 1975

The defendants called for acceptance of their offer by registered or recorded delivery letter. The plaintiffs sent an ordinary letter containing their acceptance. This arrived without delay.

Held: The acceptance was valid, since the defendants had not stipulated that this was the only method of acceptance which sufficed. The method selected by the plaintiff was equally advantageous to the defendant.

26. There must be some act on the part of the offeree to indicate his acceptance. The offeror cannot impose a condition, without the offeree's consent, that silence shall constitute acceptance.

Case: Felthouse v Bindley (1862)

The plaintiff offered by letter to buy a horse stating, 'If I hear no more about him, I consider the horse is mine at £30. 15s.' No acceptance was communicated, but the owner told the defendant, an auctioneer in whose possession the horse was at the time, not to sell the horse. When the horse was sold by mistake at auction to someone else, the plaintiff sued the defendant for conversion (a tort alleging wrongful disposal of the plaintiff's property).

Held: The offeror could not impose acceptance merely because the offeree had not rejected the offer. There had been no contract of sale and the plaintiff did not own the horse. Hence, the case for conversion failed.

27. Acceptance is not effective if communicated in ignorance of the offer. Acceptance may be effective, however, even though the offer was not the sole reason for it being made.

Case: R. v Clarke (1927)

The defendant offered a reward to anyone who found and returned his lost property. The plaintiff, not knowing about the offer, found the property and returned it of his own free will. He subsequently discovered the reward offer and sued to recover it.

Held: The plaintiff was not accepting the defendant's offer, since he was unaware of it. There was no contract and, therefore, there could be no contractual obligation to pay the reward.

Case: Williams v Carwardine (1833)

The plaintiff, an accomplice in a crime, provided information which led to the arrest of criminals. She had been aware of the existence of a reward for the provision of such information, but was motivated primarily by remorse at her own part in the crime.

Held: A contract had been formed, even though the motive for acceptance was different than that contemplated by the offeror.

• Communication of acceptance—exceptions
28. Although as a general rule there cannot be a binding contract unless acceptance has been communicated to the offeror by the offeree, two exceptions to this general rule apply:

(a) where performance of an act or the conduct of a person is deemed to constitute acceptance;

(b) where acceptance is made by post, telegram or cable and such communication is lost or delayed.

Where performance or conduct constitutes acceptance

29. A 'unilateral contract' may be established whereby the offeror includes in the offer a term providing that complete performance or conduct by the offeree will constitute complete acceptance. There is no need to give advance notice of acceptance to the offeror.

Case: Kennedy v London Express Newspapers (1931)

The publishers of an English newspaper offered a free accident insurance scheme to its registered readers. The plaintiff's wife had registered with a newsagent and on her being killed accidentally by a bus, her husband claimed the sum payable under the insurance scheme.

Held: The offer of the free insurance scheme represented a unilateral offer made to the world at large. Registration by the plaintiff's wife brought a valid contract into existence, and the publishers were legally bound by it.

Acceptance by letter or telegram

30. Whereas an offer only takes effect if and when received, an acceptance by letter takes effect when posted and an acceptance by telegram takes effect when given to the post office for transmission. Acceptance by telephone or telex follows the normal rule and is effective from the time received.

Case: Household Fire Insurance Co. v Grant (1879)

The defendant applied for shares in the plaintiff company and enclosed a deposit for those shares. The company accepted his offer by posting a letter of allotment, which never arrived, to the defendant. The company later went into liquidation and the liquidator called upon the defendant to pay the balance due on the shares.

Held: The subscriber for shares was bound by an acceptance in a letter of allotment although the letter was never delivered.

IMPORTANT CASES

Numbers in brackets refer to paragraphs of this chapter

PROGRESS TEST

Numbers in brackets refer to paragraphs of this chapter

1. Identify the essentials of a valid offer. (2)
2. Is (i) a statement of the price of goods, and (ii) a display of goods, an offer which becomes a contract if accepted? (4, 6)
3. List five methods by which an offer may be terminated. (13)
4. When will lapse of time terminate an offer? (17)
5. Outline the essentials of a valid acceptance. (23)
6. What effect does the stipulation by the offeror of the method of communicating acceptance have? (25)
7. Is acceptance effective if communicated in ignorance of an offer? (27)
8. Explain the significance of (i) unilateral contracts, and (ii) the postal rule. (29, 30)

chapter 11

CONSIDERATION *Contrepartie*

Topics covered in this chapter are:

- The nature of consideration
- Legal rules governing consideration

- The principle of promissory estoppel

Summary of the chapter

All contracts, except those made by deed under seal, require consideration to pass between the parties before they can be said to be valid. This chapter examines the concept of consideration and the rules developed by the courts which govern it.

• The nature of consideration

1. Consideration is required for all enforceable contracts, except those made by deed. A person cannot sue on a simple contract unless he can show that he gave, or promised to give, some advantage to the party he wishes to sue, in exchange for what that party promised in return. A promise, therefore, is only legally binding if it is made in return for another promise or act, i.e. it is part of a bargain.

2. In Currie v Misa (1875), consideration is defined as 'some right, interest, profit or benefit accruing to the one party, or some forbearance, detriment, loss or responsibility given, suffered or undertaken by the other'. Such a benefit accruing or detriment suffered is, of course, in return for a promise received or given.

3. The courts, therefore, do not enforce a bare promise. To prove that no consideration was given in return is a complete defence in a court action. A number of rules have been formulated by the courts in cases where the question as to the existence of consideration arises.

• Legal rules governing consideration

Consideration must be of some value, but it need not be adequate.

4. Anything of value which contributes to the bargain made is recognised in law as good consideration. It can be money, land, goods, services or any other undertaking which confers a benefit to one party or represents a loss to the other. However, in the absence of fraud or unfair dealing, the court will not assess the relative value of the contributions made by each party. The law refuses to protect a person of full capacity who makes a bad bargain.

Case: Commodity Broking Co. Ltd v Meehan (1985)

The defendant, the sole beneficial owner of a company, acknowledged that the company owed a sizeable sum of money to the plaintiffs. He intimated that the company was insolvent, but promised to pay off the outstanding debt by monthly instalments of £1,000. He made two such payments, but then refused to pay any more on the grounds that there had been no consideration for his promise to indemnify the plaintiffs.

Held: The promise to indemnify the plaintiffs was unenforceable because there had been no consideration for the defendant's promise. The plaintiffs' reason for not suing the company was the intimation that it was insolvent—not the defendant's promise to pay off the company's debts.

Case: Thomas v Thomas (1842)

The plaintiff's husband expressed a wish before his death that the plaintiff, his widow, should have the use of his house throughout her life. After his death, the executors of the husband's will allowed the plaintiff to occupy that house in return for an undertaking by her to pay a rent of £1 per annum. They later argued that no consideration had been provided for the benefit of the use of the house.

Held: The promise of a payment of £1 per annum was valuable, but not adequate, consideration. Consequently, the contract was valid and enforceable.

Consideration must not be illegal, vague or impossible to perform.

5. The court will not enforce an illegal contract, such as an undertaking to pay a reward for a criminal act, because to do so would be contrary to public policy. A court may similarly refuse to enforce a contract where the consideration relied upon is vague or impossible to perform, because this would indicate that no real agreement was reached.

Consideration must be something which the promisee is not bound to do under the general law or under an existing contract with the other party.

6. Performance of an existing obligation imposed by statute is no consideration for a promise. However, if some extra service is given then that is sufficient consideration.

Case: Collins v Godefroy (1831)

The plaintiff, a witness in a lawsuit, was promised expenses by the defendant in return for giving evidence. It turned out that the witness had already been subpoenaed, i.e. ordered to attend.

Held: The performance of an existing obligation was no consideration for a promise of expenses. The promise was, therefore, unenforceable.

Case: Glasbrook Bros Ltd v Glamorgan C.C. (1925)

The owners of a colliery asked for, and promised to pay for, a special police guard on their mine throughout a time of industrial unrest. They later reneged on their promise, claiming that the police had only been performing their public duty.

Held: The police had provided more protection than was reasonably necessary and so there was something unique given which could be regarded as good consideration. The extra protection provided, therefore, did amount to consideration for the promise to pay.

7. A promise to do something which an existing contract already requires a person to do is no consideration. There is no extra obligation and no extra rights or benefits.

Case: Stilk v Myrick (1809)

The plaintiff was a member of the eleven-man crew of a ship. During the voyage, two members deserted and the captain promised the rest of the crew that they would share the wages of the deserters if they would complete the voyage. On completion, the plaintiff requested his share, and was refused.

Held: The plaintiff was already contractually bound to complete the voyage and did not provide consideration for the promise of extra pay. The promise, therefore, was not binding.

Consideration must be provided by the promisee
8. Consideration is the price of a promise, so a person can only enforce a promise if he himself provided the consideration.

Case: Tweedle v Atkinson (1861)

The plaintiff's father and father-in-law exchanged promises that they would each pay a sum of money to the plaintiff following his marriage. The father-in-law died without making the promised payment, and the plaintiff sued his father-in-law's executor for the specified amount.

Held: The plaintiff had no enforceable rights under the agreement because he had provided no consideration for his father-in-law's promise.

9. As a general rule, only a person who is a party to a contract, i.e. has provided consideration, can sue on it. This is known as the 'privity of contract doctrine'. Any person not contributing to the consideration is not 'privy' to the contract and has no enforceable rights or obligations under it.

Case: Dunlop Pneumatic Tyre Co. Ltd v Selfridge & Co. Ltd (1915)

The plaintiff, a tyre manufacturer, supplied tyres to Dew & Co. Ltd on terms that Dew & Co. Ltd would not resell the tyres at less than the current list price, with the exception of sales to trade customers. If Dew & Co. Ltd sold the tyres wholesale to trade customers, they would have to get a written undertaking from those buyers not to sell the tyres below the current list price. The defendant purchased tyres on these conditions from Dew & Co. Ltd, and subsequently sold tyres to two customers at less than the minimum price. Dunlop Pneumatic Tyre Co. Ltd sued to recover damages.

Held: The plaintiff could not recover damages under a contract to which it was not a party. The agreement had been between Dew & Co. Ltd and Selfridge & Co. Ltd and Dunlop Pneumatic Tyre Co. Ltd were, therefore, unable to enforce the contract since no consideration had passed from them to the defendant.

Consideration must not have been provided prior to the agreement

10. Past consideration is any act which has already been performed before a promise in return is given, and, as a general rule, is not sufficient to enforce the promise. The promisor is not getting anything in exchange for his promise, since he already has it, so unless he chooses to recognise a moral obligation he can renege on his promise.

Case: Roscorla v Thomas (1842)

The plaintiff purchased a horse from the defendant. After the sale was complete, the defendant promised that the horse was not vicious. This consequently proved to be wrong, as the horse did indeed turn out to be vicious.

Held: The act put forward as consideration, i.e. the payment of the price, was complete before the promise was made. The plaintiff gave no new consideration for the promise, and, therefore, the promise was unenforceable.

Exceptions to the past consideration rule

11. Past consideration will support a bill of exchange (such as a cheque), since most of these are issued to pay existing debts.

12. Past consideration supports a later promise to pay for something done at the promisor's request. The contract is made when the 'past' consideration is requested, and the parties understand that payment will be made. The later promise to pay merely fixes the price to be paid—it does not create the agreement.

Case: Lampleigh v Braithwait (1615)

The defendant, who had killed a man, asked the plaintiff to obtain a royal pardon for him. The plaintiff incurred expense and trouble in subsequently securing such a pardon, and the defendant later promised to pay the plaintiff £100 for his services. He broke his promise and the plaintiff sued him.

Held: An implied promise to pay could be related back to the defendant's initial request for help. The promise was, therefore, held to be binding as the later promise to pay £100 was merely fixing the amount. The plaintiff's subsequent efforts amounted to consideration for the defendant's promise.

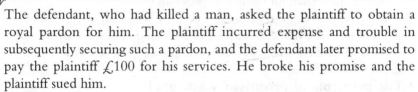

Consideration must be given to enforce the waiving of a contractual obligation

13. If a party to a contract waives existing rights which he has under the contract, he is not legally bound by such a waiver unless he has received consideration for it. This is because the waiver leads to a new agreement which must be accompanied by consideration to make it enforceable.

Case: Foakes v Beer (1889)

The defendant obtained a judgment against the plaintiff of £2,091, which attracted interest if not paid immediately. The plaintiff asked for time to discharge the debt, and they entered into a written agreement whereby the plaintiff would make an immediate payment of £500 and the remainder in agreed instalments. In return, the defendant agreed not to take 'any proceedings whatsoever' on the judgment. When the debt was paid off as agreed, the defendant sued for £360 interest which was due.

Held: The defendant was entitled to the debt with interest. No consideration had been given by the plaintiff in return for the promise to waive interest. Therefore, the claim was upheld.

BULLSHIT

14. There are a number of exceptions to the rule that the waiving of a contractual debt must be accompanied by consideration in order for the waiver to be binding:

(i) if the creditor accepts payment of a lesser sum in full settlement before the due date, the payment discharges the whole debt;

(ii) if the creditor accepts anything different to which he is already entitled, e.g. goods instead of cash, even though the value of the goods may be less than the cash value;

(iii) if the creditor accepts part payment in full settlement from a third party. The creditor will have received consideration from an individual against whom he had no previous claim;

(iv) if a group of creditors arrange that they will each accept part payment in full settlement. This will be binding between themselves;

(v) if it can be enforced under the principle of 'promissory estoppel'.

• The principle of promissory estoppel

15. Equity mitigates the hardship that could be caused to a person who relies on a promise that a debt will not be enforced in full. Under the principle of promissory estoppel, where a person makes a promise, unsupported by consideration, to waive a debt or other obligation, and where the promisee acts on his promise, the promisor is estopped (prevented) from retracting his promise.

16. It is important to note, however, that the principle prohibits the promisor from insisting on his strict legal rights when it would be unjust to allow him to do so. For example, if circumstances were to change, so as to remove the reasons for the promise, the original rights of the promisor would become enforceable again.

Case: Central London Property Trust v High Trees House (1947)

In 1939, the plaintiff leased a block of flats from the defendant for ninety-nine years at an annual rent of £2,500. Due to the war, he was unable to sublet all of the flats, so the plaintiff agreed in writing to accept a reduced annual rent of £1,250. After the war, when the flats were fully let, the plaintiff claimed the rent arrears and a full rent for the future.

Held: The plaintiff was entitled to the full rent from the end of the war and for the future, but was estopped in equity from going back on his promise and claiming the full rent back to the start of the war.

17. Two limitations to the scope of promissory estoppel are:

(a) It only applies to a promise of waiver which is voluntary.

Case: D. & C. Builders v Rees (1966)

The defendant owed the plaintiffs £482, and knowing that they were in financial difficulty offered them £300 in full settlement of the debt. The plaintiff accepted a cheque for this amount, but later sued for the balance.

Held: The promise was not voluntarily given, as it was given under threat that if they did not take this sum they would receive nothing. The plaintiff was entitled to the balance.

(b) It only applies to the waiver of existing rights. Any new rights or obligations must be supported by consideration in the usual way.

Case: Combe v Combe (1951)

A husband promised his wife during divorce proceedings to pay her an annual allowance. As a result, she did not apply to the court for a maintenance order. Subsequently, the husband paid no maintenance and the wife sued to enforce his promise. The wife succeeded in the High Court on the basis of promissory estoppel, but this was appealed to the Court of Appeal.

Held: Promissory estoppel applies only when a person who promises not to enforce his legal rights or obligations retracts his promise. It does not apply to new contracts, which must be supported by consideration. Since the wife had not provided such consideration, her action failed.

IMPORTANT CASES

Numbers in brackets refer to paragraphs of this chapter

PROGRESS TEST

Numbers in brackets refer to paragraphs of this chapter

1. Define consideration. (2)
2. If, in return for a promise, the promisee provides something which no longer has any value, is there sufficient consideration to make this promise binding? (4)
3. Is the performance of something which you are already required to do by (i) law, or (ii) an existing contract, held to be valid consideration? (6, 7)
4. Can a person enforce a contract if he is not a party to it? (8, 9)
5. Is it true that 'past consideration is no consideration'? (11, 12)
6. If a creditor accepts part payment of an existing debt in full settlement, may he still claim the unpaid balance? (13)
7. List five exceptions to the rule that the waiving of a contractual debt must be accompanied by consideration in order for the waiver to be binding. (14)
8. Explain the principle of promissory estoppel and identify two limitations to its scope. (15, 16, 17)

chapter 12

INTENTION TO CREATE LEGAL RELATIONS

Topics covered in this chapter are:

- Intention to be legally bound
- Commercial agreements
- Domestic agreements
- Collective agreements

Summary of the chapter

The parties to a contract must have intended to create a legally binding transaction before a contract can validly exist. This chapter examines a number of different types of agreements and how they fulfil such a requirement.

• Intention to be legally bound ✳

1. The law upholds agreements, not only because of the consideration involved, but also because the parties intended to create legal relations. Otherwise, there is no binding contract.

2. What matters is not whether the parties intended in their minds to be bound by what they agreed to do, but the inferences that a reasonable person would draw from their words, conduct or the circumstances of the negotiations.

3. An express statement by the parties of their intention not to create legal intentions is conclusive. When phrases such as 'subject to contract', 'agreement in principle' or 'provisional agreement' are used, the usual assumption of the courts is that such phrases indicate that the parties did not intend to be legally bound prior to the signing of a formal contract.

✳ Case: Rose & Frank Co. v Crompton Bros Ltd (1925)

An agreement was made whereby the defendant, a British manufacturer of paper tissues, appointed the plaintiff to be its sole distributors in the United States. The agreement expressly stated that it was 'not subject to legal jurisdiction in the law courts'. The defendant terminated the agreement without giving the required notice.

Held: The agreement was binding in honour only and, therefore, was not enforceable as a contract.

4. In most contracts, there is no express statement that the parties intend the agreement to be legally binding. In the absence of such an express intention, the courts have generally applied three presumptions to a case:

(a) commercial or business-type agreements are usually intended to be legally binding;

(b) domestic or social agreements are usually not intended to be legally binding;

(c) collective agreements are not usually intended to be legally binding.

• Commercial agreements

5. Where negotiations suggest that the agreement is of a commercial or business nature, it is presumed the parties intend to create legal relations. This is the normal situation and is rarely the cause of the dispute.

6. The presumption that a commercial or business agreement is not legally binding, as in Rose & Frank Co. v Crompton Bros (1925), needs to be expressly denied.

Case: Jones v Vernon Pools Ltd (1938)

The plaintiff claimed that he had sent a football pools coupon to the defendant on which the forecasts he had made entitled him to receive payment of a dividend. The agreement included a clause which stated that any transaction would be 'binding in honour only'.

Held: This clause expressly denied an intention to create legal relations, was a bar to an action in court and resulted in the agreement being invalid.

• Domestic agreements

7. An agreement between husband and wife, relatives or friends is normally presumed not to contain an intention to create legal relations.

Case: Balfour v Balfour (1919)

The defendant, an English civil servant stationed in Ceylon, promised the plaintiff, his wife, that he would pay her £30 per month to maintain her in England during his absence. The marriage subsequently ended in divorce and the plaintiff sued for the monthly maintenance allowance which the defendant no longer paid.

Held: Their agreement was unenforceable because the parties had not intended that it should be subject to legal consequences.

8. In some domestic agreements, however, the circumstances may establish that there had been an intention to create legal relations. This would be the case if the parties were in some way estranged, e.g. separated or divorced, or could be shown to have displayed 'mutuality of agreement'.

*Case: Courtney v Courtney (1923)

The married couple agreed to separate. The defendant agreed to pay his wife £150 and she agreed to return a watch and ring. The plaintiff sued her husband when he retracted his promise.

Held: In the circumstances, intention to create legal relations was to be inferred, as the parties were separated and intended to have no further dealings. The wife, therefore, succeeded in her action for breach of contract.

Case: Simpkins v Pays (1955)

Three women who lived in the same house took part in a weekly competition run by a Sunday newspaper. They agreed to send their entries on a single coupon and to share any prize money. One week, they won £750, but the plaintiff was denied her share by the others.

Held: The agreement to share had been intended to be legally binding, and was an enforceable contract.

Case: Mackey v Jones (1959)

The plaintiff laboured on his uncle's farm for no pay over a period of years. His uncle left the entire farm to another relative in his will. On the uncle's death, the plaintiff sued the personal representatives of his uncle, claiming that his uncle had verbally agreed to leave the farm to him.

Held: There was no contract to leave the farm to the plaintiff. The words of the deceased were no more than a statement of intention or wish.

• Collective agreements

9. Procedural agreements between trade unions and employers relating to a contract of employment are not usually legally binding, despite their elaborate and very legal contents. If the courts find, however, that the parties intend to create legal relations through such a collective agreement, it will hold that the contract is enforceable.

10. Whereas a trade union may be bound by such a collective contract, an individual member of the union or a non-union worker is not bound by the provisions of a collective agreement, unless they are expressly or impliedly incorporated into the employment contract.

IMPORTANT CASES

Numbers in brackets refer to paragraphs of this chapter

PROGRESS TEST

Numbers in brackets refer to paragraphs of this chapter

1. What is the effect of a 'subject to contract' statement in a commercial agreement? (3)
2. Identify three presumptions that courts have usually applied to a case in the absence of express intention by the parties for an agreement to be legally binding. (4)
3. Describe the circumstances under which a commercial agreement is not intended to be legally binding. (6)
4. What type of domestic agreement will the court regard as having been subject to an intention to create legal relations? (8)
5. Are trade unions and their members legally bound by collective agreements with employers? (9, 10)

TERMS OF A CONTRACT

Topics covered in this chapter are:

- Express terms
- Implied terms

- Conditions, warranties and exemption clauses

Summary of the chapter

Once the prerequisites of a binding contract have been established, the terms of the contract, which determine the limits to which the parties are bound, fall for examination. This chapter considers the implications of these different classes of contractual terms.

1. The contents of a contract are its terms, which define the rights, obligations and rules by which the parties are to be bound in their agreement. Contractual terms may be either express or implied.

• Express terms

2. The express terms of a contract are the words used by the parties, whether written or spoken, during negotiations leading up to a contract, and by which they intended to be bound. Such terms must be distinguished from statements, called mere representations or non–contractual representations, which help to induce the making of the contract but which are not intended to be legally binding, e.g. 'It's the best bargain in the world.' The importance of the distinction is that different remedies are available when a term is broken than when a representation is untrue.

To resolve disputes concerning the express terms of a contract, the courts have formulated 'rules of construction'. The courts will not usually look beyond the words of an express term in a contract, presuming instead that the words are possessed of their ordinary literal meaning, while legal terms are possessed of their technical meaning.

4. Disputes concerning the contents of an oral contract can only be resolved by evidence produced before the courts.

5. If the parties have expressed the terms of a contract in writing, however, the introduction of oral evidence to add to, vary or contradict the document is restricted. In certain exceptional circumstances, oral evidence may be given to assist the court in reaching a decision. Such evidence may be admitted:

(a) to explain the circumstances surrounding a term concerning trade practice or custom;
(b) to prove that the written agreement was not the whole agreement.

Case: De Lassalle v Guilford (1901)

The plaintiff signed a written lease agreement on an assurance that the drains were in order. This term was not written into the lease agreement.

Held: The term was one of a collateral contract made at the same time but not incorporated into the written contract. The parties had, therefore, agreed that their written consent should not take effect until the unwritten term had been satisfied.

(c) to correct a mistake in a written agreement drawn up subsequently.

Case: Nolan v Graves (1946)

An oral agreement was made at a public auction to purchase premises for £5,550. When drafting the memorandum of the agreement subsequently, this figure was mistakenly entered as £4,550.

Held: The memorandum of the agreement was to be corrected in favour of the seller.

6. If a term in an express contract is so ambiguous as to allow two different constructions, the court will generally choose the meaning unfavourable to the party who drew up the contract to the benefit of the other party, who is usually in the weaker economic position. This is called the *contra proferentem* rule.

• Implied terms

7. The parties to a contract may not expressly state each term of the contract, but they may choose to agree to the main purpose of the contract and some basic terms, and leave the rest to be implied from the circumstances. Additional terms of a contract may be implied by law:

(a) to give effect to the presumed intentions of the parties; or
(b) to supply a term normally implied in a particular type of contract; or
(c) to comply with statute law and the Constitution.

To give effect to the presumed intentions of the parties
8. Terms may be implied if the court decides that the parties intended these terms to apply and did not express them because they were taken for granted. The implied term must be a necessary inference from the expressed terms of the contract. The court will not imply a term simply because it is reasonable to do so. In such cases, the 'officious bystander'

test must be used; if when the parties had been making the contract, an officious bystander intervened to remind the parties that they had not mentioned a certain point, they would have answered 'Naturally, we didn't bother to state that; it's too obvious.'

Case: The Moorcock (1889)

The owners of a wharf contracted with the owners of a ship that the ship should be moored alongside in order to unload its cargo. At low tide, the ship grounded on a ridge of hard ground concealed beneath the mud and suffered damage.

Held: It was an implied term that the wharf would be a safe berth for the ship. Since both parties knew that the ship must rest on the mud, the wharf owners were held to be in breach of an implied term that the wharf was safe.

Case: Ward v Spivack Ltd (1957)

The plaintiff was appointed sole agent, on a commission basis, for the defendants' products. On termination of the agency, the plaintiff sought a declaration that he would continue to be entitled to commission on orders received from customers which he had introduced to the defendant company.

Held: To imply such a term in the contract, the court has to be satisfied that the parties would have agreed to the term had the matter been mentioned when the contract was originally being negotiated.

To supply a term normally implied in a particular type of contract

9. The reluctance of the court to imply terms does not apply, however, as regards terms normally implied by reference to a custom or practice prevailing in the particular trade to which the contract relates. Such standardised terms are always implied unless a contrary intention is expressed.

Case: Les Affreteurs etc. v Walford (1919)

It was expressly provided in an agreement for a charter of a ship, contrary to trade custom, that payment was to be made on signing the charter, and not at a later time.

Held: The contract was upheld. The express term superseded the term implied by custom.

To comply with statute law and the Constitution

10. The courts will also imply terms into contracts which have legal or constitutional connotations. Certain implied terms have been used so often by the courts that they have become formalised in statutes in an attempt to codify the law.

11. Implied terms are embodied in the Bills of Exchange Act, 1882, Sale of Goods and Supply of Services Act, 1980 and the Hire Purchase Acts, 1946–1960, which we will examine in later chapters.

12. Some terms must also be implied to comply with the Constitution. For example, under Article 40 of the Constitution, an individual's right of free association or free dissociation is guaranteed. This may lead to courts implying terms into contracts of employment.

Case: Educational Co. of Ireland v Fitzpatrick (1961)

Some employees of the company, who were union members, picketed the premises in an attempt to force the employer to employ only trade union labour and to compel all employees to join the union.

Held: Picketing to coerce workers to join associations was unlawful. The courts implied a term into the employment contract that employees, who when being employed had not been required to belong to a union, had the constitutional right to dissociate (i.e. to refuse to join a union).

• Conditions, warranties and exemption clauses

13. The terms of a contract may be classified into conditions, warranties, exemption from liability clauses or limitation of liability clauses. Where there is difficulty in classifying a term as a condition or a warranty, it is known as an 'innominate, or intermediate, term'.

Conditions

14. A condition is a vital term of a contract, breach of which entitles the injured party to rescind the contract, but he has the option to affirm it. In either case, the injured party may also recover damages for losses incurred.

Case: Poussard v Spiers (1876)

The plaintiff contracted to sing in a London operetta throughout a series of performances. She failed to perform during the first week, due to an illness. A replacement was engaged, who insisted that her services be retained for the entire run. Thus, on the recovery from the illness, the producer of the operetta declined to accept the plaintiff's services for the remaining performances.

Held: Failure to sing for the first week of the operetta was a breach of condition which entitled the producer to rescind the contract.

15. A contract may be made subject to a 'condition precedent', whereby the contract will not come into being in the absence of a specified condition being fulfilled. Similarly, it may be made subject to a 'condition subsequent', whereby the contract will be dissolved without either party incurring any liability in the event of the specified condition occurring.

Warranties

16. A warranty is a minor term subsidiary to the main purpose of a contract, breach of which merely entitles the injured party to claim damages. He is still bound by the contract.

Case: Bettini v Gye (1876)

The plaintiff, an opera singer, contracted to sing in a series of performances. The contract included a clause whereby the plaintiff was obliged to attend rehearsals six days before the opening performance. He missed the first three days, owing to illness, at which time he was informed that his services were no longer required.

Held: The singer had breached a warranty only, because the clause regarding rehearsals was subsidiary to the main purpose of the contract. The producer was obliged to accept the plaintiff's services and could not rescind the contract. He could, however, claim damages for failure to attend the six days' rehearsals, if he could prove any resultant loss.

Innominate terms

17. Instead of the traditional classification of terms into conditions and warranties, the tendency in recent years has been to consider a term of a contract in its context as to whether or not in itself it is vital to the existence of the contract. If a term is considered of such importance and is broken, the injured party is entitled to rescind the contract.

18. The significance of not classifying the relevant term until the seriousness of a breach can be judged is that a breach of a condition means that the entire contract is breached, while breach of a warranty means that damages only may be recovered.

Exemption clauses

19. An exemption clause is a term of a contract which seeks to exempt one of the parties from a liability which might arise out of the adoption or performance of the contract, or which seeks to limit his liability to a specific sum if certain events occur, such as a breach of warranty or negligence. These are also known as 'exclusion clauses'.

20. Exemption clauses are a legitimate device between parties negotiating their contract from positions of more or less equal bargaining strength. There has, however, been strong criticism of the use of exemption clauses by large organisations to abuse their bargaining power. The courts have developed various rules of case-law designed to restrain the effect of such clauses.

21. An exemption clause may become a term of the contract by signature or by notice. If a person signs a contractual document, he is bound by the terms even if he does not read them, unless the other party misrepresented its terms.

Case: L'Estrange v Graucob (1934)

The plaintiff, who was the owner of a café, purchased a cigarette vending machine. She signed, without reading, an agreement which contained conditions that excluded her normal rights under the Sale of Goods Act, 1893. The machine proved defective, and the plaintiff sought a legal remedy.

Held: The conditions of the contract were binding of the plaintiff because she had signed the written agreement.

Case: Curtis v Chemical Cleaning Co. (1951)

The plaintiff took her wedding dress to be cleaned. She was given a form to sign on which there were conditions by which the company disclaimed liability for all damage. Before signing it, she asked about its contents and was told that it excluded the cleaner's liability for damages to the beads and sequins. The dress was badly stained during the course of the cleaning process.

Held: The defendants could not rely on their exemption clause since they had misled the plaintiff as to the effect of the form.

22. Where a contractual document is not signed, the exemption clause will only apply if the party adversely affected by it knows of the clause, or if reasonable steps are taken to bring the clause to his notice before the contract is made.

Case: Olley v Marlborough Court (1949)

The plaintiff and her husband booked in at the defendant's hotel and paid for a room in advance. When they reached their bedroom they saw a notice on the wall by which the hotel disclaimed liability for articles lost or stolen unless they were handed to the management for safekeeping. The plaintiff left furs in the room, locked the door and handed in the key at the reception desk. The key was taken by a thief and the plaintiff's furs were stolen.

Held: The disclaimer of liability was too late, since the contract was completed at the reception desk when the room was booked and paid for. The hotel, therefore, could not rely on the notice disclaiming liability.

Case: Chapelton v Barry UDC (1940)

The plaintiff came upon a pile of deck chairs and a notice which read 'hire of chairs 2*d.* per session of 3 hours'. He took two chairs, paid for them and received two tickets as a receipt. One of the chairs subsequently collapsed and caused injury to the plaintiff. The defendant, when sued, attempted to rely on a notice on the back of the tickets disclaiming liability for any injury.

Held: It was unreasonable to communicate the disclaimer of liability on a receipt, when the notice advertising chairs for hire gave no such notice of limiting conditions. The disclaimer, therefore, was not binding on the plaintiff.

23. If an exemption clause cannot be eliminated from a contract, the courts will strictly construe it against the party seeking to use it to avoid liability. For example, where there is a fundamental breach of contract (i.e. the fundamental obligation is not fulfilled), the party responsible cannot seek the protection of the exemption clause to escape liability.

IMPORTANT CASES

Numbers in brackets refer to paragraphs of this chapter

PROGRESS TEST

Numbers in brackets refer to paragraphs of this chapter

1. Distinguish between the express terms of a contract and mere representations. (2)
2. Under what circumstances may oral evidence add to a written contract? (5)
3. When may additional terms, not expressed in the contract, be implied by law as part of it? (7)
4. Explain the 'officious bystander' test. (8)
5. Differentiate between a condition and a warranty. (14, 16)
6. What is the significance of an 'innominate' term? (18)
7. Compare a limitation of liability clause and an exemption of liability clause. (19)
8. List, and describe, the ways by which an exemption clause may become a term of a contract. (21, 22)
9. Explain what is meant by strict construction of an exemption clause. (23)

chapter 14

FORM OF A CONTRACT

Topics covered in this chapter are:

- Contracts which must be by deed
- Contracts which must be in writing
- Contracts which must be evidenced in writing
- The equitable doctrine of part performance

Summary of the chapter

The form of a contract is generally a matter to be decided by the parties. This chapter considers a number of special cases in which the law requires a special form to be used.

1. The general rule is that there are no formalities required for the creation of a contract; it may be made in writing, orally or even by implication from conduct. There are, however, some exceptional cases where the law demands some formality, without which the contract may still be valid but unenforceable.

2. The three categories of exceptions are:

(a) contracts which must be by deed (i.e. under seal);
(b) contracts which must be in writing;
(c) contracts which must be evidenced in writing.

• Contracts which must be by deed

3. Certain contracts, such as those unsupported by consideration or the promise of a gift, are required to be in the form of a deed and are not binding unless they are in that form. A deed is a written document, the essentials of which are that it be signed by the contracting parties, impressed with a seal and delivered by the person executing the deed. Other contracts, which need not be made by deed, may also be created under seal in this way to give them extra effect.

• Contracts which must be in writing

4. Some contracts (mainly commercial), are required by statute to be in the form of a written document, but not necessarily under seal. They are invalid if they are not in that form. This category includes:

(i) bills of exchange and promissory notes (Bills of Exchange Act, 1882);

(ii) share transfers (Stock Transfer Act, 1963);

(iii) leases greater than ones from year to year (Deasy's Act, 1860);

(iv) marine insurance contracts (Marine Insurance Act, 1906); and

(v) hire-purchase agreements.

• Contracts which must be evidenced in writing

5. Certain contracts do not have to be in writing, but only need to be evidenced in writing to be enforceable in a court of law.

6. The Statute of Frauds (Ireland) Act, 1695, section 2, provides that the following contracts must be evidenced in writing:

(i) a contract of guarantee, in which a person promises 'to answer for the debt, default or miscarriages of another person';

(ii) a contract made in consideration of marriage;

(iii) a contract relating to the sale of land or any interest in land;

(iv) a contract which is not to be performed within the space of one year of it being made.

7. No legal action can be brought in a court of law to enforce these contracts 'unless the agreement upon which such action shall be brought, or some memorandum or note thereof, shall be in writing, and signed by the party to be charged therewith, or some other person thereunto by him lawfully authorised'.

8. The memorandum or note must contain the names or identities of both parties to the contract, subject matter of the agreement and the consideration provided. It need not be prepared for the purpose of satisfying the statutory requirements—it can be any writing, made after the oral contract and before the action is brought, which sets out the terms of the agreement. If the memorandum consists of two or more documents, these must be joined together.

9. The memorandum must be signed by the person to be charged, or his agent. The signature may be stamped or printed, or even initials will suffice.

Case: Hynes v Hynes (1984)

The parties entered into an agreement to transfer a business from one brother to the other. The contract was not performed within a year, and the defendant attempted to avoid it on the grounds that some memorandum or note of the agreement in writing was required for it to be enforceable.

Held: The parties had intended at the time of contract that it should be completed within the space of a year. Hence, the contract remained enforceable, even in the absence of a memorandum or note in writing.

• The equitable doctrine of part performance

10. In some cases the Statute of Frauds caused hardship, particularly when an oral contract had been wholly or partly performed. Equity, therefore, developed the principle that if the plaintiff could prove that the defendant allowed him to do acts which were in part performance of a contract consistent with the one alleged, it would enforce the contract, even though there was not written evidence of it. The contract of part performance must point clearly to a contract consistent with the one the plaintiff seeks to enforce.

Case: Rawlinson v Ames (1925)

The plaintiff agreed orally to lease a flat to the defendant. It was part of the agreement that the plaintiff would make several alterations to the flat, which he did under the defendant's supervision. The defendant then refused to take the lease. The plaintiff sued for specific performance.

Held: The defendant had requested and supervised the alterations, thereby indicating that she had agreed to take the lease. Although a written memorandum did not exist, the order for specific performance was made (i.e. the defendant had to take and pay rent under the lease).

IMPORTANT CASES

Numbers in brackets refer to paragraphs of this chapter

Hynes v Hynes (1984) ....(9)
Rawlinson v Ames (1925)..(10)

PROGRESS TEST

Numbers in brackets refer to paragraphs of this chapter

1. What are the three categories of exceptions where the law demands some formality for the creation of contracts? (2)
2. State the essentials of a valid deed. (3)

3. Give three examples of contracts which must be in writing in order to be valid. (4)
4. How may a contract for the sale of an interest in land be enforced? (7)
5. List the essentials of a valid memorandum. (8)
6. Explain the doctrine of part performance and the circumstances in which it may be applied to an otherwise unenforceable contract. (10)

chapter 15

MISREPRESENTATION

Topics covered in this chapter are:

- Nature of misrepresentation
- Types of misrepresentation
- Negligent misrepresentation
- Loss of the right of rescission

Summary of the chapter

Many statements are made during negotiations leading to the formation of a contract. This chapter looks at those false statements of fact which induce the other party to enter into a contract, and the different remedies available.

• **Nature of misrepresentation**

1. A misrepresentation is a false statement of material fact, made innocently or otherwise by one party to the other, before the contract is made, in order to induce the latter to enter into the contract, which is relied on by the party misled.

It must be a false statement of material fact

2. A false statement of opinion, intention, law or mere 'sales talk' is not a misrepresentation. It is not meant to be a legally binding statement. The extent of the speaker's knowledge, as much as the words he uses, determines the category to which the statement belongs.

Case: Bisset v Wilkinson (1927)

The seller of a farm in New Zealand, which both parties knew had not previously been grazed by sheep, stated that it could support about 2,000 sheep. This proved to be untrue.

Held: This was merely a statement of opinion, which did not constitute misrepresentation.

3. It is usually necessary for the statement to be expressed, though silence can amount to a misrepresentation where there is a failure to reveal changes in circumstances relevant to the contract. Silence is not usually a misrepresentation except when a statement of fact made in the course of negotiations subsequently becomes false and is not corrected, or when silence distorts a literally true statement.

Case: With v O'Flanagan (1936)

A doctor disclosed the turnover of his practice to a potential purchaser. Between the time of this disclosure and the eventual contract, there was a significant deterioration in the value of the practice, which the vendor failed to reveal.

Held: There was misrepresentation by way of omission or silence.

The false statement must have induced the person to enter into the contract, and must have been relied upon.

4. To be actionable, a misrepresentation must have induced the person to enter into the contract. The injured party, therefore, cannot avoid the contract if he did not know there had been a misrepresentation, if he knew the statement was untrue or if he did not allow the statement to affect his judgment.

Case: Horsfall v Thomas (1862)

The plaintiff made a gun to be sold to the defendant. The plaintiff had concealed a defect in the breach of the gun by inserting a metal plug in the hole (misrepresentation by conduct). The defendant purchased the gun without inspecting it, and, when it exploded, refused to pay for it, on the grounds that he had been misled into purchasing it by a misrepresentation that it was sound.

Held: The defendant had not examined the gun, so the concealing of the defect could not have affected his decision as to whether or not to purchase it. The metal plug, therefore, could not have been a misleading inducement. As a consequence, the defendant had no grounds to refuse to pay for the gun.

5. The person to whom a misrepresentation is made is under no obligation to check upon its truth or relevance, even if given the opportunity.

• Types of misrepresentation

6. A misrepresentation may be classified as:

(a) fraudulent;
(b) innocent; or
(c) negligent.

for the purpose of determining what remedies are available. The classification depends on the state of mind of the person making the false statement.

Fraudulent misrepresentation

7. A misrepresentation is fraudulent when a false statement is made knowingly, or without belief in its truth, or recklessly, without regard to whether it is true or false.

Case: Derry v Peek (1889)

A company had a statutory power, conferred by a special Act of Parliament, to run trams in Plymouth by animal power and, with Board of Trade consent, by steam power. The defendant and other directors of the company issued a prospectus inviting applications for shares from the public. The prospectus stated that the company had power to run trams by steam power, assuming that a licence would be granted whenever they might apply for it, but, in the event, it was not. The directors were sued for fraud.

Held: The directors honestly believed their statement to be true and, therefore, were not liable for fraudulent misrepresentation.

Case: Fenton v Schofield (1966)

In selling a fishery, the vendor claimed that an average of three hundred fish had been caught in the previous four years. He also claimed that he had spent a large sum of money renovating the property.

Held: The vendor was guilty of fraudulent misrepresentation because both statements were false.

8. The party misled may:

    (i)   rescind the contract (since it is voidable);
    (ii) refuse to perform his part of the contract; and/or
    (iii) recover damages for any loss suffered by him.

Innocent misrepresentation

9. A misrepresentation is innocent when a false statement is made in the belief that it is true, and with reasonable grounds for that belief.

Case: Smelter Corporation of Ireland v O'Driscoll (1977)

The defendant was reluctant to contract to sell her land to the plaintiff. She did so eventually, after being told by an agent of the company that she had no real choice as her property would be otherwise acquired by compulsory purchase by the local authority. The plaintiff sued for specific performance.

Held: The agent of the company had believed what he said to be true, but it was, in fact, false. He was, therefore, liable for innocent misrepresentation. The court held that it would be unjust to order specific performance, and the defendant could refuse to perform the contractual obligations.

Case: Gahan v Boland (1984)

On inspection of the defendant's property, the plaintiff enquired as to whether a proposed motorway would affect the property in any way. The defendant assured him that it would not, and, based on this assurance, the plaintiff agreed to purchase the property. The plaintiff subsequently discovered that the motorway was in fact routed to pass through the property and sought to rescind the contract.

Held: By acting on the defendant's innocent misrepresentation, the plaintiff was entitled to rescind the contract.

10. The parties misled may:

  (i) rescind the contract, subject to being awarded damages in lieu of rescission by the court; or
  (ii) refuse to perform his part of the contract.

• Negligent misrepresentation

11. A misrepresentation is negligent when a false statement is made in the belief that it is true, but without reasonable grounds for that belief.

12. The misrepresentation must be in breach of a duty of care which arose out of a 'special relationship'. Anyone with special knowledge or skill, who applies it for the assistance of another, owes a duty of care to that person, or to persons likely to be affected by it. This duty exists only where the person who makes the statement foresees that it may be relied on.

Case: Hedley Byrne & Co. Ltd v Heller & Partners Ltd (1964)

The plaintiffs, advertising agents, requested credit references from the defendants, bankers, on a mutual client, E. Ltd. The defendants stated that E. Ltd was a respectably constituted firm and was considered good, but they also stated that this statement was made without responsibility on their part. As a result of this statement, the plaintiff granted credit to E. Ltd on several advertising contracts. Shortly afterwards, E. Ltd went into liquidation, and the plaintiffs were unable to recover £17,000 owed to them. The plaintiffs, therefore, sued the defendants on their negligent statement.

Held: The defendants owed the plaintiffs a duty of care, because the plaintiffs relied on the skill and judgment of the defendants, and the defendants knew, or ought to have known, of this reliance. However, although the defendants had broken their duty, they were not held to be liable, because the reference was given with a disclaimer of responsibility.

13. The party misled may:

(i) rescind the contract, subject to being awarded damages in lieu of rescission by the court;

(ii) refuse to perform his part of the contract; or

(iii) recover damages for any loss suffered by him.

• Loss of the right of rescission

14. Rescission allows the parties to a contract to be restored to their position as it was before the contract was made. This remedy is not available when:

(a) the party misled affirms the contract after discovering the true facts;

(b) a court awards damages in lieu of rescission;

(c) restoration to the pre-contract state of affairs is impossible;

(d) lapse of time, in the case of innocent misrepresentation, implies affirmation; or

(e) the rights of third parties, such as creditors of an insolvent company, would be prejudiced.

IMPORTANT CASES

Numbers in brackets refer to paragraphs of this chapter

PROGRESS TEST

Numbers in brackets refer to paragraphs of this chapter

1. Define a misrepresentation. (1)
2. Distinguish between a false statement of opinion and a misrepresentation. (2)
3. When may silence be construed as misrepresentation? (3)

4. Can a person avoid a contract if he did not know there had been a misrepresentation? (4)
5. Explain the difference between fraudulent and negligent misrepresentation. (7, 11)
6. What are the remedies available to a party who has been misled by innocent misrepresentation? (10)
7. Describe the circumstances which may lead to negligent misrepresentation. (12)
8. When may a party misled by misrepresentation be unable to rescind the contract? (14)

chapter 16

MISTAKE IN CONTRACT

Topics covered in this chapter are:

- Mistake as to the identity of the subject matter
- Mistake as to the identity of the other party
- Mistake as to the existence of the subject matter
- Mistake as to the existence of a fundamental state of affairs
- Mistake as to the nature of a document

Summary of the chapter

As a general rule, mistake will not justify rescinding a contract concluded under such a misapprehension. This chapter considers the circumstances under which a contract may be void or voidable for mistake.

1. In general, a mistake made by one, or both, parties to a contract will not affect its validity. Offer and acceptance establish the terms of the contract; what the parties think or intend should not override those terms. However, in certain restricted circumstances, a contract may be rendered void or voidable. This will only apply if the parties contract under a fundamental mistake of fact, such that there was never any real agreement between them.

• Mistake as to the identity of the subject matter

2. If *A* believes that the contract refers to something, and *B* believes it refers to something else of the same nature, then the contract is void, as the terms are uncertain.

Case: Raffles v Wichelhaus (1864)

The plaintiff agreed, in London, to sell to the defendant a cargo of cotton, which was to arrive 'Ex *Peerless* from Bombay'. There happened to be two ships called *Peerless* with a cargo of cotton from Bombay; one in October and the other in December. The defendant intended the contract to refer to the October sailing, and the plaintiff to the December sailing.

Held: The defendant was able to show that there was ambiguity, and that he intended to refer to the October sailing. The contract was, therefore, void.

3. Mistake as to quality of subject matter does not make the contract void. If each party is unaware that the other intends subject matter of a different quality, he may perform his side of a contract according to his intention, regardless of the other party expecting something different.

Case: Smith v Hughes (1871)

The plaintiff was shown a sample of oats by the defendant. Believing them to be old oats, he bought them. The defendant was, in fact, selling new oats, and he was unaware of the plaintiff's impression. When the plaintiff discovered his mistake, he refused to accept the new oats.

Held: The mistake was one of quality, and as such did not make the contract void. Although the parties were at cross purposes, it was not to such an extent that there was no agreement. The defendant, therefore, was entitled to deliver and to receive payment for his oats.

- **Mistake as to the identity of the other party**

4. Unless identity of the parties is essential to the contract, mistaken identity does not render a contract void.

5. Where a buyer fraudulently adopts the identity of another existing person known to the seller, with whom the seller intends to make the contract, the sale to the actual buyer is rendered void.

Case: Cundy v Lindsay (1878)

The plaintiff received an order for handkerchiefs from a dishonest person called Blenkarn, who gave his address as 37 Wood Street. He signed the letter so that his name appeared to be Blenkiron & Co., a respectable firm known to the plaintiff, who traded at 123 Wood Street. The plaintiff dispatched the handkerchiefs to Blenkiron & Co. on credit at 37 Wood Street, where Blenkarn possessed them. Blenkarn sold the handkerchiefs to the defendant, and absconded with the proceeds, without paying the amount due to the plaintiff. The plaintiff subsequently sued the defendant to recover the value of the handkerchiefs.

Held: The plaintiff intended to deal with Blenkiron & Co. and, therefore, no title could pass to Blenkarn. So, he could not pass title to the defendant. The mistake over the address was considered reasonable, so the defendant was liable to the plaintiff for the value of the handkerchiefs.

6. Where a buyer fraudulently adopts the identity of a non-existent person, the seller cannot make a mistake as to identity. The contract, therefore, is only voidable for fraud.

Case: King's Norton Metal Co. v Elderidge Merrett & Co. (1897)

The plaintiff received an order for wire from Hallam & Co, an alias for a dishonest person called Wallis. The letterhead indicated that Hallam & Co. had substantial premises and overseas branches. The plaintiff dispatched the wire on credit to Hallam & Co. Wallis possessed the wire and resold it to the defendant. The plaintiff sued the defendant for the value of the wire.

Held: The plaintiff had, in fact, intended to contract with the writer of the letter, since Wallis and Hallam & Co. were one and the same. Thus, the contract was only voidable for fraud. Wallis acquired title of the wire and passed it to the defendant before the contract between the plaintiff and Wallis was rescinded. The defendant, therefore, was not liable for the value of the wire.

7. Mistake as to identity cannot be made when the parties deal face to face. There is a presumption that the parties do intend to deal with each other. In such a situation, a person can only make a mistake as to the attributes of the other party. So, the contract will only be voidable for misrepresentation, and the aggrieved party must avoid the contract at the earliest opportunity or else suffer the loss.

Case: Lewis v Averay (1972) UNILATERAL MISTAKE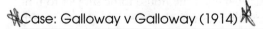

A dishonest person proposed to purchase a car from the plaintiff and to pay for it by cheque. He claimed to be a well-known television actor, and produced a false pass from the studios bearing a photograph which resembled the aforementioned actor. The plaintiff then accepted the cheque and allowed him to take away the car. When the cheque was dishonoured, the plaintiff attempted to recover the car from the defendant who had purchased it in good faith from the dishonest person.

Held: The plaintiff could not recover the car. The contract between the plaintiff and the dishonest person was not void, but only voidable, as a result of the fraudulently induced mistake. The dishonest person had transferred the voidable title to the defendant.

• Mistake as to the existence of the subject matter
8. If the parties make a contract relating to subject matter which, unknown to them both, does not exist, or which no longer exists, e.g. it has been destroyed prior to the contract, there can be no contract. It is void.

Case: Galloway v Galloway (1914)

A man and woman entered into a separation agreement, believing that they were married. Neither of them knew that, at the time of their marriage ceremony, the man's first wife was still alive.

Held: The separation agreement was void for mistake, because the 'marriage', which formed the basis of the agreement, was null and void.

Case: Couturier v Hastie (1852)

The plaintiff made a contract in London with the defendant to purchase a cargo of corn, which was being shipped from Salonika. Unknown to either party, the cargo of corn had, in fact, been sold in transit at the time the contract was made, as it was deteriorating due to the weather.

Held: There was no contract between the plaintiff and the defendant, because it had related to non-existent subject matter.

9. A contract is also void if, by mistake, a party purports to buy his own property. In such cases, a contract is void because there is nothing to buy.

Case: Cochrane v Willis (1865)

The defendant was entitled, under a family settlement, to inherit property on his brother's death. His brother had become bankrupt and, to prevent the property from being sold to a third party, the defendant agreed to buy the property from his brother's bankrupt estate. Unknown to the defendant and the plaintiff, his brother's trustee, the property had already passed to the defendant by inheritance, because his brother had died before the contract was made.

Held: The defendant could not buy what already belonged to him. The contract, therefore, was void.

• Mistake as to the existence of a fundamental state of affairs

10. If both parties are equally mistaken on some fundamental point, such that had this state of affairs not existed, the contract would not have been made, the contract is void.

11. However, if both parties are equally mistaken concerning some quality in the subject matter bargained for, such contracts are voidable rather than void, and may be set aside on such terms as the court sees fit.

Case: Grist v Bailey (1967)

The plaintiff bought a house, which was occupied by a tenant, from the defendant for £850. Both parties believed the house to be subject to rent control. It later turned out that this was not the case, and so was worth £2,250.

Held: The contract was voidable. The defendant was entitled to rescind the contract, with the condition attached that the plaintiff should get first option to buy the house at the current market price.

12. Moreover, if subsequent facts become known which, although relevant, do not affect the subject matter of the contract when it was first made. The contract remains valid.

✳Case: Bell v Lever Bros Ltd (1932) ✳

The defendants wished to terminate the employment of the plaintiff, its managing director. The plaintiff negotiated a payment of £30,000 in consideration for the cancellation of his employment contract. At a later stage, the defendants discovered that the plaintiff had used inside information to make profits on his own account. This was serious misconduct, which would have entitled the defendants to dismiss him without compensation. The defendants claimed that there had been a mistake as to the existence of a fundamental state of affairs, since the employment contract for which they had paid £30,000 was, in fact, valueless to the plaintiff. They sued to recover the compensation paid.

Held: The defendants could not recover compensation paid to the plaintiff, because there was not a sufficiently fundamental mistake on the part of either party at the time of the contract.

• Mistake as to the nature of a document✳

12. In general, if a person signs a document, he is bound by it, even if he does not read or understand the document. However, if a contract is signed by one party in the mistaken belief that he is signing a document of a fundamentally different nature, such a mistake will render the contract void. The mistaken party will be able to successfully plead *non est factum* (it is not my deed).

13. The following conditions must be satisfied in repudiating a signed document as *non est factum*:

(a) the signature must have been induced by fraud;
(b) there must be a fundamental difference between the legal effect of the document signed and that which the person who signed it believed it to have; and
(c) the party who signed the document must prove that he acted with reasonable care.

Case: Foster v Mackinnon (1869)

The defendant, an elderly man of feeble sight, was asked to sign a guarantee. The document put before him was a bill of exchange for £3,000, which he mistakenly signed as acceptor. The bill of exchange was subsequently negotiated to the plaintiff. The defendant repudiated it, raising a defence of *non est factum*.

Held: As the defendant was not negligent in endorsing the bill of exchange, and the document signed was so different from what he believed it to be, he was not liable.

Case: Lewis v Clay (1897)

The defendant was asked to sign two documents as a witness. Apart from the spaces for the signatures, the rest of the documents were covered. The reason given to the defendant for this was that the documents were of a private nature. The defendant, in fact, signed two promissory notes, which he later repudiated, claiming a defence of *non est factum*.

Held: Although the defendant was unable to say what type of document he thought he had signed, the defence of *non est factum* applied. He was held not liable.

IMPORTANT CASES

Numbers in brackets refer to paragraphs of this chapter

Raffles v Wichelhaus (1864) ....(2)
Smith v Hughes (1871) ....(3)
Cundy v Lindsay (1878) ....(5)
King's Norton Metal Co. v Eldridge, Merrett & Co. Ltd (1897).......(6)
Lewis v Averay (1972)..(7)
Galloway v Galloway (1914) ....(8)
Couturier v Hastie (1852)..(8)
Cochrane v Willis (1865) ....(9)
Grist v Bailey (1967)..(11)
Bell v Lever Bros Ltd (1932)...(12)
Foster v Makinnon (1869) ....(13)
Lewis v Clay (1897) ....(13)

PROGRESS TEST

Numbers in brackets refer to paragraphs of this chapter

1. Does mistake as to (i) identity, or (ii) quality of the subject matter render a contract void? (2, 3)

2. What are the consequences of a buyer fraudulently adopting the identity of a non-existent person while entering into a contract with a seller? (6)
3. If the subject matter of a contract no longer exists, is agreement between the unsuspecting parties binding? (8)
4. Can a person contract by mistake to buy his own property? (9)
5. Explain what is meant by the defence of *non est factum*, and outline the conditions which must be satisfied in order for such a claim to be successful. (12, 13)

chapter 17

DURESS AND UNDUE INFLUENCE

Topics covered in this chapter are:

- Duress
- Undue influence
- Unconscionable bargains

Summary of the chapter:

A contract may be voidable if the consent of one of the parties is not freely given. This chapter examines the circumstances under which force and pressure may render a contract voidable.

1. It is presumed in law that any agreement between contracting parties is made voluntarily. Consequently, if an agreement is brought about by improper force or pressure, this will undermine the agreement, making the contract voidable.

Duress

2. Duress is the actual or threatened violence to, or the unlawful imprisonment of, the contracting party, his or her spouse, parents or children. Its effect, if proved, is that the contract is voidable.

Case: Cumming v Ince (1847)

An old woman was induced to make a settlement of her property in favour of a relative by a threat of lawful detention in a mental home.

Held: The contract was voidable on the grounds of duress.

Case: Griffith v Griffith (1944)

A young man was induced into marrying a young woman he was alleged to have made pregnant. The woman's mother, his own father and the local priest pressed him into entering a contract of marriage. Under a threat of imprisonment, the young man agreed to the marriage. Later, it became known that he was not the child's father and he petitioned for a decree of nullity.

Held: The contract of marriage was voidable for duress, but would have been upheld were he the father of the child.

3. In older cases, a threat to a person's goods or property has been held to be insufficient grounds for duress. In some recent English decisions, however, the courts have set aside contracts made under economic duress.

Case: The Atlantic Baron (1979)

The parties had agreed upon a price to be paid for a ship. Shortly afterwards, a currency devaluation prompted the seller to claim a ten per cent increase in the original price. When the purchaser refused to pay, the seller threatened to terminate the contract. As a result of this threat, the purchaser reluctantly agreed to the price increase.

Held: The threat by the seller amounted to economic duress, a form of undue influence, thereby rendering the contract voidable.

• Undue influence

4. The equitable doctrine of undue influence enables a court to set aside contracts where an agreement has been reached by excessive pressure, which falls short of duress, being brought to bear on an individual by a potential beneficiary or third party.

5. There is a presumption of undue influence where the parties to a contract are in a special relationship with each other, such that one of them, by reason of the confidence placed in him, is able to take unfair advantage of the other. Undue influence is presumed in contracts between a parent and child, an accountant and client, a trustee and beneficiary, a doctor and patient, a religious adviser and disciple, a guardian and a ward, among others.

6. Where the presumption of undue influence is made, the onus of proof is on the person in the dominant position to show that the other party expressed free and independent judgment. He can do this by showing that the weaker party had independent legal advice, that there was a full disclosure of all the relevant facts and that the consideration was adequate.

Case: White v Meade (1840)

The plaintiff, an eighteen-year-old girl, entered a religious institution as a lodger. The defendants induced the plaintiff to take vows, without taking guidance from her brother, and to transfer property to the religious order. The deed for the transfer of property was prepared by the legal adviser to the religious institution.

Held: The plaintiff was able to set aside the transfer of property.

Case: Croker v Croker (1870)

A son transferred property in favour of his father and subsequently sought to have the transfer set aside.

Held: The father was unable to prove that his son had exercised free will in transferring the property, so the contract was set aside.

7. Even if the presumption of undue influence does not arise automatically, it is possible to prove from the conduct of the parties in their dealings that one, in fact, did have undue influence.

Case: Williams v Bayley (1866)

A father mortgaged property to a bank because a bank official had hinted at prosecuting his son for forgery of promissory notes with the father's signature.

Held: There had been undue influence, and, as a result, the agreement to execute the mortgage was set aside.

• Unconscionable bargains

8. A court will intervene in a contract, or other transaction, in cases in which one party is in a position to victimise the weaker party. Where an advantage is taken of a weak, distressed or mentally deficient person in negotiating a contract, the court will give relief against such unconscionable bargains.

9. The party wishing to uphold the contract must justify its fairness. Otherwise, the court will regard it as an unconscionable bargain, and will set it aside.

Case: Grealish v Murphy (1946)

An elderly, illiterate and mentally deficient man transferred his farm, after consulting a solicitor, at under its value in favour of a younger man, who was unrelated.

Held: The bargain was invalid, because it was so improvident that no reasonable person would have entered into it. The solicitor had not done everything to advise fully on the implications of the transaction, since he was unaware of all the material facts and of the extent of his client's mental deficiency.

Case: Smyth v Smyth (1978)

A young man, with a drink problem, sold part of the property of his trust to his trustee. The sale took five years to complete and one solicitor acted for both parties.

Held: The bargain was neither improvident nor unconscionable, because the seller first raised the question of sale, the consideration paid was adequate and the length of time to complete the sale gave the seller plenty of time for reflection. The contract was, therefore, valid.

IMPORTANT CASES

Numbers in brackets refer to paragraphs of this chapter

PROGRESS TEST

Numbers in brackets refer to paragraphs of this chapter

1. What is the difference between duress and undue influence? (2, 4)
2. Explain how a presumption of undue influence is established. (5)
3. How can the dominant party prove that the other party expressed free and independent judgment in making the bargain? (6)
4. Describe how a court may grant relief against unconscionable bargains. (8, 9)

chapter 18

CONTRACTS ILLEGAL OR CONTRARY TO PUBLIC POLICY

Topics covered in this chapter are:

- Contracts void by statute
- Contracts illegal and void at common law

- Contracts in unreasonable restraint of trade
- Contracts in restraint of trade

Summary of the chapter

The law refuses to give effect to a contract for an illegal purpose, or for a purpose which offends public policy. This chapter examines the different types of such contracts.

1. A court will not enforce some types of contract because they are invalidated by statute or because they are prohibited under common law, since these are contrary to public policy. The most important examples of the latter type are those in unreasonable restraint of trade.

• Contracts void by statute

2. Some contracts are proscribed by statute. The following examples provide a sample of such contracts:

(a) Contracts of insurance which fail to disclose an insurable interest are void under the Insurance Act, 1936.

(b) Contracts of hire-purchase which are not evidenced in writing are void under the Hire Purchase Acts, 1946–80.

(c) Contracts by way of wagering or gambling are void under the Gaming and Lotteries Act, 1956.

(d) Contracts for the conveyance of the family home, without the prior consent in writing of the other spouse, are void under the Family Home Protection Act, 1976.

• Contracts illegal and void at common law

3. Contracts which will not be enforced because they are contrary to public policy include:

    (i)   contracts to commit a crime, tort or fraud;
    (ii) contracts promoting sexual immorality;
    (iii) contracts which detract from the institution of marriage;

(iv) contracts which impede the administration of justice;
(v) contracts which serve to defraud the Revenue Commissioners;
(vi) contracts which serve to corrupt public officials;
(vii) contracts in unreasonable restraint of trade.

Contracts to commit a crime, tort or fraud

4. Such agreements are obviously contrary to public policy.

Case: Everett v Williams (1725)

Both parties to the contract were highwaymen who turned to the courts seeking assistance concerning a 'partnership' arrangement.
Held: The contract was originally illegal and, therefore, void.

Case: Daly v Daly (1870)

The defendant had been declared bankrupt, but had obtained such an order by fraud. The plaintiff, one of his creditors, aware of this fact, agreed not to attempt to have the bankruptcy set aside on condition that his debt was paid in full. A cheque for the full amount was given to the plaintiff, but was subsequently dishonoured.
Held: The contract was contrary to public policy, as the consideration, i.e. the undertaking not to attempt to have the bankruptcy set aside, was illegal.

Contracts promoting sexual immorality

5. Even if the conduct contemplated by the contract is not in itself illegal, a contract which promotes sexual immorality will be held to be illegal.

Case: Pearce v Brooks (1866)

The plaintiff hired out a carriage to a prostitute who, to the knowledge of the owner, intended to parade along the streets in the carriage as a means of soliciting clients, and would pay for the carriage out of her immoral earnings. She later refused to pay the agreed amount and the plaintiff sued to recover it.
Held: The plaintiff's knowledge of the immoral purpose behind the contract rendered the contract illegal and void.

Contracts which detract from the institution of marriage

6. The courts regard it as a matter of public interest to uphold the sanctity of marriage. This is enforced by Article 41 of the Constitution. Contracts in restraint of marriage, contracts for future separation and marriage brokage contracts, whereby one person agrees to procure a marriage for a money payment, are void.

Case: Williamson v Gihan (1805)

The plaintiff contracted to pay £500 to the defendant in return for assistance in helping a young lady to elope so he, the plaintiff, could marry her. The money was to be paid from his wife's estate, and when the plaintiff rescinded his promise, the defendant sued for the amount agreed.

Held: The plaintiff was not entitled to fetter his wife's property. In these circumstances, the contract was void because it was illegal at common law.

Contracts which impede the administration of justice

7. Contracts which serve to frustrate the administration of justice are not of themselves criminal, but they are illegal and cannot give rise to enforceable contractual obligations.

Case: Brady v Flood (1841)

The plaintiff paid a sum of money to the defendant in return for a promise to have criminal charges of conspiracy against the plaintiff's son dropped. The plaintiff later sued to recover the amount.

Held: The judge refused to hear litigation on the transaction. He stated, 'I will not try this case. You are parties to an illegal contract and, whoever has got the money, I will allow him to keep it.'

Contracts which serve to defraud the Revenue Commissioners

8. The courts will not enforce a contract which defrauds the Revenue Commissioners through, for example, a misstatement of consideration, or a collective arrangement between an employer and an employee in order to reduce his liability to PRSI contributions, because it is void as illegal at common law.

Case: Lewis v Squash Ireland Ltd (1983)

The plaintiff brought an action for unfair dismissal against the defendants, his former employers. The employers and employee had been party to an agreement whereby the payment of salary was treated in the company's books as 'expenses', in an attempt to avoid the payment of income tax and social insurance contributions.

Held: The claim for unfair dismissal was not upheld because this collusive arrangement had been designed to defraud the Revenue Commissioner, and was consequently void as illegal at common law.

Contracts which serve to corrupt public officials

9. A contract to promote corruption in public life is void as being illegal at common law.

Case: Dublin Corporation v Hayes (1876)

The defendant, on being appointed Marshall of the City of Dublin, a position which also gave him the post of Registrar of Pawnbrokers, agreed to accept a fixed salary and to hand over to the treasure of the plaintiffs those fees he was entitled to collect. He was subsequently sued by the plaintiff for failure to comply with the arrangement.

Held: The promise to transfer the fees was void because the appointment was adjudged by the court to have been made in exchange for the defendant's promise to pay over the aforementioned monies, thereby promoting corruption among public officials.

• Contracts in unreasonable restraint of trade

10. A contract in restraint of trade is one whereby the action of one party to a contract restricts the other party from freely exercising his trade, profession or calling in such a way and with such persons as he chooses. Such contracts are prima facie void, as they are contrary to public interest.

11. We shall now examine in detail the circumstances under which a restraint of trade can be justified and be enforceable.

• Contracts in restraint of trade

12. A restriction on the freedom of an individual to trade will be upheld if it is shown to be in the interest of both parties and the public. The onus of proof in any action in respect of contracts, or, more correctly, clauses in restraint of trade lies with the party trying to enforce it.

13. A restraint of trade clause may be justified and enforceable if:

   (i) the person who imposes it has a genuine interest to protect;
  (ii) the restraint is reasonable between the parties as a protection of that interest; and
 (iii) the restraint is also reasonable to the public at large.

14. The main categories of contracts in restraint of trade which may be upheld as being reasonable are as follows:

(a) restrictions imposed on ex-employees;
(b) restrictions imposed on the sellers of a business;
(c) solus (exclusive dealing) agreements;
(d) resale price maintenance agreements.

Helen Joy

Restrictions imposed on ex-employees

15. Any restraint imposed upon an employee's freedom to take up other employment, or to carry on business on his own account, after leaving the employer's service, will not be upheld unless it can be justified.

16. A restraint must be no wider than is necessary to protect the employer's trade secrets or business connections. Therefore, if a restraint is imposed on an employee who is not in a position to gain the confidence of his employer's customers or who has no access to his employer's secrets, it will be void. Furthermore, if it is excessive as regards the prohibited trades, the geographical area to which it applies, or the time for which the restraint is to last, it is also void. The reasonableness of the extent and duration of the restraint depends on the type of business to be protected.

Case: Mulligan v Corr (1925)

The defendant, a solicitor's apprentice, agreed that on leaving the plaintiff's employment he would not practise within thirty miles of Ballina and Charlestown, and within twenty miles of Ballaghaderreen. The plaintiff sought an injunction to compel the defendant to abide by the terms of the agreement.

Held: Even if severance of the restriction regarding practice within twenty miles of Ballaghaderreen were to take place, the geographical area was too large and went far beyond what was reasonably required for the protection of a solicitor's practice.

Case: Fitch v Dewes (1921)

The defendant, a former law clerk, had qualified as a solicitor while being employed by the defendant. On the commencement of his employment he had contracted not to practise as a solicitor within seven miles of the Town Hall at Tamworth. The plaintiff sought an injunction to prevent the defendant from a breach of the employment contract.

Held: The restraint on the employee was reasonable in the above circumstances because, though unlimited as to the duration, it confined the restraint to a reasonable space.

Case: Macken v O'Reilly (1978)

The plaintiff, an international show-jumper, challenged a rule of the Equestrian Federation of Ireland which obliged competitors representing Ireland in international competitions to ride only Irish-bred horses.

Held: This rule was not an unreasonable restraint, since it was designed to protect the public interest, i.e. to protect the Irish half-bred horse industry.

Case: ECI European Chemical Industries Ltd v Bell (1981)

The defendant was an industrial chemist who, in the process of training and employment, acquired trade secrets from his employer. He had agreed that if he were to leave the employment, he would abstain from using these trade secrets for his own or another competitor's profit for a period of two years. After over six years, he gave notice of termination of his employment with the plaintiffs and proposed to commence employment immediately with one of the plaintiff's competitors. The plaintiff sought an injunction to prevent this course of action.

Held: An interlocutory injunction was granted. The restraint of trade was prima facie valid, since the aforementioned interests were ones which an employer is entitled to protect.

Restrictions imposed on the sellers of a business
17. A restraint on the seller of a business from doing business with his old customers or clients will be more readily upheld in favour of the buyer, because he has paid goodwill for it. The restraint will only be effective if there is a genuine sale of the goodwill of the business and the restraint is not excessive.

Case: Nordenfelt v Maxim Nordenfelt Guns and Ammunition Co. Ltd (1894)

The defendants, owners of an armaments business, sold it to the plaintiff and agreed in writing not to carry on a similar business anywhere in the world for a duration of twenty-five years, except on behalf of the purchasers.

Held: The restraint was neither excessive nor contrary to public policy, and was, therefore, held to be valid.

Case: British Concrete Co. v Scheiff (1921)

The defendants, who carried out a small business of making a single type of steel road reinforcement, sold his business to the plaintiffs, manufacturers of road reinforcements used throughout the U.K. The defendant agreed in writing not to compete with the plaintiffs in the sale or manufacture of road reinforcements in any part of the U.K.

Held: The restraint was too wide, because it attempted to protect the plaintiffs from more than what they had bought. The restraint of trade was, therefore, void.

Solus (exclusive dealing) agreements

18. A solus agreement is the name given to a contract by which a trader agrees to restrict his orders to one supplier.

19. In general, such exclusive dealing agreements are valid since the parties bargain in a position of equal strength and do not create a market structure detrimental to the public. The duration, therefore, of such restraints is usually the most important factor in assessing the reasonableness of these agreements.

Case: McEllistrem v Ballymacelligot Co-operative Agricultural and Dairy Society (1919)

The plaintiff was a member of a Kerry co-op., which had been formed to develop and improve dairy farming in the district. The members of the co-op. were bound by its rules to supply all their milk to the co-op., and were precluded from supplying any other local creamery.

Held: The restraint of trade went further than necessary in protecting the supply of milk to the co-op. The contract was therefore invalid due to its unreasonableness.

Resale price maintenance agreements

20. Agreements between producers or retailers, which keep the price of goods or services at a certain level, are valid unless such agreements are designed to produce a monopoly or the price level maintained is unreasonable.

Case: Cade & Sons Ltd v John Daly & Co. Ltd (1910)

The members of the South of Ireland Mineral Water Manufacturers and Bottlers Trade Protection Association agreed that no member would sell alcohol or minerals below fixed prices for a period of six months, within sixteen miles of the city of Cork. The defendant, a member of the Association, sought to have this arrangement overturned as being unreasonable.

Held: The restraint was binding on the defendant. The agreement was reasonably made with the intention of protecting local trade and, therefore, valid at common law.

IMPORTANT CASES

Numbers in brackets refer to paragraphs of this chapter

PROGRESS TEST

Numbers in brackets refer to paragraphs of this chapter

1. Give three examples of contracts which are void by statute. (2)
2. What is the implication of a contract which serves to frustrate the administration of justice? (7)
3. Define a contract in restraint of trade. (10)
4. What must be shown to justify and enforce a restraint of trade? (13)
5. How can a restriction imposed on an ex-employee's freedom to take up other employment, or to carry on business on his own account, be justified? (16)
6. Why will a restriction on the seller of a business from trading with his old customers be more readily upheld in favour of the buyer? (17)
7. What is a solus agreement, and how is the doctrine of restraint of trade applied to such a contract? (18, 19)
8. When will a price maintenance agreement be invalid? (20)

chapter 19

CAPACITY TO CONTRACT

Topics covered in this chapter are:

- Minors
- Corporations
- Mental patients and drunks

Summary of the chapter

The law seeks to protect certain persons by limiting their legal capacity to enter contracts. This chapter examines those legal persons who are unable to contract freely.

1. In order that an agreement be a valid contract, both parties must have capacity to contract. In general, all persons have full capacity to enter into legally binding contracts. Different rules apply, however, to minors, corporations, mental patients and drunks. These have only restricted capacity and contracts made by them may be valid, voidable or void.

• Minors

2. A minor (or infant) is, by virtue of the Age of Majority Act, 1985, an unmarried person who has not reached the age of eighteen.

Valid contracts of a minor

3. A minor may enter binding contracts for necessary goods and services, and they may enter beneficial contracts of employment or apprenticeship.

4. Necessary goods, or 'necessaries', are defined as goods suitable to the condition in life of the particular minor and to his actual requirements at the time of sale and delivery. The goods (or services) must, therefore, satisfy a double test of 'suitability' and 'need' if they are to be necessaries. The test in each case is what is reasonable for that particular minor, and the burden of proof rests with the seller.

5. The seller must first prove that the goods are capable of being necessaries. An item of 'mere luxury', for example, a racehorse, cannot be a necessary. However, a luxurious item of utility, such as a gold watch, may be defined as such. This broad definition of necessaries has been adopted to give protection to suppliers who give credit to minors from wealthy families.

6. The seller must then prove that the goods are, in fact, necessary for the particular minor in question. Necessaries do not include goods with which the minor is already well supplied, and so does not need any more. A minor is not liable if he has an adequate supply of the goods, even if the supplier did not know this.

Case: Nash v Inman (1908)

The plaintiff, a tailor, sued the defendant, a Cambridge undergraduate, for the price of clothes, including eleven fancy waistcoats, which he had supplied to the minor over a period of nine months.

Held: The clothes were suitable for the defendant's use, but the plaintiff was unable to show that the minor was not adequately supplied at the time. The clothes, therefore, were not necessaries, and the plaintiff could not recover the monies due to him.

7. Beneficial contracts of employment or apprenticeship are also binding on a minor if they may reasonably be regarded as for the benefit of the minor. If the terms, on the whole, are too harsh or oppressive, they will be invalid.

Case: Doyle v White City Stadium (1935)

Jack Doyle, who was a minor, obtained a licence to compete as a professional boxer from the British Boxing Board of Control. The terms of the licence provided that should the licensee be disqualified for a foul blow (as, in fact, happened) his portion of the purse would be forfeited. The plaintiff challenged the terms of the licence, alleging that as the contract was not for his benefit, they could not bind him.

Held: The terms of the licence were beneficial as a whole, since it was generally in the plaintiff's interests that illegal blows be prohibited. This was true even though on this occasion the terms operated against him. Therefore, the contract was held binding on the defendant.

Case: De Francesco v Barnum (1890)

A minor entered into an apprenticeship for stage dancing with the plaintiff. The terms of the contract provided that she was entirely at the disposal of the plaintiff; that she would only get paid if he actually employed her; that she could not get married during the apprenticeship and that his consent was required before she could accept any other professional engagement with the defendant without obtaining the plaintiff's consent. The minor subsequently accepted a professional engagement with the defendant, who was sued by the plaintiff in the tort of inducing a breach of contract.

Held: The contract was, on the whole, unreasonably harsh and oppressive and, as such, could not be described as being beneficial to the minor. It was held to be invalid.

Voidable contracts of a minor

8. Certain long-term contracts will be binding on both parties, unless they are avoided by the minor before, or within a reasonable time after, reaching the age of eighteen. The other party cannot avoid the contract.

9. Contracts voidable by a minor are contracts whereby a minor acquires interests of a continuing nature and undertakes obligations incidental to them. These include:

(a) contracts involving land—e.g. leases;
(b) purchases of shares in a company;
(c) partnership agreements; and
(d) marriage settlements.

10. Although a minor may repudiate such contracts, he may not be able to recover money or property which he has paid or transferred under the contract, unless he has received no consideration whatsoever for it.

Case: Steinberg v Scala (1925)

The plaintiff, a minor, applied for and was allotted shares in the defendant company. When she was requested to pay the balance of the purchase price, she attempted to avoid the contract and recover the money that she had already paid.

Held: The plaintiff had the right to rescind the contract and be removed from the register of members. However, she could not recover what she had already paid, because she had received some consideration, such as the right to receive dividends and the right to vote at company meetings.

Case: Blake v Concannon (1871)

The defendant, a minor, had leased land from the plaintiff and enjoyed its use up until the time he reached the age of majority, whereupon he repudiated the contract and refused to pay rent due.

Held: The defendant was entitled to repudiate the lease, but was liable for the rent up to the date of the repudiation.

Void contracts of a minor

11. Certain types of contract which are entered into by a minor are held to be absolutely void. Such contracts cannot be confirmed by the minor or enforced against him.

12. The Infants Relief Act, 1874 states that the following contracts are absolutely void:

(a) contracts for the repayment of money lent, or to be lent, to an infant (minor);
(b) contracts for goods supplied, or to be supplied (other than necessaries), to an infant.

13. The Betting and Loans (Infants) Act, 1892 makes void any new agreement by a person after he reaches the age of majority to repay a previous loan contracted during minority.

14. As with voidable contracts which are avoided, the minor cannot recover money or property under a void contract which has been performed, unless there has been total failure of consideration.

Case: Valentini v Canali (1889)

The plaintiff, a minor, contracted to lease a house and to buy the furniture therein for £102. He paid part of the sum agreed, namely £68, on account, and after living in the house and using the furniture for some time, he subsequently sued to recover the money he had paid.

Held: The plaintiff had taken the benefit of a void contract for the sale of goods. He could not, therefore, retain the goods and recover the money he had paid for them.

• Corporations

15. Companies formed under the Companies Acts and statutory corporations are limited by their constitutions, contained in the objects clause of the Memorandum of Association, and incorporating statutes respectively, to entering only certain types of contracts. If they make contracts outside these limits, the contracts are said to be *ultra vires* (beyond the power) and void.

Case: In re Bansha Woollen Mill Co. Ltd (1888)

A shareholder and director loaned money to the company, which was empowered by its Memorandum to borrow money but restricted by its Articles as to the amount of such borrowing. He later sought the recovery of his money but was refused on the grounds that the company had been acting *ultra vires*.

Held: The party who loaned the money was privy to the activities of the company, and ought to have known the objects of the company. Since the shareholder and director, therefore, ought to have known that the company was acting *ultra vires*, he was not entitled to recover his money.

16. The harshness of the *ultra vires* doctrine preventing a third party, honestly dealing with a company, from being able to sue on a contract, has led towards certain statutory reform.

17. Under s.8, The Companies Act, 1963, a company cannot defeat the claim of a third party contracting with it, unless it can be shown that the third party was actually aware that the company was acting *ultra vires*.

18. This provision has since been joined by the European Communities (Companies) Regulations, 1973, whereby contracts made in good faith with directors of companies are deemed to be valid. Where the contract is *ultra vires*, it will still be binding on the company, but the director(s) will be personally liable to the company for any loss suffered as a result of entering into such a contract.

19. A contract may still be *ultra vires* and void where the third party is supplied with a copy of the Memorandum and mistakenly believes it to authorise the transaction.

Case: Northern Bank Finance Corporation Ltd v Quinn and Achates Investment Co. (1979)

The plaintiffs contracted to loan the first defendant money on the condition that an officer of the second defendant would guarantee the loan by the mortgage of some of the company's property. An officer of the plaintiffs inspected the Memorandum and Articles of Association, but failed to appreciate that the company was not empowered to guarantee loans. When the first defendant defaulted, the company argued that the transaction, namely signature of a guarantee, was *ultra vires*.

Held: The plaintiffs were aware of the contents of the Memorandum, but failed to appreciate their significance. The plaintiffs' action against the company was dismissed.

• Mental patients and drunks

20. If a person is insane or drunk when he enters into a contract, the contract is voidable if it can be shown that:

(a) he was at the time incapable of understanding the nature of the contract; and
(b) the other party knew, or ought to have known, of his disability.

21. The burden of proof is on the party suffering from the incapacity to prove the knowledge of the other party.

22. A contract made by a drunk or mentally disordered person may be ratified on recovery to a sober or lucid state, and thereby become completely valid.

Case: Matthews v Baxter (1873)

The defendant, while in a drunken state, contracted to buy some houses from the plaintiff. He later ratified the contract when he became sober.

Held: The contract was binding on the defendant.

Case: Hassard v Smith (1872)

The plaintiff leased property, which included land, a house and garden, to the defendant for a period of five years. The plaintiff later attempted to have the lease set aside on the grounds that he was of unsound mind at the date of the lease and had let the property at an undervalue.

Held: The contract was an honest and bona fide transaction, and was completely executed. Assuming that the plaintiff was insane at the time of the contract, there was no evidence to show that the defendant had any actual knowledge of this fact.

23. The Sale of Goods Act, 1893 provides that when necessaries are supplied, with the intention of obtaining payment, to a mental patient or drunk, he must pay a reasonable price for them in any case. Necessaries, as outlined before, are goods suitable to the condition in life of such a person and to his actual requirements at the time of sale and delivery.

IMPORTANT CASES

Numbers in brackets refer to paragraphs of this chapter

PROGRESS TEST

Numbers in brackets refer to paragraphs of this chapter

1. Define a minor. (2)
2. When may a minor be bound to pay for goods? (3, 4, 5, 6)
3. Under what circumstances may a minor be bound by a contract for employment or apprenticeship? (7)
4. Give three examples of contracts which are voidable by a minor. (9)
5. Explain the circumstances under which a contract entered into by a minor can be held to be absolutely void. Can a minor recover money or property under such a contract? (12, 13, 14)
6. What is the doctrine of *ultra vires*? (15)
7. When is a mental patient or drunk not bound by his contract? (20)

chapter 20

DISCHARGE OF CONTRACT

Topics covered in this chapter are:

- Discharge by performance
- Discharge by agreement
- Discharge by frustration
- Discharge by acceptance of breach

Summary of the chapter

Once the requirements of a valid contract have been established, the parties to the contract proceed to fulfil their obligations. This chapter considers the ways by which the parties may be discharged from those obligations.

1. There are four ways by which the rights and obligations of the parties to a valid contract may be terminated, i.e. extinguished, determined or discharged, by:

(a) performance;
(b) agreement;
(c) frustration;
(d) acceptance of breach.

• Discharge by performance

2. In general, when both parties have performed their contractual obligations, the contract is extinguished or discharged. The performance must be complete and be exactly in accordance with the terms of the contract. A party who does not precisely perform the contract will be in breach and may not be able to sue on the contract to recover payment or other benefits.

Case: Re Moore v Landauer (1921)

A supplier of canned fruit contracted to supply 3,100 cases of the goods, packed thirty tins to a case. When he delivered the goods, the number of tins met the contract requirement, but about half the shipment was packed in cases of twenty-four tins each. The market value of the goods supplied was unaffected, but the buyer attempted to reject the entire consignment because of the failure to meet the contract description.

Held: The buyer was entitled to rescind the contract because the goods were not of the contract description. There had been a breach of contract, and so it was not discharged by performance.

Case: Coughlan v Moloney (1905)

The plaintiff, a builder, agreed in July 1902 to build a house for the defendant for £200, and to have it completed by December 1902. The building was left incomplete at that date and, the following November, the defendant engaged another builder to finish the work. The original builder sued for the value of the work completed.

Held: The defendant had no option but to accept a partially constructed house built on his own land. Since an agreement to pay for the work completed could not be inferred from such an acceptance, the action for such work done failed. The claim was, therefore, dismissed because the contract was dependent on complete performance.

3. Where prompt performance is an essential condition in a contract, it is said that 'time is of the essence', and that late performance will not discharge obligations.

4. Time will be of the essence where it is an express or implied term of the contract, or if time is vital considering the particular nature of the contract. However, even if time was not originally of the essence, either party to the contract could make it so, once the time of performance has been reached, by serving a notice to complete within a reasonable time on the other party.

5. There are a number of exceptions to the general rule that unless both parties have performed their obligations completely and exactly, the contract is not extinguished.

Partial performance
6. Where a contract may be divided into several parts, payment for parts that have been completed may be claimed. Or, if performance is by instalments, it is possible to recover payment for each instalment completed unless the intention of the parties is to treat the contract as an entire agreement.

Case: Taylor v Laird (1856)

The plaintiff contracted to captain a ship up the River Niger. The terms of the contract allowed for him to be paid a wage of £50 per month, but when he abandoned the job before it was completed, the defendant refused to pay him any wages for the months completed.

Held: The contract had provided for performance and payment in monthly instalments, and the plaintiff was thereby entitled to payment for each complete month.

7. Where partial performance of the contract is accepted by both parties, then the contract is discharged. The law assumes thereby a willingness and intention to make a reasonable payment for the work done, and an action may otherwise be brought on a *quantum meruit* (explained in Chapter 21).

8. A person may also sue on a *quantum meruit* where completion of the contract is prevented by the other party.

Case: Planche v Colburn (1831)

The plaintiff contracted to write a book to be published by instalments in the defendant's periodical. After the plaintiff had carried out some research, and written some of the book, the defendant ceased publication of his periodical, and repudiated the contract.

Held: The plaintiff had been wrongfully prevented from performing the contract and could therefore recover on a *quantum meruit* for the work he had carried out under the contract.

Substantial performance
9. The doctrine of substantial performance states that where a contract has been performed as completely as a reasonable person could expect, the person is entitled to sue on the contract for the contract price, less a reduction for the cost of rectifying any defects. This removes the inequity of depriving a person, who has substantially performed what he contracted to do, of all remuneration.

Case: Hoenig v Isaacs (1952)

The plaintiff undertook to furnish and decorate the defendant's flat for a price of £750, to be paid in instalments as the work was being completed. The defendant made regular payments, totalling £400, in the course of the execution of the contract, but then, in objection to the quality of work which had been performed, refused outright to pay the outstanding amount. It was estimated at the trial that the cost of making good any defective work and completing the job was £56.

Held: The plaintiff was entitled to receive the balance outstanding of the total contract price, less a deduction of £56 damages to cover the costs of rectifying the defects.

• Discharge by agreement
10. A contract being formed by agreement, may also be varied or terminated by agreement. It may be discharged by the agreement of the parties to the contract by:

(a) the conditions contained in the contract;
(b) waiver of the contract;
(c) release of one of the parties;
(d) novation of the old contract.

Conditions contained in the contract

11. A condition precedent, designed to prevent a contract coming into effect prior to the condition being met, or a condition subsequent, whereby a contract will no longer remain in effect following the later happening of an event, are means by which the contract may include provisions for its own discharge.

12. Examples of conditions subsequent are to be found in some contracts of a continuing nature, such as franchise or employment contracts, which may be discharged by agreement when the required notice is given by one or other of the parties.

Waiver of the contract

13. Where the contract remains wholly unperformed by either party, they may agree to cancel the contract by a simple waiver. However, this agreement to discharge the contract is itself a new contract which must be accompanied by consideration. Under this type of discharge by agreement, the consideration will be the waiving of rights and obligations by both parties to the contract. This is a bilateral discharge.

Case: McKillop v McMullen (1979)

The defendant contracted to sell land to the plaintiff before a specified date, subject to the plaintiff acquiring planning permission and the defendant acquiring a right of way over a road to be built on the land. Although the planning permission had not been acquired by the specified date, the defendant did not rescind the contract. Planning permission was eventually acquired, but shortly afterwards the defendant attempted to rescind the contract.

Held: The defendant was not allowed to rescind this particular contract, because he had waived his right to terminate the contract for failure to acquire planning permission by the specified date. The court also held, however, that this waiver need not be unqualified—the right to terminate the contract could still be exercised upon giving reasonable notice of a new date.

Release of one of the parties

14. One party to the contract who has wholly or partly performed his obligations, may discharge the contract by releasing the other party from his obligations. This unilateral discharge also requires consideration so as to make it effective. This usually takes the form of a cancellation fee, which is termed 'accord and satisfaction' for the obligations foregone.

Novation of the old contract

15. Where the parties to an unperformed contract substitute it with a new one, this is referred to as novation of the old contract. The necessary consideration is provided in the new contract. An example of novation would arise in an agreement to transfer one party's obligations to some other third party, thereby replacing the old contract with a new one.

• Discharge by frustration

16. If some event occurs during the course of the contract, without the fault of either party, which renders the contract fundamentally different in its nature from the contract originally entered into by the parties, it may be discharged by frustration.

17. A contract may be discharged by frustration owing to:

(a) destruction of the subject matter of the contract;
(b) non-occurrence of an event upon which the contract is dependent;
(c) incapacity to perform a contract for personal services;
(d) government intervention or subsequent illegality.

Destruction of the subject matter of the contract

18. Where the subject matter of the contract is destroyed, and this renders the contract impossible to perform, the contract may be discharged by frustration.

Case: Taylor v Caldwell (1863)

The defendant let a music hall for a number of concerts to take place on specified dates. The hall was completely destroyed by fire before the first of these, and the plaintiff sued the owner of the music hall for damages arising out of breach of contract.

Held: The contract was discharged by frustration: performance of the contract was impossible due to the destruction of the subject matter and, therefore, the defendant could not be held liable for damages.

Non-occurrence of an event upon which the contract is dependent

19. Where further performance of a contract would be in appearance only, as the real or substantial purpose cannot be fulfilled, the contract may be discharged by frustration.

Case: Krell v Henry (1903)

The defendant rented a room overlooking the route of the coronation procession of Edward VII for the day of the ceremony so as to view the procession. Upon cancellation of the ceremony, due to the illness of the King, the defendant refused to pay on request and was subsequently sued by the plaintiff in an attempt to recover the agreed fee.

Held: The coronation procession was the sole occasion of the contract, and the non-occurrence of this event thereby frustrated the contract. In such circumstances, the defendant was held not liable for payment for the room.

Incapacity to perform a contract for personal services

20. A contract to perform personal services may be frustrated by illness (where personal incapacity is established), death, imprisonment or a call-up for military service. If vicarious performance is possible, however, there will be no frustration.

Case: Condor v Barron Knights (1966)

The plaintiff, under contract to perform as a drummer with the defendant pop group, became seriously ill and was advised by his doctor to restrict his performances to four nights per week. His contract was terminated.

Held: Personal incapacity did not allow the plaintiff to perform his duties in the manner as originally envisaged by the parties, and the contract was therefore correctly discharged by frustration.

Government intervention or subsequent illegality

21. A contract may be frustrated where a government intervenes to restrain or suspend its performance, or where a subsequent change in the law renders the contract illegal.

Case: O'Crowley v Minister for Justice (1934)

The plaintiff made a claim in respect of pension rights relating to a judicial office which had been abolished by statute.

Held: The contract was frustrated by the intervention of the legislature in suspending its performance.

22. There will, however, be *no* frustration, where:

(a) the contingency has been provided for in the express terms of the contract;
(b) the event was foreseen, or reasonably foreseeable, so that it should have been covered by a contractual term;
(c) mere inconvenience, hardship or loss has arisen; or
(d) an alternative means of performance is still possible.

Case: McGuill v Aer Lingus & United Airlines (1983)

The plaintiff booked a holiday with the defendants. Due to strike action by the defendants' employees, the plaintiff was carried on another flight by a different airline, but at a higher price. The plaintiff sued for breach of contract, and the defendants argued that the contract had been frustrated by the strike.

Held: The defendants were aware of the possibility of a strike, but entered into the contract without including an exemption clause to safeguard their position in the event of a strike taking place. Consequently, the defendants were not able to use a defence of frustration and were liable for breach of contract.

23. When a contract is discharged by frustration, the parties may recover payments made under the terms of the contract to the extent that there has been a total failure of consideration. If either party, however, has received a valuable benefit (other than money) under the contract, prior to it being discharged, the court may order him to pay all or part of that value to the other party.

• Discharge by acceptance of breach
24. A contract may be terminated by:

(a) actual breach; or
(b) anticipatory breach.

Actual breach
25. If a party to a contract breaks a condition, the injured party may treat the contract as discharged. We have already seen in Poussard v Spiers (1876) that breach of a condition is sufficiently serious to entitle the injured party to repudiate the contract. Mere breach of warranty is not enough.

Case: Robb & Co. v James (1881)

The plaintiffs purchased fabrics at an auction held by the defendant. A condition of the contract was that the price be paid and the goods collected within twenty-four hours. A dispute arose as to the price to be paid, and the plaintiffs refused to pay the requested amount and remove the goods. The defendants sold the fabrics to a third party, and the plaintiffs sued for breach of contract.

Held: The plaintiff had failed to perform the most essential term of the contract, i.e. to pay for and remove the fabrics within twenty-four hours. The defendants, therefore were perfectly entitled to treat the contract as abandoned by the plaintiff, and to detain and resell the goods.

26. The injured party, on the other hand, may prefer to ignore the breach and to tender performance on his own part, and merely claim damages for the loss suffered.

Anticipatory breach

27. A party to a contract may break a condition merely by declaring in advance that he is unable or unwilling to fulfil his obligations under the contract. In such circumstances, the other party may take this as 'anticipatory breach' of contract, thereby allowing him to treat the contract as discharged and to bring an action for damages immediately, even before the time agreed for performance.

Case: Hochster v De La Tour (1853)

The plaintiff was employed as a courier to accompany the defendant on a tour commencing on 1 June. The defendant, however, wrote to the plaintiff on 11 May, saying that his services were no longer required. The plaintiff immediately commenced legal proceedings on 22 May for breach of contract, to which the defendant objected on the grounds that the breach was not actionable until 1 June.

Held: Although the previously agreed commencement date of employment was in the future, the plaintiff was entitled to instigate legal proceedings once the anticipatory breach had happened on 11 May.

28. The injured party may, at his option, ignore the anticipatory breach and, instead, allow the contract to continue until such a time as there is an actual breach. Under such circumstances, the opportunity is afforded to the party guilty of anticipatory breach to change his mind and fulfil his obligations under the contract after all.

IMPORTANT CASES

Numbers in brackets refer to paragraphs of this chapter

Re Moore v Landauer (1921) ....(2)
Coughlan v Moloney (1905) ....(2)
Taylor v Laird (1856)...(6)
Planche v Colburn (1831)..(8)
Hoenig v Isaacs (1952)..(9)
McKillop v McMullan (1979)..(13)
Taylor v Caldwell (1863) ....(18)
Krell v Henry (1903) ....(19)
Condor v Barron Knights (1966) ....(20)
O'Crowley v Minister for Justice (1934) ....(21)
McGuill v Aer Lingus & United Airlines (1983)......................(22)
Robb & Co. v James (1881) ....(25)
Hochster v De La Tour (1853) ....(27)

PROGRESS TEST

Numbers in brackets refer to paragraphs of this chapter

1. List the ways by which the rights and obligations of the parties to a valid contract may be terminated. (1)
2. Under what circumstances will late performance of a contract fail to discharge obligations? (3, 4)
3. When may a party to a contract be entitled to payment without having performed their obligations completely and exactly? (6, 7, 8, 9)
4. How can a contract be discharged by agreement? (10)
5. Differentiate between a condition precedent and a condition subsequent. (11, 12)
6. When will a contract be discharged 'in accord and satisfaction'? (14)
7. List and describe the circumstances under which a contract may be discharged by frustration. (17–23)
8. What is anticipatory breach? What options does it offer the injured party on its occurrence? (27, 28)

chapter 21

REMEDIES FOR BREACH OF CONTRACT

Topics covered in this chapter are:

- Damages
- Rescission
- Specific performance
- Injunction
- *Quantum meruit*

Summary of the chapter

Where a contract has been breached, the injured party may seek a legal remedy from the court for the loss he has incurred by not having the contract performed. This chapter examines the remedies available to the injured party and the circumstances under which each will be used.

1. When one party to a contract breaches the agreement, the injured party may apply to the court for a legal remedy for the loss he has incurred by not having the contract performed, provided he acts without delay.

2. The right to a legal remedy for breach of contract is subject to time-limits. Under the Statute of Limitations, 1957, the right to sue for breach of a simple contract becomes statute barred after *six* years from the date when the cause of action arose, or after *twelve* years where the contract was by deed. An action consisting of, or including damages for, personal injuries, however, must be commenced within *three* years.

3. The limitation period may be extended where the plaintiff is a minor or under some other contractual disability, such as being of unsound mind, or where the breach was not discovered by the plaintiff because of fraud, concealment or mistake.

4. The following remedies may be applied for to the court on the occasion of a breach of contract:

(a) Damages;
(b) Rescission;
(c) Specific performance;
(d) Injunction;
(e) *Quantum meruit.*

• Damages

5. Damages are a common law remedy, the purpose of which is to put the injured party, by an award of monetary compensation, into the same position he would have been in if the contract had been performed.

6. Every breach of contract gives rise to an action for damages. Where there is a breach of *warranty,* but the injured party sustains no loss, he will receive only nominal damages so as to acknowledge that his legal rights have been infringed. However, where there is a breach of *condition,* the injured party may regard the contract as discharged or reduce the breach to a breach of warranty, claim damages and continue with the contract. If he opts for a discharge of the contract, he will be unable to take an action for damages, but will be able to sue for reasonable expenses incurred by him prior to the date of breach of the condition.

7. The parties to a contract may agree in the contract itself that, in the event of a breach of contract, damages shall be fixed at a sum certain or to be calculated in a certain manner. Such *liquidated damages* will only be enforced by the courts if it is a genuine pre-estimate of loss, and not merely a penalty to secure performance. An amount could be held to be a penalty where the specified sum is extravagant compared with the conceivable loss, where the same sum is to be paid irrespective of the nature of the breach or number of the breaches, or where the specified sum is greater than a money debt due under the contract. In such cases, the penalty intends to frighten a party into compliance with the terms of the contract, and will be void and unenforceable.

Case: Toomey v Murphy (1897)

The defendant agreed to pay 'a penalty as liquidated damages' of £5 per week if construction work which he had undertaken was not completed by a specified date. Due to the work being incomplete at the end of the agreed duration, the plaintiff subsequently sued for damages relating to thirty-two weeks.

$$\begin{array}{r} 32 \times \\ 1\,5 \\ \hline 160 \end{array}$$

Held: This was a valid liquidated damages clause, and the defendant was obliged to pay the £160.

Case: Kemble v Farren (1829)

The defendant, an actor, had agreed to pay the plaintiff, his manager, a sum of £1,000 in the event of a breach of contract by him. The plaintiff subsequently sued for such 'liquidated damages'.

Held: Since the actor's daily fee was less than £4, the specified sum was extravagant in comparison with the greatest loss that could result from the breach, and was but a penalty clause. The sum of £1,000, therefore, was not recoverable.

8. Where a contract makes no provision for the quantification of damages on the occasion of a breach, or where such a sum is void as a penalty, then the injured party will sue for *unliquidated damages*, and the court will decide what losses resulting from the breach are compensatable.

9. Damages may be recovered from the court for losses, financial or non-financial, resulting naturally from the breach of contract, or which may reasonably have been in the minds of the parties on making the contract, as likely to result from a failure to complete the contract.

10. As a general rule, the amount awarded as damages by a court is assessed on the basis of what is considered as a reasonable and fair estimation of the injured party's loss due to non-performance of the contract. This amount may be arrived at by a comparison with market prices. Furthermore, the injured party may be compensated for incidental expenses arising out of the breach, as well as for normal loss of profits, but under no circumstances may be compensated for special unspecified profits. Finally, the injured party may also be entitled to damages for physical inconvenience, such as loss of enjoyment or mental distress arising from the breach of contract.

Case: Hadley v Baxendale (1854)

The plaintiffs owned a flour mill. When the crank-shaft of their steam-engine broke, they had to dispatch it for repair. The defendants, carriers, promised delivery by a certain date, but were unreasonably late in returning it to the plaintiffs. The flour mill was unable to operate without the crank-shaft, and was stopped for the entire duration. The plaintiffs sued the defendants for damages arising out of the loss of profits caused by the delay.

Held: The plaintiffs were not entitled to damages, since the consequences of the breach of contract had not been made known to the defendants who might, had they contemplated them, have wished to have made arrangements under the contract.

11. In assessing the amount of damages, the courts assume the injured party will have taken any reasonable steps to moderate or 'mitigate' his loss. Otherwise, the amount of compensation will be reduced.

12. Other factors may influence the amount of damages awarded. The court may take inflation into account where inflationary loss was a foreseeable consequence of the breach of contract. It may also reduce the amount to take account of sums claimed for, out of which taxation would have been paid.

Case: Hickey & Co. Ltd v Roches Stores (Dublin) Ltd (1980)

The plaintiffs contracted in 1969 to sell retail fashion fabrics in the defendants' store on a profit-sharing basis. In 1972, the defendants broke the contract on the assumption that, even after paying agreed compensation for breach of contract, they would profit from continuing the business alone. The assessment of damages was not finalised until 1980. Consequently, the plaintiffs sought an upward adjustment of the amount to account for inflation, and the defendants sought a downward adjustment to account for the burden of taxation on it.

Held: The defendants were not liable to compensate the plaintiffs for the consequences of inflation, since the parties could not have reasonably foreseen the delay in the award of damages at the time the contract was originally entered into. Furthermore, as the damages receivable by the plaintiff are chargeable to tax, it was not appropriate to make any deduction from the total amount.

• Rescission

13. The injured party may rescind a contract upon breach of a condition. This remedy terminates the rights and obligations of both parties to the contract at the time of rescission, unlike a case of misrepresentation where the contract is held never to have existed if rescission is allowed.

14. The application to the court for an order of rescission may be made by the injured party if he is in doubt as to his entitlement to be relieved from further liability to perform his obligations, or where he requires the return of a deposit.

Case: Grist v Bailey (1966)

The plaintiff bought a house, which was occupied by a tenant, from the defendant for £850. Both parties believed the house to be subject to rent control. It later turned out that this was not the case, and so was worth £2,250.

Held: The contract was voidable. The defendant was entitled to rescind the contract, with the condition attached that the plaintiff should get first option to buy the house at the current market price.

15. Where rescission is allowed by the court, any benefits received must be restored by the parties to the contract, unless it is given as a guarantee of performance. If the injured party is unable to restore the benefits received under the contract, he may lose the right of rescission and have to be content with damages.

16. Whether or not the injured party rescinds the contract, he will be entitled to claim in addition for damages.

• Specific performance

17. Specific performance is a court decree ordering a contracting party to perform his duties under a contract he has made. It is an equitable remedy, and will only be ordered in circumstances where the common law remedy of damages is inadequate.

18. Contracts for the sale of land are enforced by an order for specific performance, because the land may be needed for a particular purpose and the loss of the bargain could not be adequately compensated by an award for damages.

19. Contracts for the sale of goods, however, are not usually enforced in this way, unless the goods in question are rare and unique (such as a rare stamp), and, therefore, no substitute is available.

20. A decree for specific performance will not be made to enforce a contract of a personal nature, such as a contract of employment or of personal service, since such a decree would require performance over a period of time, and the court could not properly supervise its enforcement.

Case: Rawlinson v Ames (1925)

The plaintiff agreed orally to lease a flat to the defendant. It was part of the agreement that the plaintiff would make several alterations to the flat, which he did under the defendant's supervision. The defendant then refused to take the lease. The plaintiff sued for specific performance.

Held: The defendant had requested and supervised the alterations, thereby indicating that she had agreed to take the lease. Although a written memorandum did not exist, the order for specific performance was made i.e. the defendant had to take and pay rent under the lease.

21. Since an order for specific performance is an equitable remedy, such a decree will not be made unless the injured party has behaved fairly. Where the injured party has been in default of his obligations, or where the contract involves an attempt to defraud the revenue authorities, specific performance will be refused.

22. Damages may be awarded as well as, or instead of, a decree for specific performance.

Case: Vandeluer & Moore v Dargan (1981)

The plaintiffs contracted to sell land for £320,000 to the defendant, who subsequently refused to complete the sale. The defendant had only paid a deposit of £20,000, and the plaintiffs sought and obtained an order for specific performance of the contract. The defendant failed to comply with this order, and the plaintiffs sought to collect damages in lieu of specific performance.

Held: The plaintiffs were entitled to apply to the court for enforcement of the court order, or to apply to the court to dissolve the order and ask the court to discharge the contract. Upon discharge of the contract, the plaintiffs would be entitled to damages appropriate for a breach of contract.

• Injunction

23. An injunction is another example of a discretionary court decree, ordering a party to a contract to perform, or not to perform, a certain act. It may be mandatory, prohibitory or interlocutory.

24. A mandatory injunction is a court decree for a party to the contract to perform a definite act, while a prohibitory injunction is a court decree restraining a party to the contract from doing something which is unlawful. Both are suitable in contracts of an ongoing nature. Finally, an interlocutory injunction is a court decree which preserves the status quo between the parties to a contract pending a court hearing.

25. An injunction will not be ordered by the court, however, where damages would be an adequate remedy, or where it would be unfair to the parties to the contract. It will normally only be granted in circumstances in which a decree for specific performance might have been made, except in a case to enforce a contract of personal service, for which a request for a decree for specific performance would be refused by the court.

Case: Lumley v Wagner (1852)

The defendant agreed to sing at a series of concerts organised by the defendant, and undertook that she would not sing for anyone else during the period of the agreement without the plaintiff's written consent. The plaintiff subsequently sued for an injunction to restrain the defendant from breaking this undertaking.

Held: The injunction was granted, since it did not force her to sing for the plaintiff, but rather encouraged her to do so. Similarly, it did not prevent her from obtaining different types of work.

• *Quantum meruit*

26. Where a contract is discharged because of breach by one of the parties, the injured party may make a claim on a *quantum meruit* (as much as he deserved) for the work he has done, or services he has provided, in performance of the contract, as an alternative to the remedy of damages.

Case: Hoenig v Isaacs (1952)

The plaintiff undertook to furnish and decorate the defendant's flat for a price of £750, to be paid in instalments as the work was being completed. The defendant made regular payments, totalling £400, in the course of the execution of the contract, but then, in objection to the quality of work which had been performed, refused outright to pay the outstanding amount. It was estimated at the trial that the cost of making good any defective work and completing the job was £56.

Held: The plaintiff was entitled to receive the balance outstanding of the total contract price, less a deduction of £56 damages to cover the costs of rectifying the defects.

Cutter v Powell (1795)

The defendant agreed to pay the plaintiff's husband a wage of thirty guineas for acting as second mate upon a ship sailing from Jamaica to Liverpool. The plaintiff's husband died at sea while the ship was approximately nineteen days short of its destination, and his widow sued in respect of the work he had done during the previous forty-nine days of sailing from Jamaica.

Held: She was unable to recover a proportionate part of the agreed wages, because her husband had failed to do what he had expressly agreed to do.

27. Similarly, if the contract is unenforceable because either it was only partially completed by the plaintiff, or because it did not comply with the Statute of Frauds, but the defendant accepted the work done, a claim may be made on a *quantum meruit*. Such an award would be in restitution for the work done, as opposed to being in compensation.

IMPORTANT CASES

Numbers in brackets refer to paragraphs of this chapter

PROGRESS TEST

Numbers in brackets refer to paragraphs of this chapter

1. When may the right to sue for breach of contract become statute barred? (2, 3)
2. What remedies are available for breach of contract? (4)
3. Under what circumstances will a court refuse to enforce liquidated damages? (7)
4. How is the amount awarded by a court as damages assessed? (10, 11, 12)
5. What are the implications of rescission as a remedy for breach of contract? (15, 16)
6. A decree of specific performance will not usually be used to enforce what types of contracts? (19, 20)
7. Differentiate between mandatory, prohibitory and interlocutory injunctions. (24)

EXAMINATION QUESTIONS

Section 3: Law of Contract

1. Explain, with reasons, whether a valid contract has been formed between Sidney and Brian in each of the following situations:

   (a) Sidney agrees to sell goods to Brian on the usual terms.
   (b) Sidney offers to sell goods to Brian for £500.
        Brian says he will pay £400 but Sidney refuses to reduce his price. Brian then says he will pay £500.
   (c) Sidney agrees to deliver goods to Brian on the condition that Tom pays him £200.

(d) Sidney offers to sell goods to Brian and gives him ten days to decide whether he wishes to buy them. After five days Sidney sells the goods elsewhere. Two days later, Brian says that he accepts the offer.

C.I.M.A. (November 1988)

2. 'Consideration must:

(a) be sufficient though it need not be adequate;
(b) move from the promisee.'

Discuss with reference to case law.

I.C.S.A. (December 1990)

3. Explain when and how mistake will affect a contract.

C.I.M.A. (November 1989)

4. In relation to the law of contract, write a note on ANY TWO of the following:

(a) undue influence;
(b) offer and acceptence;
(c) exemption clauses.

I.A.T.I. (Summer 1990)

5. Describe and explain the nature of the equitable remedies which may be available in respect of a breach of contract.

A.C.C.A. (June 1990)

section **4**

COMMERCIAL LAW

Negotiable instruments
Bills of exchange
Cheques and promissory notes
Agency
Sale of goods
Hire-purchase and leasing
Insurance

chapter 22

NEGOTIABLE INSTRUMENTS

Topics covered in this chapter are:

- Choses in action
- Definition of a negotiable instrument
- Negotiability of an instrument

Summary of the chapter

Negotiable instruments are transferable commercial documents. This chapter outlines the means by which such a document can be freely transferred, and in respect of which a transferee can acquire a better title to it than the transferor.

• Choses in action

1. A chose in action is a property right which cannot be reduced into physical possession, but which can only be enforced by legal action. It is, therefore, an intangible form of personal property, such as a debt, patent, copyright or share.

2. The owner of such property usually has some document of title to prove that he has such a valuable right and to facilitate the transferability of his title. Such documents of title are known as 'instruments', and these include cheques, bills of exchange, promissory notes, share certificates, debentures and dividend warrants.

3. The transfer of a chose in action is referred to as an 'assignment'. At common law, a chose in action was non-transferable, though, in time, equity law allowed transfer subject to two restrictions:

(a) Notice in writing of the assignment had to be given to the person against whom the right operated; to the debtor, for example, in the case of a debt. Otherwise, if this person paid the assignor (the original creditor), he could not be called upon to pay the assignee.

(b) The assignee could obtain no better rights than the assignor. The assignment was, therefore, subject to whatever defects existed at the time of the transfer. For example, the debtor might dispute his liability to the original creditor. Investigation of the past history of the debt was, therefore, required by the assignee, so as to avoid uncertainty as to his own rights.

4. These restrictions were disliked by the business community, however, who needed an unrestricted means of giving credit, and of transferring debts as a method of paying for goods and services. The practice has grown through custom and usage, therefore, whereby certain types of choses in action have evolved to which these restrictions do not apply. These are known as 'negotiable instruments'.

• Definition of a negotiable instrument

5. A negotiable instrument is defined as: 'a chose in action, the full and legal title to which is transferable by mere delivery of the instrument with the result that complete ownership of the instrument and all the property it represents passes free from equities to the transferee, provided the latter takes the instrument in good faith and for value'.

6. The essential characteristics of a negotiable instrument are:

(a) Title is passed by delivery (if the instrument is payable to 'bearer'), or by delivery and a signature (endorsement) of the previous holder on the back of it.

(b) A transferee has an unqualified right to payment of the full amount. He can obtain a good title even though the transferor had no title or a defective title, provided the instrument was in a negotiable state and the transferee took it in good faith, for value and without notice of any defect in title.

(c) The transferee is entitled to sue on the instrument in his own name.

• Negotiability of an instrument

7. The negotiability of certain instruments has been established by statute and custom, i.e. by proof that it is universally regarded as such by mercantile usage. Negotiable instruments, therefore, include:

(a) bills of exchange;
(b) cheques;
(c) promissory notes, including bank notes;
(d) debentures payable to bearer;
(e) share warrants; and
(f) bankers' drafts.

8. Negotiable instruments, however, do not include IOUs (which are merely acknowledgments of a debt), postal orders or money orders.

PROGRESS TEST

Numbers in brackets refer to paragraphs of this chapter

1. Define a chose in action. (1)
2. Explain what is meant by an 'assignment'. (3)
3. Identify the restrictions under equity of the transfer of a chose in action. (3)
4. What are the essential characteristics of a negotiable instrument? (6)
5. Is an IOU a negotiable instrument? Why? (8)

chapter 23

BILLS OF EXCHANGE

Topics covered in this chapter are:

- The purposes of a bill of exchange
- Definition
- Types
- Acceptance

- Negotiation and endorsement
- Holder
- Liabilities of the parties
- Dishonour
- Discharge

Summary of the chapter

The Bills of Exchange Act, 1882, which codified the existing common law rules, distinguished a bill from other negotiable instruments. This chapter examines how a bill of exchange works in practice, and sets out the obligations of the parties to this instrument.

• The purposes of a bill of exchange

1. Nowadays, the use of bills of exchange in domestic transactions is comparatively uncommon. Cheques (which are a particular type of bill of exchange) are, of course, widely used both in commercial and consumer transactions, but these only developed in popularity in the twentieth century.

2. The Bills of Exchange Act, 1882, therefore, is mainly concerned with a different kind of financial document, which is now most frequently used in foreign trade. The purposes of a bill of exchange can best be illustrated by an example:

3. If O'Brien, in Dublin, supplies goods to Smyth, in London, who requires a sixty-day credit period, O'Brien will draw a bill of exchange on Smyth, ordering him to pay in sixty days.

4. The bill of exchange may be drawn as follows:

£5000   Dublin 1 June 1990

Sixty days after date pay to my order the sum of five thousand pounds (£5,000) value received.

To John Smyth   Patrick O'Brien Ltd
  London

---

5. If Smyth agrees to the terms of this bill of exchange, he shows his acceptance by signing his name on the face of it and returning it to O'Brien.

6. O'Brien may keep the bill of exchange until the agreed date, i.e. until maturity, and then present it to Smyth for payment. Alternatively, O'Brien may sell (i.e. negotiate) it to a bank, or anyone else, at its face value less a small discount, because the buyer will have to wait until maturity to collect the money. The buyer is said to have 'discounted' the bill of exchange.

7. The bill of exchange may be negotiated many times before payment. This is done by the holder simply signing his name on the back of the bill of exchange. This is referred to as 'endorsement'.

8. Therefore, O'Brien has his money, while Smyth has credit for sixty days as requested. O'Brien has the facility of transferring the bill of exchange to another party, so that when it matures the holder may seek payment from Smyth, who hopefully will have the funds to make the payment.

• Definition of a bill of exchange
9. The Bills of Exchange Act, 1882 defines a bill of exchange as: 'an unconditional order in writing, addressed by one person to another, signed by the person giving it, requiring the person to whom it is addressed to pay on demand, or at a fixed or determinable future time, a sum certain in money, to, or to the order of, a specified person, or to bearer'.

10. The definition refers to, and requires that there shall be, three parties to a bill of exchange:

The *drawer* is the person who orders money to be paid on his behalf.
The *drawee* is the person to whom the order to pay is addressed. If, and when, he signs his name on it, he becomes the acceptor.
The *payee* is the person to whom payment is ordered to be made. If no payee is specified, the order may be expressed to be payable to 'bearer', and so it is payable to any person in possession of it.

11. To comply with the definition, the instrument must fulfil the following conditions:

(a) it must be an order and not a mere request;
(b) the order must be unconditional as between the drawer and drawee;
(c) the order must be in writing;
(d) the order must be addressed by one person to another;

(e) the order must be signed by the drawer;

(f) the order must be to pay on demand or at a fixed or determinable future time;

(g) the order must be in respect of a sum certain in money;

(h) the bill must be payable to, or to the order of, a specified person or to the bearer.

It must be an order and not a mere request

12. A bill of exchange must be phrased imperatively. However, words of courtesy or politeness, such as 'please pay', are permissible.

The order must be unconditional as between the drawer and the drawee

13. If payment under the document is to be made only on either the occurrence of a contingency or the fulfilment of a condition, the document will not qualify as a bill of exchange.

Case: Bavins & Simms v London & South Western Bank (1900)

The order contained an instruction to pay 'provided the receipt form at the foot hereof is duly signed'.

Held: The order to the drawee was conditional, and was therefore not a bill of exchange.

Case: Nathan v Ogdens (1905)

At the foot of the document, an instruction stated 'the receipt on the back must be signed'.

Held: This was a valid bill of exchange. Such an order was addressed to the payee, rather than the drawee, who was ordered to pay unconditionally.

The order must be in writing

14. 'Writing' includes printing or typing. It also includes orders made by pencil, although payment is frequently refused in practice, since this obviously facilitates fraudulent alterations. The writing may be done on any substance which is capable of delivery. For example, a cheque, which is a type of bill of exchange, need not necessarily be drawn on a preprinted numbered form issued by a bank. It could be written on any piece of paper, but must, of course, be stamped.

The order must be addressed by one person to another

15. The word 'person' includes legal persons, and not merely individuals. It includes both limited companies and partnerships.

16. The drawer and the drawee, however, may be the same person. For example, a bank may address an order to itself, known as a banker's draft. This is frequently used to pay for a purchase of land, because the amount of money involved is such that the seller would not be prepared to accept a cheque. As the order is signed by the bank itself, this makes it a safer means of payment than an order signed by any other person.

17. Similarly, when a cheque is drawn payable to the drawer by name or 'self', the drawer and the payee will be the same person.

Case: North & South Insurance Corporation v National Provincial Bank Ltd

A cheque was drawn with the words 'pay cash or order' on it. The defendants refused to honour it, saying that it was not a valid bill of exchange.

Held: The document remained a valid order to the banker to whom it was addressed, even though the words 'pay cash or order' deprived it of its character as a bill of exchange.

The order must be signed by the drawer
18. The drawer need not sign at the time the bill of exchange is drawn, but until such a time as this is done, the bill of exchange will be of no effect.

19. The statutory requirement of a signature may be interpreted liberally. As well as an ordinary signature by his own hand, the initials or mark of the drawer or a mechanically produced signature will also be acceptable.

20. The drawer may also have an order signed on his behalf by a duly authorised agent. Where an agent signs a bill of exchange in his own name, he is personally liable on the bill unless he adds words to indicate that he signs in the capacity of agent. For example, if he signs the bill of exchange:

> Sean Farrell, Director
> For and on behalf of Patrick O'Brien Ltd

he will be exempt from personal liability.

21. However, if he merely specifies his position:

> Sean Farrell, Director
> Patrick O'Brien Ltd

he will be treated as signing in a personal capacity, and will be liable accordingly.

The order must be to pay on demand or at a fixed or determinable future time

22. A bill of exchange is payable *on demand* if it is so expressed, or if nothing is written on it to establish a time for payment.

23. A bill of exchange may also be made payable at a fixed future time after the date of the bill or after the date of presentation for acceptance (the latter being referred to as the period 'after sight' of the bill of exchange).

24. Finally, the bill may be made payable on or at a fixed period after the occurrence of a specified event which is certain to happen, though the time of happening may be uncertain.

25. For example, an order to pay a bill of exchange three months after a person's death will be valid, because this person's death is inevitable, but an order to pay a bill of exchange three months after a person's marriage will be invalid, because occurrence of the event is not certain.

The order must be in respect of a sum certain in money

26. Where the order demands that anything be done other than pay a sum of money, it will not qualify as a bill of exchange.

27. A bill of exchange may provide for payment of a sum certain in money, even if it is required to be paid by stated instalments, with interest, or according to a stated or ascertainable rate of exchange.

28. The sum payable need only be expressed in figures. Where, however, the sum payable is expressed in both words and figures, and there is a discrepancy between the two, the sum denoted by the words is the amount payable.

The bill must be payable to, or to the order of, a specified person or to the bearer

29. The payee must be named or indicated with reasonable certainty, unless the bill of exchange is payable to bearer. A bill may be payable to two or more persons jointly, to the holder of a particular office, e.g. 'Collector General' or to a person by the name under which he trades, e.g. 'Irish Commercial Academy'.

30. The bill of exchange is payable to the bearer if it is drawn as such, or if the only or last endorsement is in blank. (Endorsement is explained later in the chapter.)

• Types of bills of exchange

Order bill

31. An order bill is one payable to order, or which is expressed to be payable to a particular person, and does not contain words prohibiting transfer. For example, 'Pay Tom' or 'Pay Tom or order' means that Tom is entitled to payment, but he may, if he wants, order (by endorsement) that payment will be made to someone else.

Bearer bill

32. A bearer bill is one payable to bearer originally, or an order bill which the only or last endorsement is an endorsement in blank, which is where the endorser merely signs his own name without specifying the endorsee.

33. A bearer bill is also one payable to a fictitious or non–existent person. It may appear to be an order bill, but in reality it is not.

34. The essential distinction between a bearer bill and an order bill is that a bearer bill is negotiated (transferred) by delivery alone, whereas an order bill can only be negotiated by an endorsement by the holder coupled with delivery. Delivery without endorsement does not transfer ownership—only possession.

Inchoate bill

35. Where a bill of exchange is lacking in any material particular, the person in possession of it has prima facie authority to fill up the omission in any way he thinks fit.

36. Moreover, where a person signs a blank piece of paper with the intention that it may be converted into a bill of exchange, it can operate as authority to complete it for any amount, using the signature already on it as that of the drawer, endorser or acceptor.

• Acceptance

37. The drawee is under no liability on a bill of exchange, unless he accepts it by signing his name on the front of the bill and, as is usual but not legally necessary, by adding the word 'accepted' and possibly the date.

38. In general, it is not necessary for the holder to present the bill of exchange for acceptance. This duty of presentation for acceptance only arises when the holder receives a bill of exchange which has not already been accepted. He usually presents such a bill to the drawee for his acceptance, and presents it again when payment falls due. However, if the bill of exchange is one payable on demand, it can never be presented for acceptance, since, by its nature, it is due for payment as soon as it is presented.

39. Presentation of a bill of exchange for acceptance is only necessary in three specific cases:

(a) where the bill is payable at a specified time 'after sight';
(b) where the bill expressly requires that it be presented for acceptance; or
(c) where the bill is drawn payable elsewhere than at the place of business or residence of the drawee.

40. An acceptance may be either general or qualified. A *general* acceptance assents without qualification to the bill of exchange as drawn. A *qualified* acceptance varies in some way the effect of the bill of exchange as drawn. There are five types of qualified acceptance:

(a) conditional acceptance—this makes a condition of acceptance (e.g. by writing 'accepted, provided goods delivered by 1 June 1990');
(b) partial acceptance—acceptance is made in respect of only part of the amount of the bill (e.g. on a £1,000 bill, by writing 'accepted for £800 only');
(c) local acceptance—acceptance is made for the bill to be paid in one particular place, and not elsewhere (e.g. by writing 'accepted, to be paid in Galway only');
(d) acceptance qualified as to time—acceptance is made for payment at a time different from that expressed in the bill of exchange (e.g. by writing 'accepted, payable in sixty days', whereas the bill specified thirty days);
(e) acceptance by some, but not all, of the drawees—acceptance for a bill drawn on two or more persons jointly is made by one or more of the drawees, but not all of them.

41. On receiving a qualified acceptance, the option to take or refuse it rests with the holder.

42. Where the holder assents to a qualified acceptance, he should give notice to the drawer and any endorser. They are discharged from liability, unless they have assented to the qualification. Moreover, they are deemed to assent if, within a reasonable time after notification, they do not dissent.

43. Where the holder does *not* assent to a qualified acceptance, he may regard the bill of exchange as dishonoured (rejected) by non-acceptance.

• Negotiation and endorsement
44. A bill of exchange may be negotiated when it is transferred from one person to another so as to constitute the transferee the legal holder of the bill.

45. If the bill of exchange is payable to bearer, it may be negotiated by delivery, but if it is payable to order, it must be negotiated by endorsement of the holder coupled with delivery.

46. The endorsement must be written on the bill of exchange itself. It must be signed by the endorser. An endorsement of the entire amount is required to operate as a negotiation. A partial endorsement, which attempts to transfer to the endorsee part of the sum payable, on the other hand, will not qualify as a negotiation.

47. The four main types of endorsement are:

(a) endorsement in blank;
(b) special endorsement;
(c) restrictive endorsement;
(d) conditional endorsement.

Endorsement in blank
48. An endorsement in blank is a simple signature of the holder on the bill of exchange, without the endorsee being specified. For example,

> (signed) Michael Dunne

49. An order bill so endorsed becomes payable to bearer, since it authorises payment to anyone to whom the bill of exchange is delivered.

Special endorsement
50. A special endorsement includes both the signature of the holder plus instructions to pay a particular person, known as the 'endorsee'. For example,

> Pay John O'Neill
> (signed) Michael Dunne

51. The bill remains an order bill. If the bill of exchange is delivered to John O'Neill, he becomes the holder and may in turn negotiate the bill to another person by endorsement (special or in blank) plus delivery. If the bill of exchange comes into possession of anyone other than John O'Neill, that person is not the holder. The bill is not payable to the possessor alone, nor is it payable to bearer.

Restrictive endorsement

52. A restrictive endorsement prohibits further negotiation of the bill of exchange, or merely gives directions, without transferring ownership. For example,

---

Pay John O'Neill only

or

Pay John O'Neill for the account of Liam Tierney

Conditional endorsement

53. A conditional endorsement makes the transfer of the property in a bill of exchange subject to the fulfilment of a specified condition. For example,

---

Pay Gregory Browne, if he delivers the goods on order.

---

54. Such a condition will exist between the endorser and endorsee alone. It can be disregarded by the payer, and payment to the endorsee will be valid whether the condition has been fulfilled or not.

• Holder of a bill of exchange

55. A holder of a bill of exchange is the payee or endorsee in possession of it, or the bearer of a bearer bill. He will usually be the person legally entitled to possession of the bill, although a thief or finder of a bearer bill is technically also a holder. The rights of a holder will depend on whether he is a holder for value or a holder in due course.

Holder for value

56. A holder for value is a holder who has given, or is deemed to have given, valuable consideration for a bill of exchange, and where some previous holder has given value for the bill.

57. For example, if Tom issues a cheque to Richard in respect of a supply of goods, then Richard gives, and Tom receives, value. If Richard then endorses the cheque and delivers it to Harry as a present, Harry, who has given no value himself for the bill of exchange, is none the less a holder for value.

58. A holder for value receives no better title to a bill of exchange than that of his immediate transferor. Therefore, although a holder for value is entitled to sue in his own name to enforce a bill of exchange against those liable on it, his enforcement rights may be defeated, since his title to the bill will have been taken subject to any defects in title arising because of fraud or illegality.

59. For example, if John steals a bearer bill, for which value has been given, and delivers it to Michael as a present, Michael, as a holder for value, has no better title than John, i.e. no title at all.

60. The rights of a holder for value are against the latest party to the bill of exchange who received value, and all parties previous to that latest party, whether or not they received value.

61. For example, suppose Alan gives a cheque to Barry as a gift, and Barry negotiates it for value to Ciaran: Ciaran negotiates it for value to Declan, and Declan gives it to Enda as a gift. If the cheque is not paid, Enda can sue Alan, Barry or Ciaran, but not Declan, who has received no value from him. Alan is liable because value, although not received by himself, was given after he issued his cheque.

Holder in due course

62. A holder in due course is a person who has taken a bill of exchange which is complete and regular on the face of it, before it is overdue, without notice of any previous dishonour, in good faith, for value, and without notice of any defect in the title of the person who negotiated it to him.

(a) The bill of exchange must be complete and regular on the face of it.

It will not be complete and regular if the name of the payee or signature of the drawer is absent, if it has an alteration which is apparent or if it has an endorsement which is irregular.

(b) The bill of exchange must not be overdue for payment.

The bill of exchange may be negotiated when overdue for payment, but will be subject to any defects in title which existed at the date of maturity.

(c) There must be no notice of any previous dishonour or a defect in title of the person who negotiated it to him.

Only when some irregularity is established in the history of the bill of exchange must the holder show that he had no knowledge or strong grounds of suspicion of the facts in question.

(d) The bill of exchange must be taken in good faith.

As long as the bill of exchange is taken honestly, it it irrelevant as to whether or not there was any negligence.

(e) The bill of exchange must be taken for value.

The value given for a bill need not be equal to the full amount of the bill. It is usually money or property, but it may take any other form.

63. A holder in due course holds a bill of exchange free from any defect of title of previous parties. In other words, he always takes a better title than the transferor had to it.

64. Finally, a holder in due course may negotiate his enforcement rights to any person, other than one who was a party to a fraud, illegality or other unlawful act on the bill.

Differences between a holder in due course and a holder for value

65. Certain distinct differences exist between a holder for value and a holder in due course, the most important of which are:

(a) A holder for value takes the bill of exchange 'subject to equities', while a holder in due course takes the bill of exchange 'free of equities'.
(b) A holder for value is the holder of a bill of exchange for which value has at some time been given, but not necessarily by the holder. A holder in due course must have given value for the bill of exchange himself.
(c) A holder for value can enforce the bill of exchange against previous parties down the sequence as far as the last to receive value. A holder in due course has rights against all previous parties.

• Liabilities of the parties to a bill of exchange

66. By signing a bill of exchange as drawer, acceptor or endorser, a person becomes a party to whom special liabilities apply.

Liabilities of the drawer

67. By issuing a bill of exchange ordering payment, the drawer undertakes that the bill will be accepted and paid at the due date, and that, if it is dishonoured, he will compensate the holder or any endorser who is compelled to pay it, provided the necessary proceedings on dishonour are taken.

68. The drawer may not deny payment to a holder in due course on the grounds that the payee does not exist or because of the payee's lack of capacity.

Liabilities of the drawee

69. The drawee is the person to whom the order in the bill of exchange is given. The drawee will, however, only have liability as a party to the bill after acceptance, thereby becoming acceptor.

70. The acceptor undertakes that he will pay in accordance with the terms of the acceptance.

71. The acceptor may not deny payment to a holder in due course on the grounds that the drawer does not exist, that the drawer's signature is a forgery or because of the drawer's lack of capacity or authority to issue the bill of exchange.

Liabilities of the endorser

72. A person who endorses a bill of exchange undertakes that it will be accepted and paid at the due date, and that, if it is dishonoured, he will compensate the holder or any person who endorses the bill subsequent to himself who is compelled to pay it.

73. An endorser may not deny payment to a holder in due course on the grounds of invalidity of the drawer's signature and all previous endorsements.

74. Neither may he deny to an immediate or subsequent endorser that the bill of exchange was valid at the time of his endorsement.

• Dishonour of a bill of exchange

75. A bill of exchange can be dishonoured (rejected) by:

(a) non-acceptance;
(b) non-payment.

Non-acceptance

76. A bill of exchange will be treated as dishonoured by *non-acceptance* when the drawee fails, for whatever reason, to accept the bill when presented for acceptance.

Non-payment

77. A bill of exchange will be treated as discharged by *non-payment* either when it is presented for payment at the proper place and is not paid, or when presentment for payment is excused and the bill is overdue and unpaid.

78. In case of dishonour by non-acceptance or non-payment, the holder of the bill of exchange must give notice of the dishonour to the drawer and every endorser whom he may wish to hold liable within a reasonable time of dishonour (normally within twenty-four hours). Otherwise, they are discharged.

79. No special form of notice is required. It may be oral or in writing, so long as it clearly identifies the bill of exchange which has been dishonoured.

80. The duty to give notice of dishonour is dispensed with altogether in a number of specified circumstances:

(a) when after the exercise of reasonable diligence, notice cannot be given (e.g. the drawer or endorser cannot be found);
(b) where the person entitled to notice has waived it;
(c) where the drawer has countermanded payment;
(d) where the drawee is a fictitious person; or
(e) where the drawee has insufficient contractual capacity.

81. When a foreign bill (i.e. one which is either drawn or payable outside Britain or Ireland) is dishonoured by non-acceptance or non-payment, formal notice of dishonour must be given by the procedure of noting and protesting. Noting involves a public notary re-presenting the bill of exchange for payment, and if it is again dishonoured, noting the relevant facts on the bill. Protesting, thereafter, involves the formal declaration by the notary of what he has done on a certificate of dishonour referred to as the protest.

82. Either the drawer or any endorser may insert on the bill of exchange a *referee in case of need* to whom the holder may apply for payment, should the drawee fail to accept the bill of exchange. This is an *acceptance for honour,* and serves to maintain the reputation of the drawer and any endorsers.

• Discharge of a bill of exchange

83. A bill of exchange is said to be discharged when all rights of action on it are extinguished. This will be so when nobody has any outstanding claims arising from it.

84. A bill of exchange is discharged:

(a) by payment in due course by, or on behalf of, the drawer or acceptor. 'Payment in due course' means payment is made at, or after, the maturity of the bill of exchange to the holder of the bill in good faith and without notice of any defect in his title;
(b) where the acceptor of a bill of exchange is, or becomes, the holder of the bill at, or after, its maturity;
(c) where the holder renounces in writing his rights against the acceptor, or delivers the bill of exchange to him at, or after, its maturity;
(d) where the holder, or his agent, intentionally makes a cancellation of the bill of exchange which is 'apparent';
(e) where there is a material alteration of the bill of exchange, without the consent of all the parties liable on it (e.g. alteration to the date, time of payment or sum payable).

IMPORTANT CASES

Numbers in brackets refer to paragraphs of this chapter

IMPORTANT STATUTES

Bills of Exchange Act, 1882

PROGRESS TEST

Numbers in brackets refer to paragraphs of this chapter

1. Define a bill of exchange. (9)
2. Who are the parties to a bill of exchange? (10)
3. List and describe three types of bills of exchange. (31–6)
4. What is the difference between general and qualified acceptance of a bill of exchange, and how may acceptance be qualified? (40)
5. Identify the four main types of endorsement. (47)
6. Explain the differences between a holder for value and a holder in due course. (65)
7. Outline the specific liabilities of a drawer (67, 68), a drawee (69, 70, 71) and an endorser (72–4) of a bill of exchange.
8. How may a bill of exchange be dishonoured? (75) Will notice of dishonour always be required? (80)
9. Describe five ways by which a bill of exchange may be discharged. (84)

chapter 24

CHEQUES AND PROMISSORY NOTES

Topics covered in this chapter are:

- Definition of a cheque
- Crossing a cheque
- Relationship between banker and customer
- Protection of banks
- Differences between cheques and other bills of exchange
- Promissory notes

Summary of the chapter

The Bills of Exchange Act, 1882 also defines cheques and promissory notes. This chapter examines their unique features, and the obligations of the parties to these instruments.

• Definition of a cheque

1. A cheque is a bill of exchange drawn on a banker payable on demand.

2. Combined with the definition of a bill of exchange, a cheque may be further defined as: 'an unconditional order in writing addressed by one person *to a bank*, signed by the person giving it, requiring the *bank* to pay *on demand* a sum certain in money to, or to the order of a specified person, or to bearer'.

3. Suppose Gerry O'Connor, in Dublin, supplies goods to John Kelly, in Limerick, who does not wish to pay by cash, he may accept a cheque drawn as follows:

South Western Bank Ltd,   1 June 1990
Patrick St, Limerick.

Pay Gerry O'Connor, or order
five hundred pounds only   £500.00

                                                            John Kelly

---

4. When Gerry O'Connor, or his endorsee, wishes to get payment of this cheque, he may present it at the South Western Bank Ltd, Patrick St, Limerick, and get payment across the counter. Alternatively, he may lodge the cheque in his own bank, which will present the cheque to the South Western Bank Ltd for payment.

5. If John Kelly has funds in his bank account, or he has permission to overdraw on his account, the South Western Bank Ltd will pay on the cheque, debit John Kelly's account and cancel the instrument. The bank which has collected payment will then credit the bank account of Gerry O'Connor, or his endorsee.

• Crossing a cheque

6. A cheque is crossed so as to convey instructions to the drawer's bank that it is to be paid in a particular manner. This is done through a bank, thereby making fraud more difficult.

7. If a bank fails to obey the instructions and makes payment in a manner other than that demanded, this may leave the bank open to an action by the drawer.

General crossing

8. A general crossing is made by drawing two parallel lines across the face of the cheque with, or without, the addition of the words 'and company', or any abbreviation thereof (e.g. '& Co.') between the lines.

9. The effect of a general crossing is to make the cheque payable only through a collecting bank, and not across the counter.

10. In addition to the ordinary general crossing, two common general crossings are often used:

(a) if the words 'not negotiable' are inserted between the traverse lines, the person into whose hands the cheque may come does not have (and cannot give to his transferee) any better title than that which the transferor to him had. The cheque is still transferable, but it is not negotiable.
(b) if the words 'account payee' or 'account payee only' are inserted between the parallel lines, they serve as an instruction to the collecting bank (i.e. the bank holding the account of the payee to the cheque) to credit the payee's bank account alone with the proceeds of the cheque.

Special crossing

11. A special crossing is made by an addition of the name of a bank across the face of the cheque, with or without the addition of two traverse lines.

12. The effect of a special crossing is that the cheque should only be paid to the bank named in the crossing (or another bank with authority to act as an agent for the named banker).

• Relationship between banker and customer

13. The relationship between a banker and a customer is a simple contractual relationship of debtor and creditor. Many of the terms of the contract are not expressed, but are implied by banking practice.

Duties of the banker

14. A banker, therefore, has an obligation to the customer:

(a) to honour his cheques; and
(b) to maintain secrecy over his affairs.

Duty to honour the customer's cheques

15. A banker owes a duty to a customer (but not to a holder) to pay on a cheque presented for payment, provided the customer's account is in credit or within the overdraft limits allowed by the banker.

Case: Dublin Port & Docks Board v Bank of Ireland (1976)

A drawer drew cheques on his bank in favour of the plaintiffs. At that time, his account was in credit. When the cheques were presented for payment, there were insufficient funds in the drawer's account and the bank refused to honour the cheques. The plaintiffs sued for amounts owing to them.

Held: The banker was completely entitled to refuse to honour the cheques, since it owed no duty to the payee, but to the customer alone.

16. If, however, a banker wrongly refuses to honour a cheque, the customer, if he is a *trader,* can claim damages, without proof of the actual loss, for breach of contract. A *private customer,* however, can only claim nominal damages, unless he can prove actual loss. The bank may also be liable to pay damages for the tort of defamation as a result of injuring the customer's reputation.

17. The banker's duty to honour the customer's cheques will be ended by notice of:

(a) countermand of payment being given to the correct branch of the bank on which the cheque is drawn;
(b) an act of bankruptcy on the part of the customer;
(c) a petition for compulsory liquidation, or of a resolution for voluntary liquidation, of a company customer;
(d) the customer's death or insanity;
(e) a court order, whereby the customer's bank balance is frozen.

Case: Reade v Royal Bank of Ireland (1922)

The plaintiff issued a cheque in payment of a gambling debt. He notified the plaintiffs by telegram, before presentment, that he wished to have the cheque cancelled. The defendants, however, chose to ignore this instruction and paid the cheque on presentment. He sued the defendants for breach of duty.

Held: The plaintiff was entitled to recover the amount of the cheque, as the defendants had failed to follow his instructions.

Duty to maintain secrecy over the customer's affairs

18. A banker owes a general duty to the customer to keep information about his customer's affairs secret. This duty extends to include all information acquired in his position as banker, and not just the state of the bank account. It continues even after the closure of the account.

19. The duty of secrecy does end, however, where disclosure is:

(a) under compulsion by law;
(b) in the public interest;
(c) in the interest of the bank, such as when the bank sues a customer on an overdraft;
(d) by express or implied consent of the customer, such as when the customer gives his banker's name to a third party as a reference.

Duties of the customer

20. The customer owes a duty to the banker:

(a) to take those precautions in drawing a cheque which are usual, such as writing a cheque in ink and not in pencil;
(b) to inform the bank of any forgeries of which he is aware.

• Protection of banks

21. A bank has no authority to pay a cheque (and if it does so may not debit the customer's account) if:

(a) its authority has been terminated;
(b) the apparent signature of the drawer has been forged; or
(c) the cheque is void for material alteration.

22. Banks process a huge volume of cheques each day, and this means that each cheque cannot be given the careful scrutiny in the light of their knowledge of customers' affairs.

23. Therefore, both the paying banker and the collecting banker are given statutory protection against liability subject to certain conditions.

Protection of the paying banker

24. A paying bank is deemed to have paid a cheque in due course, i.e. to the person entitled, in spite of any forged, unauthorised or irregular endorsement, or the absence of any endorsement provided he pays:

(a) in good faith; and
(b) in the ordinary course of business.

25. A payment will be made *in good faith*, so long as it is made honestly, whether or not it has been made negligently.

26. A payment will be made *in the ordinary course of business*, so long as normal banking procedure is followed, even though there was negligence in doing this. However, for example, a payment outside banking hours, or a payment of a large sum to a suspicious person not known to the banker, could not be classified as being made in the normal course of business, and, therefore, statutory protection against liability could not be provided.

Protection of the collecting bank

27. A collecting bank is protected from liability where he receives payment for a customer who has no title, or a defective title, provided he acts:

(a) in good faith; and
(b) without negligence.

28. *Negligence* by a collecting bank has been established in cases where:

(a) an account was opened for a previously unknown customer without proper enquiry;
(b) payment was obtained for a customer of a cheque for an abnormally large amount in relation to his circumstances;
(c) payment was obtained for a customer of a cheque drawn by his employer in favour of a third party, or drawn by a third party in favour of his employer, and in either case endorsed over to the customer, without enquiring as to the customer's title to that cheque;
(d) payment was obtained for a customer of a cheque drawn by him as agent for a third party, but payable to himself, without enquiring as to the customer's title to that cheque.

• Differences between cheques and other bills of exchange

29. The rules governing cheques and other bills of exchange, subject to some exceptions, are identical. However, there are a number of important differences:

(a) a cheque must always be drawn on a bank;
(b) a cheque must always be payable on demand;
(c) cheques are rarely negotiated;
(d) cheques may be crossed;
(e) delay in presenting a cheque for payment does not discharge the drawer, unless loss is suffered by that delay;
(f) a banker is protected against a forged or unauthorised endorsement of a cheque drawn on him (Cheques Act, 1959).

• Promissory notes

30. A promissory note is an unconditional promise in writing made by one person to another, signed by the maker, engaging to pay, on demand or at a fixed or determinable future time, a sum certain in money to, or to the order of, a specified person or to bearer.

31. A promissory note may be drafted as follows:

Dublin
1 June 1990

I promise to pay Mary White or order (or bearer) the sum of five thousand pounds (£5,000) on 1 December 1990, value received.

Signed: Anne Browne

---

32. The main differences between promissory notes and bills of exchange are that:

(a) whereas a promissory note has two parties to it—the promisor (maker) and the promisee (payee), a bill of exchange has three parties to it—the drawer, the drawee and the payee;
(b) a promissory note is a promise to pay, while a bill of exchange is an order to pay;
(c) a promissory note is not complete until such a time as it is delivered to the promisee, whereas a bill of exchange is complete once it has been drafted and signed.

IMPORTANT CASES

Numbers in brackets refer to paragraphs of this chapter

Dublin Port & Docks Board v Bank of Ireland (1976).....................(15)
Reade v Royal Bank of Ireland (1922)...(17)

IMPORTANT STATUTES

Bills of Exchange Act, 1882

PROGRESS TEST

Numbers in brackets refer to paragraphs of this chapter

1. Define a cheque. (1, 2)
2. Differentiate between a general and special crossing. (8–13)
3. What are the duties of a banker to a customer, and under what conditions may such duties end? (14–19)
4. Identify those duties owed by a customer to a banker. (20)
5. Describe the statutory protection against liability given to (a) the paying banker (24–6), and (b) the collecting banker. (27, 28)
6. List six differences between cheques and other bills of exchange. (29)
7. Define a promissory note. (30)
8. What are the main differences between promissory notes and bills of exchange? (32)

chapter 25

AGENCY

Topics covered in this chapter are:

- Definition of agency
- Classification of agents
- Creation of agency
- Duties of an agent
- Rights of an agent

- Effects of contracts made by agents
- Termination of agency
- Special types of agent

Summary of the chapter

Business activities are frequently conducted through the medium of agents. This chapter examines the distinctive characteristics of the persons who are used to effect contractual relations between the principals and third parties.

• Definition of agency

1. Agency is the relationship which arises when one person, called an 'agent', has legal authority to bind another person, called a 'principal', by entering into contracts with others on the principal's behalf.

2. The legal usage of the word 'agent' must be distinguished from its usage in everyday language. For example, the word 'agent' is often used to describe a person who buys and sells a particular manufacturer's products. These are merely traders on their own account who buy and sell a particular manufacturer's goods under a special contract known as a 'franchise' or 'concession'. Such traders cannot usually contract with their customers so as to create legal relations between the customers and the manufacturer. Therefore, they cannot be known as agents of the manufacturer in the narrow legal sense, and the manufacturer cannot be described as their principal.

3. An agent, therefore, is a person employed to bring his principal into contractual relations with a third party. The most important feature of the relationship is that the agent has the power to make a binding contract between his principal and a third party without himself becoming a party to the contract.

4. Since an agent does not contract on his own behalf, he need not possess full contractual capacity. He may, for example, be a minor. However, his principal must have full capacity to enter into contractual relations.

• Classification of agents

5. There are many different types of agent. All agents, however, fall into one of three main categories:

(a) general agents;
(b) special agents;
(c) universal agents.

General agent

6. A general agent has implied authority to enter into any contracts which are normally within the scope of the trade, business or profession he has been appointed to by the principal.

7. The principal, therefore, appoints the general agent to represent him in all matters of a particular kind. For example, an agent appointed to manage a public house would have implied authority to enter into contracts on behalf of the principal to purchase alcohol, cigarettes and cigars.

Special agent

8. A special agent has authority to enter into any contracts relating to one specific purpose. For example, an estate agent may be appointed to find a purchaser for the principal's house.

Universal agent

9. A universal agent has unlimited authority to enter into any contracts for which his principal has contractual capacity. He can even execute a deed on his principal's behalf. This type of agency is very rare, although it may be used where a person is going to live abroad for some considerable time.

10. A universal agent is appointed by a deed known as a 'power of attorney'.

• Creation of agency

11. Agency may be created in the following ways:

(a) express authority;
(b) implied authority;
(c) ratification (retrospective);
(d) necessity (operation of law);
(e) estoppel.

Express authority

12. Agency is usually created under a contract of agency. This determines the rights and duties of the principal and agent, and is enforceable between them.

13. To create agency by express authority, no particular formalities are legally necessary. The agent may be appointed verbally or in writing. But if the agent is to execute a deed on behalf of the principal, he must be appointed by a power of attorney, which is itself a deed.

14. The extent of the agent's express authority depends on the true construction of the words of the appointment. The principal may be bound by these words, if they are vague or ambiguous, in the event of the agent interpreting them in a sense not intended by the principal.

Implied authority

15. Agency may be created from the conduct or relationship of the parties, i.e. by implication.

16. The express appointment of the agent need not define his authority in express terms. Every agent has implied authority, in the absence of express provisions to the contrary, to make those contracts which are a necessary or normal incident of the agent's activities. The principal may, of course, limit this implied authority by express definition, but any such restrictions are only effective if the principal communicates them to those with whom the agent deals on his behalf.

Case: Watteau v Fenwick (1893)

The defendant, an owner of a public house, employed the previous owner, *H*, to manage it. He expressly forbade *H* to purchase cigars on credit, but *H* ignored this and proceeded to purchase cigars from the plaintiff, who believed that *H* still owned the public house. *H* was unable to pay for the cigars.

Held: The purchase of cigars on credit was within the implied usual authority of a manager of a public house, and it was this authority upon which the plaintiff was entitled to rely. The defendant was therefore bound by the contract.

17. A wife has implied authority to pledge her husband's credit for necessaries, i.e. goods or services appropriate to the life-style of the spouses and required by her. This is based on a presumption that the wife is expressly or by implication the agent of her husband for this purpose, but is restricted as follows:

(a) The husband and wife must be living together, or if they live apart, it must not be through any fault on the wife's part. Since cohabitation is the legal basis, this implied authority extends also to a man's mistress or housekeeper.

(b) Agency will not be implied for purchases by the wife which, although perhaps 'necessary', such as a motor car, are not usually under the wife's control as manager of the household.

(c) The husband may rebut this presumption of implied agency by:

(i) telling traders not to supply goods to the woman on his credit;
(ii) forbidding the woman to pledge his credit in this way;
(iii) providing her with the means to pay without having to pledge his credit, such as a housekeeping allowance or joint bank account.

Ratification

18. If an agent exceeds his authority, or a person having no authority purports to be an agent, the 'principal' will not be bound by the contract. The third party could, therefore, take action against the 'agent'.

19. Alternatively, the 'principal' may retrospectively give him the authority or status he lacks, by ratification of the contract. The contract then takes effect, and is binding from the time when the agent makes the contract. Ratification, therefore, is a case of express authority given after the contract has been made.

20. A contract can only be ratified if:

(a) The agent expressly informed the third party that he was contracting as an agent, and named his principal.

Case: Keighley Maxted & Co. v Durant (1900)

An agent had authority to buy wheat at 45s. 3d. per quarter from the defendant, who would not sell for less than 45s. 6d. The agent contracted to buy at the latter price, without disclosing that he was buying for the principal, i.e. the plaintiffs. The plaintiffs later purported to ratify the contract. When they failed to pay the agreed price, the defendants sued for breach of contract.

Held: The undisclosed principal could not adopt and ratify the contract. It was, therefore, the agent who was personally liable to pay for the wheat.

(b) The principal existed, and had contractual capacity, at the date of both the contract and the ratification.

Case: Kelner v Baxter (1866)

The defendant, purporting to be an agent of a company which was about to be formed, contracted to buy wine from the plaintiff. The company, when formed three weeks later, took over and sold the wine, but refused to pay the plaintiff.

Held: The defendant was personally liable to pay for the wine, because the company could not by ratification bind itself to a contract made before it existed.

(c) The principal has full knowledge of all material terms of the contract, or is prepared to ratify in any event.

(d) The principal ratifies the contract within the time period specified under the purported contract, or within a reasonable time after the agent has made the contract for him and, at latest, before the time fixed for performance.

(e) The principal ratifies the whole contract, and not merely parts of it.

Necessity

21. An agency of necessity will be created, in certain circumstances, whereby the law will automatically confer an authority on one person to act as the agent of another, without requiring the principal's consent. This rule is of very restricted application, and will usually only apply to a party who acts to save the property of another, or to perform some obligation of another.

22. The courts will only uphold the actions of an agent by necessity provided:

(a) There was an emergency, which necessitated the agent taking the action he did.

Case: Prager v Blatspiel (1924)

The defendant purchased skins as agent for the plaintiff, but was unable to send them to the plaintiff, because of prevailing war conditions. The defendant then sold the skins before the end of the war without communicating with the plaintiff.

Held: There was no real emergency, since the defendant could have stored the skins until the end of the war. The defendant, therefore, was not an agent of necessity.

(b) It was practically impossible to get instructions from the principal.

Case: Springer v Great Western Railway (1921)

The defendant found a consignment of fruit, which it was carrying on behalf of the plaintiff, going bad, and sold it locally instead of delivering it to its ultimate destination.

Held: The defendant could have obtained new instructions from the owner of the fruit, and consequently was not an agent of necessity. The defendant, therefore, was personally liable in damages to the plaintiff.

(c) The agent acted in good faith in the principal's interests, and not merely for his own convenience.

Case: Walsh v Bord Iascaigh Mhara (1981)

The defendants' boat, whose engine had failed, and was drifting towards rocks in stormy conditions, was saved by the crew of the Valentia lifeboat.

Held: Although the crew of the Valentia lifeboat was unable to communicate with the defendants, so as to obtain their instructions within the time available, they had taken action which was reasonable to protect the interests of the defendants. The plaintiffs were, therefore, deemed to be agents of necessity, and were awarded £1,500 salvage.

Estoppel

23. Agency by estoppel may be created where a person, by his words or conduct, represents to a third party that another person is his agent to make contracts on his behalf, even though in fact no agency really existed.

24. The alleged principal will be bound by such contracts as if he had expressly authorised them, i.e. he is 'estopped' from denying the existence of an agency.

Case: Kett v Shannon (1987)

The defendant was given the use of a car by a garage owner whilst his own car was being repaired. On returning the car, and discovering that his own was still unavailable, the defendant obtained the use of a different car from a mechanic, an employee of the aforementioned garage owner. The defendant subsequently collided with the plaintiff, a pedestrian, who sued him for damages. The defendant argued that the garage owner's insurance should cover any expense involved.

Held: The defendant had been driving without the consent of the owner, since there was no evidence to suggest that the mechanic had been acting with express or implied authority when he lent the car to the defendant. Therefore, he was not covered by the garage owner's insurance and was personally liable for damages.

Case: Pickering v Busk (1812)

The plaintiff, a merchant, employed a broker to buy hemp on his behalf. The broker, at the request of the plaintiff, retained the purchased hemp at his own wharf, but later sold it to the defendant.

Held: The plaintiff had represented that the agents had authority to act for him. The plaintiff, therefore, was estopped by his conduct from denying the existence of an agency, and the defendant was held to have obtained a good title to the hemp.

• Duties of an agent

25. An agent is a person appointed by a principal to arrange transactions between the principal and a third party. Since an agent is in a position to injure his principal by committing him to over-ambitious obligations, or by abusing his position to his own advantage, the law has prescribed various general duties which the agent owes his principal:

(a) The agent must 'perform' his agreed task in accordance with the principal's instructions, unless he is acting gratuitously (i.e. without reward).

Case: Turpin v Bilton (1843)

The defendant, an insurance broker, was engaged as an agent, in return for a fee, to arrange insurance on the plaintiff's ships. The defendant failed to do so, and a ship was subsequently lost at sea.

Held: The defendant was personally liable to make good the loss suffered by his principal.

(b) An agent for payment must maintain a standard of 'skill and care' expected of a person in his trade or profession. An unpaid agent must display the standards of skill and care which people ordinarily use in managing their own affairs.

Case: Chariot Inns Ltd v Assicurazioni Generali SPA (1981)

The plaintiffs employed insurance brokers as agents, who advised their principal not to disclose information regarding a previous loss on a proposal form for insurance. After a fire in the plaintiffs' premises, the defendant insurance company avoided the policy.

Held: The insurance company was entitled to avoid the contract, and the agent insurance brokers were later held liable in negligence.

(c) An agent must not delegate the performance of his duties, unless the principal expressly or impliedly authorises the agent to appoint a subagent. This is sometimes referred to as the maxim *delegatus non potest delegare* (a delegate cannot delegate). An agent, however, is not deemed to be delegating by instructing his own employees to perform necessary acts in connection with the performance of his own duty.

Case: John McCann & Co. v Pow (1974)

The defendant employed the plaintiff firm of estate agents as 'sole agents' to find a purchaser for his flat. The plaintiffs passed details of the flat to another firm of estate agents, who advised a Mr Rudd that the flat was for sale. When Mr Rudd went to see the flat, the defendant enquired as to whether he had been referred to him by the plaintiffs, and was told that he had not. The defendant and Mr Rudd agreed a sale between themselves. The plaintiffs subsequently sued the defendant for commission for introducing the purchaser of the flat.

Held: The claim for commission failed, since the plaintiffs were not entitled to delegate the agency without the express or implied authorisation of the defendant.

(d) An agent must both disclose all material information to his principal of his agency transactions and provide accounts, when requested, for all moneys arising from such transactions. An agent should keep his principal's property and money separate from his own, so that they will be easily identifiable.

(e) An agent must not let his own interests conflict with those of his principal. An agent who is appointed to sell cannot sell to himself, and an agent appointed to buy cannot buy from himself, in the absence of full disclosure to his principal.

Case: Armstrong v Jackson (1917)

The defendant, a stockbroker, was employed by the plaintiff to buy shares for him. The defendant sold his own shares to the plaintiff, who subsequently sued to have the contract rescinded.

Held: The stockbroker, as agent, had a conflict of interest and duty. His interest as seller was to sell at the highest possible price, while his duty as agent was to buy at the lowest possible price. As a result, the contract was set aside.

(f) An agent must not make a secret profit or accept an inducement to do business with one person rather than another, without the principal's permission. A principal, on discovering that his agent has accepted a bribe, may dismiss him, recover the bribe from him, refuse to pay him his agreed remuneration, rescind the contract and sue the third party who paid the bribe to recover damages for any loss.

Case: Boston Deep Sea Fishing & Ice Co. v Ansell (1888)

The defendant, who was employed as managing director of the plaintiff company, contracted with a shipbuilding company for the supply of ships, taking a secret commission from the suppliers. This was duly discovered by the plaintiffs, who dismissed the defendant and sued to recover the commission.

Held: The defendant's action was a breach of his duty to his principal. The company was therefore justified in dismissing him and was entitled to recover the amount of the commissions from him.

(g) The agent must not disclose or misuse confidential information regarding his principal's affairs.

• Rights of an agent

26. An agent is entitled to be paid any agreed commission or remuneration for his services by his principal. If it is agreed that an agent is to be remunerated, but the amount has not been settled, the agent is entitled to what is customary in the particular business, or in the absence of custom, to a reasonable amount.

Case: Way v Latilla (1937)

The plaintiff undertook to provide information on gold mines in West Africa to the defendant. He later sued the defendant for remuneration.

Held: Agreement that there should be remuneration was inferred by the court in these specific circumstances, and an amount of £5,000 was awarded as being reasonable.

27. An agent is also entitled to be indemnified by the principal for losses and liabilities incurred in the course of the agency. If an agent acts negligently, or outside the limits of his authority, he loses this entitlement. However, if an agent makes a payment on behalf of his principal, which is not legally enforceable by the third party, but which is made as a result of some moral pressure (e.g. payment of a betting wager), he may reclaim this expense from his principal.

• Effects of contracts made by agents

28. The legal consequences of a contract made by an agent will depend on whether:

(a) the agent discloses the identity of the principal;
(b) the agent discloses the existence, but not the identity, of the principal;
(c) the agent does not disclose the existence of the principal;
(d) the principal is non-existent.

Identity of the party disclosed by the agent

29. When an agent discloses to the third party that he (the agent) is acting for a principal whose identity is also disclosed, the agent will generally have no liability under the contract and no right to enforce it. The agent drops out of the transaction and privity of contract exists between the principal and the third party.

30. An agent may be liable, however, in some such cases:

(a) if he executes a deed or a negotiable instrument without indicating that he does so on behalf of a principal;
(b) if trade custom makes him liable;
(c) if he contracts for himself and is liable as the principal.

Existence, but not identity, of the principal disclosed by the agent

31. When an agent discloses to the third party that he (the agent) is acting for a principal whose identity is *not* disclosed, again the general rule is that the agent can neither sue nor be sued on the contract.

32. However, the agent may still be personally liable, regardless of whether or not the principal is identified, in the exceptional circumstances identified above (30).

Existence of the principal **not** disclosed by the agent

33. When an agent enters into a contract with a third party apparently on his own behalf, but actually on behalf of a principal, the undisclosed principal may sue and be sued on the contract, provided:

(a) the agent was authorised to make the contract;
(b) the third party cannot show that he wanted to deal with the agent for reasons personal to the agent, such as his skill, or that he would not have contracted with the agent if he knew who he was acting for;
(c) the contract made by the agent cannot be construed as having an express term in it that the agent is really the principal.

34. On discovering the principal, the third party may elect to treat him as the other party to the contract. However, he cannot sue both the agent and principal, but must elect for one or the other. The commencement of legal proceedings against either does not necessarily amount to a conclusive election so as to bar proceedings against the other, but if he obtains judgment against one on the breach of contract he is barred from suing the other.

• Termination of agency

35. Agency may be terminated by:

(a) acts of the parties;
(b) operation of law.

Acts of the parties

36. Agency ends when the purpose for which it was created, such as the purchase of a house, is completed. Similarly, agency for a fixed period ends with the expiry of the period.

37. The parties may at any time mutually agree to end the contract, or the principal may revoke the agent's authority, subject to the following restrictions:

(a) if the agent has been given an authority coupled with an interest, such as where he is authorised to collect debts on behalf of his principal and retain a part of the sum collected, the principal cannot withdraw his authority without sufficient notice;
(b) if the agent is also an employee of the principal, then proper notice must be given to terminate the agent's contract of employment;
(c) if the principal does not give notice of the revocation to third parties with whom the agent has dealt, he will be estopped from denying the capacity of the agent, should the agent make subsequent contracts with these third parties.

38. Agency will be terminated without notice if an agent commits a serious breach of an express or implied duty. The principal may also be entitled to sue for damages.

Operation of law

39. Agency is automatically terminated in any one of the following circumstances:

(a) death, insanity or bankruptcy of the agent or principal;
(b) frustration or intervening illegality of the subject matter or operation of the agency agreement.

• Special types of agent

Auctioneer

40. An auctioneer is an agent employed to sell property at a public auction. He is primarily an agent for the seller, and has authority to sell to the highest bidder.

41. If the seller fixes a reserve price (i.e. a minimum price below which the auctioneer is not authorised to sell), but nothing is said to the bidders, and if the auctioneer accepts a bid below the reserve price, the seller is contractually bound.

42. But, if the bidders are informed that the auction takes place 'subject to reserve', and the auctioneer accepts a bid below the sale price, then the seller is *not* contractually bound since he has given notice that his agent has only limited authority. The auctioneer, however, may be sued by the successful bidder for breach of warranty of authority in accepting his final bid with the implication that he, the auctioneer, had the authority to sell at that price.

43. On the sale of the property by auction, an auctioneer has an implied authority to accept payment of the price and to sign the memorandum of sale on behalf of both the seller and buyer.

Broker
44. A broker is an agent who is employed to buy or sell goods in the principal's name, but does not have possession of the goods or of documents of title to them. The compensation paid to such agents for their services is known as 'brokerage'.

45. A stockbroker is a member of the stock exchange who has an implied authority to make contracts for his principals, subject to the rules of the exchange. These rules bind the principals, irrespective of whether or not they are aware of them, as long as they are neither unreasonable nor illegal.

Factor
46. A factor is an agent entrusted with possession of goods or documents of title to goods for purposes of sale in either his own name or his principal's name.

47. A factor also has a lien (this term will be explained at a later stage) on the goods for his charges, and has an insurable interest in the goods.

Estate agent
48. An estate agent negotiates the purchase or sale of land or buildings on behalf of his principal. An estate agent has no usual or implied authority to conclude a sale for his principal, or to prepare a memorandum of sale. He will only be entitled to receive commission from his principal when he does exactly what he was employed to do.

Del credere agent

49. A *del credere* agent undertakes to indemnify his principal should the third party purchasers of his principal's goods fail to pay for them. He usually receives a higher commission than normal in return for this indemnity.

50. He does not guarantee, however, that a buyer will accept delivery of the goods. In the event of the buyer not accepting delivery of the goods, the agent incurs no personal liability to the principal.

IMPORTANT CASES

Numbers in brackets refer to paragraphs of this chapter

PROGRESS TEST

Numbers in brackets refer to paragraphs of this chapter

1. Define agency. (1)
2. List three main categories under which the different types of agents may be classified. (5)
3. How may agency be created? (11)
4. In what circumstances may a person retrospectively give authority to another who has purported to contract on his behalf? (20)
5. When will the courts uphold the actions of an agent by necessity? (22)

6. What are the general duties which an agent owes his principal? (25)
7. When may an agent be liable for a contract made on behalf of a disclosed principal? (30)
8. How may agency be terminated? (35–9)
9. Differentiate between:

   (a) an auctioneer and an estate agent; and
   (b) a broker and a factor. (40–48)

chapter 26

SALE OF GOODS

Topics covered in this chapter are:

- Contract for the sale of goods
- Terms of the sale of goods contract
- Transfer of property in the goods to the buyer
- Performance of the sale of goods contract
- Remedies for breach of a sale of goods contract
- Supply of services

Summary of the chapter

A contract for the sale of goods is like any other contract, except that statutory provisions may apply to it. This chapter examines how the ordinary principles of contract law apply to such contracts, and how the statutory provisions, for the most part, merely set out the rules which will apply when some detail of their arrangement is not covered by express agreement.

Introduction
1. A sale of goods is the most common type of commercial transaction. A contract for the sale of goods is regulated by the principles of contract law as modified by the Sale of Goods Act, 1893 (the 1893 Act) and the Sale of Goods and Supply of Services Act, 1980 (the 1980 Act).

2. A contract for the sale of goods, therefore, is like any other contract in law where, in addition to the statutory rules, the ordinary principles of contract law, e.g. the rules relating to offer, acceptance, mistake and mis-representation, still apply. Statutory rules for the most part will merely apply where some detail of the contracting parties' arrangement has not been covered by express agreement.

• Contract for the sale of goods
3. The 1893 Act defines a contract for the sale of goods as 'a contract whereby the seller transfers or agrees to transfer the property in goods to the buyer for a money consideration called the price'.

4. The definition of a contract for the sale of goods includes two distinct transactions: a 'sale' and an 'agreement to sell':

(a) Where ownership (called 'property' in the 1893 Act) is transferred immediately from the seller to the buyer, the contract is called a 'sale' (s.2(4)).

(b) Where ownership of the goods is to be transferred at a future time, or subject to some condition later to be fulfilled, the contract is called an 'agreement to sell' (s.2(5)).

5. The distinction is important because several consequences follow from the passing of property:

(a) unless otherwise agreed, the risk of accidental loss or damage passes with the property;

(b) once the property has passed to the buyer, the seller can sue for the price, even if there has been no delivery, i.e. no transfer of possession;

(c) if the property has passed to the buyer, he may claim the goods if the seller becomes a bankrupt if a person, or goes into liquidation if a company;

(d) if the seller resells the goods after the property has passed to the buyer, no title is acquired by the second buyer unless he is protected, by one of the exceptions to the *nemo dat quod non habet* rule (see 50 below).

6. A contract for the sale of goods must be one for 'goods' which are defined as 'all chattels personal other than things in action and money'. Things in action include debts, shares, patents, cheques, bills of exchange and promissory notes.

7. 'Consideration' in a contract for the sale of goods must be money. If the consideration is goods alone, then the contract is one of exchange or barter and the Act will not apply. However, the consideration need not be exclusively money, and a contract for the sale of goods will be valid if the consideration is partly goods and partly money.

Formation of a contract for the sale of goods
8. The ordinary rules of contract govern the formation of a contract for the sale of goods. There must be agreement between the parties to the contract, an intention to create legal relations and consideration.

9. The 1893 Act provides that, subject to statutory exception, the contract may be made by deed, in writing, by word of mouth, by the conduct of the parties, or a mixture of these (s.4).

10. The 1980 Act provides that the Minister for Industry and Commerce may order that contracts relating to goods of a specified type must be in writing.

11. Where goods are valued at £10 or over, the contract cannot be enforced unless one of the following conditions is fulfilled:

(a) there has been acceptance and receipt of part of the goods by the buyer; or

(b) the buyer has given something in earnest (i.e. as a deposit) to bind the contract or in part payment; or

(c) there is a written note or memorandum containing the essential terms of the contract, and signed by the party to be sued or his agent.

• Terms of the sale of goods contract

12. The contents of a contract for the sale of goods are determined by the normal principles of contract law. Statements will become terms of a sale of goods contract if the maker of them, expressly or by implication, warrants them to be true. A sale of goods contract, therefore, like all contracts, may contain both express and implied terms.

Express terms

13. Typically, the parties to a sale of goods contract will agree verbally and/or in writing on the basic terms of their agreement. Such terms will normally include the amount and quality of the goods, the price to be paid and maybe the time and method of delivery. However, in the absence of express agreement some of these terms are provided by the 1893 Act.

14. The parties to a contract need not expressly agree to the price, provided they agree on a feasible method of fixing the price, such as the ruling market price on the day of the delivery. If a price is not determined as above, then the buyer must pay a price which is found to be reasonable in the circumstances of the case (s.8).

Implied terms

15. The Sale of Goods Acts, 1893 and 1980 imply certain conditions and warranties into contracts for the sale of goods. These give extensive protection to the buyer, and cannot, except in certain circumstances, be excluded.

16. A condition is a vital term, breach of which normally entitles the innocent party to repudiate the contract and claim damages. A warranty is a subsidiary term, breach of which only entitles the innocent party to damages. However, a buyer may waive a breach of condition by the seller, or elect to treat it as a breach of warranty.

Title (seller's right to pass good title to the goods)

17. Under s.12(1) of the combined Acts, there is an implied condition that the seller has, or will have, at the time when property in the goods is to be transferred, a right to sell the goods. If a buyer purchases goods from a seller who has not a good title to the goods, he must generally return the goods to the true owner. The buyer, however, may recover the entire price he paid for the goods, without any allowance for the use of the goods, on the grounds that there has been a total failure of consideration.

Case: Rowland v Divall (1923)

The defendant sold a car, which unknown to him had been stolen, to the plaintiff, who subsequently sold it to a third party. The true owner of the car later recovered it from the third party, who was fully reimbursed by the plaintiff. The plaintiff then sued the defendant to recover the full price originally paid by him, but the defendant argued that allowance should be made for the use of the car before it had been returned to the true owner.

Held: The plaintiff was entitled to recover the whole purchase price, without any set off for the use of the car. Since the contract was for the transfer of ownership of the car and not merely the right to use it, there had been a total failure of consideration.

18. Under s.12(2) of the combined Acts, there is an implied warranty that the goods are free from any charge in favour of a third party which was not made known to the buyer either before, or at the time the contract was made, and that the buyer will enjoy quiet possession of the goods, except so far as it may be disturbed by any person entitled to the charge disclosed.

Description (goods to correspond with description)

19. Under s.13(1) of the combined Acts, there is an implied condition that where goods are sold by description, then the goods shall correspond with that description.

20. The courts tend to construe this condition widely. A sale may be 'by description' even if the buyer inspects the goods before buying them, provided he relies essentially on the description, and any discrepancy between the description and the goods is not apparent. Moreover, if the buyer asks for the goods by stating his requirements and the seller then supplies them to those requirements, this is also the case.

Case: T.O'Regan & Sons Ltd v Micro-Bio (Ireland) Ltd (1980)

The plaintiffs informed the defendants that they required a product in order to vaccinate day-old broiler chickens against infectious bronchitis. The defendants recommended that the plaintiffs purchase a vaccine, called H-120, from them. The plaintiffs subsequently purchased and administered the vaccine, only to discover that a large number of the treated chickens had died. Tests later proved that the vaccine supplied by the defendants had in fact been H-52, a much stronger product used to vaccinate adult fowl.

Held: There had been a breach of the condition as to description, since the vaccine sold under the description H-120 did not correspond with that description because of its greater potency.

21. Under s.13(2) of the combined Acts, there is also an implied condition that where goods are sold by sample, as well as by description, then it is not sufficient that the bulk of the goods shall correspond with the sample, if the goods do not correspond with the description.

Merchantable quality

22. Under s.14(2) of the combined Acts, there is an implied condition that where goods are sold *in the course of a business*, the goods will be of a reasonable standard and suitable for the purpose or purposes for which goods of that kind are commonly bought, and as durable as is reasonable to expect having regard to any description applied to them, the price (if relevant), and all other relevant circumstances.

Case: McCullough Sales Ltd v Chetham Timber Co. (Ireland) Ltd (1983)

The plaintiffs sold a man-made building material, known as Celuform, to the defendants. This plastic substance, designed as an alternative to timber, was supplied with special nails to affix the material to masonry. The nails proved unsuitable to be applied to concrete walls in the Republic of Ireland, and the defendants refused to pay for those materials supplied.

Held: The plaintiffs were familiar with the purpose for which the defendants required the materials. The materials supplied were not of merchantable quality and not fit for the purpose for which they were required.

Case: Egan v McSweeney (1956)

The plaintiff purchased coal from the defendant. When ignited, some of the coal exploded and the plaintiff was struck by flying particles, which led to the loss of her left eye. She sued the defendant for damages.

Held: The goods did not meet the implied condition of merchantable quality, in that the coal was not fit for its ordinary use, i.e. to burn in a domestic fire. The defendant was therefore liable to compensate the plaintiff for personal injuries suffered by her.

23. The condition that the goods supplied under a contract of sale are of merchantable quality is *excluded* if:

(a) any defects are brought specifically to the buyer's attention before the contract is made; or
(b) the buyer examines the goods before the contract is made as regards defects which that examination ought to reveal.

Case: Thornett & Fehr v Beers & Sons (1919)

The plaintiffs purchased several barrels of glue from the defendants. The barrels themselves were examined at the time of purchase, but no inspection was made of their contents. The glue subsequently proved defective.

Held: The defendants were not held liable because the plaintiffs could have discovered the defects when making the examination of whether the goods were of merchantable quality.

Fitness of goods for a disclosed purpose

24. Under s.14(3) of the combined Acts, there is an implied condition that where goods are sold *in the course of a business*, and the buyer expressly, or by implication, makes known to the seller any particular purpose for which the goods are being bought, then the goods supplied under the contract shall be reasonably fit for that purpose, whether or not that is a purpose for which such goods are commonly supplied.

25. There is no such implied condition of fitness of goods for a disclosed purpose where the circumstances show:

(a) that the buyer did not rely on the seller's skill and judgment; or
(b) that it would have been unreasonable for the buyer to rely on the seller's skill and judgment.

26. Where there is only one obvious purpose for which the goods are required, it need not be made known expressly to the seller since it is clearly implied. But if the goods can be used for more than one purpose or there are special circumstances which affect their suitability, there is no breach of an implied condition of fitness unless the buyer has made an express disclosure.

Case: Godley v Perry (1960)

The plaintiff purchased a catapult from the defendant. It broke whilst being used by the plaintiff and resulted in him losing an eye.

Held: The purpose of the purchase was known by implication. Because it was not an effective catapult, it was in breach of s.14(3).

Sale by sample
27. Under s.15 of the combined Acts, there are implied conditions that:

(a) the bulk shall correspond with the sample in quality;
(b) the buyer shall have a reasonable opportunity of comparing the bulk with the sample; and
(c) the goods shall be free from any defect rendering them unmerchantable, which would not be apparent from a reasonable examination of the sample.

Case: Nichol v Godts (1854)

The plaintiff entered into a contract to purchase from the defendant 'foreign refined rape oil warranted only equal to sample'. However, the sample had not been 'foreign refined rape oil' in the first place, so although the bulk corresponded with the sample when delivered, it did not meet the plaintiff's described requirements. He sued the defendant for breach of condition.

Held: The defendant was in breach of s.13(2) and s.15, and the plaintiff was therefore not liable to pay the price.

Sale of motor vehicle
28. Under s.12 of the 1980 Act, there is an implied warranty in a contract for the sale of a motor vehicle, except where the buyer is a person whose business it is to deal in motor vehicles, that the seller will make available for the specified period if any, such spare parts and 'adequate aftersale service' as are stated in any offer, description or advertisement given by the seller, or given by him on behalf of the manufacturer. The Minister for Industry and Commerce is empowered to define by order what a reasonable period will be in relation to any class of goods.

29. Under s.13 of the 1980 Act, there is an implied condition in a contract for the sale of a motor vehicle, except when the buyer is a dealer, that at the time of delivery the vehicle is free from any defect which would render it a danger to the public, including persons travelling in the vehicle. This condition is not implied when, in a fair and reasonable agreement, the parties agree that the vehicle is not intended for use in the condition in which it is to be delivered to the buyer, and a certificate to that effect is signed by the seller, or someone on his behalf, and the buyer, and given to the buyer prior to, or at the time of, delivery.

Exclusion of implied terms

30. The 1893 Act permitted the implied conditions and warranties to be excluded, or limited, in contracts for the sale of goods. Therefore, one of the parties to a contract was able to exclude or diminish his liability by way of an exemption clause, thereby rendering these valuable protections meaningless.

31. It is no longer possible for a seller of goods to totally exclude the statutory implied conditions and warranties from a contract for the sale of goods.

32. Under s.55 of the combined Acts, any term in a contract for the sale of goods which excludes all, or any of the provisions of s.12, concerning the seller's title to the goods, is void.

33. Under s.55(4) of the combined Acts, any term in a contract for the sale of goods which excludes all, or any of the provisions, of s.13, concerning the description of the goods, s.14, concerning the quality and fitness of the goods and s.15, concerning the sale of goods by sample, is void where the buyer deals as a consumer, and in any other case will be unenforceable unless such exclusion is shown to be fair and reasonable.

34. A consumer is defined as a party who does not make the contract in the course of a business, while the other party does, and the goods sold are of a type ordinarily sold for private use or consumption.

Case: O'Callaghan v Hamilton Leasing (Ire.) Ltd (1983)

The plaintiff, owner of a take-away restaurant, leased a drink-dispensing machine from the defendants. The machine produced drinks which were dispensed by the plaintiff to the customer. After two payments, the machine proved defective and the plaintiff sued the defendants for breach of condition.

Held: The plaintiff had not dealt as a 'consumer' within the meaning of the Sale of Goods and Supply of Services Act, 1980. The defendant, therefore, could not be held liable for a breach of condition.

35. In considering whether a term is to be judged fair and reasonable, it is up to the court to have regard to the circumstances which were, or ought reasonably to have been known to, or in the contemplation of, the parties when the contract was made. Particular regard should be taken of the relative bargaining power of the parties, any inducement received by the customer to agree to the term, the customer's knowledge of the existence and extent of the term and whether any of the goods supplied were manufactured, processed or adapted to the special order of the customer.

Guarantees

36. S.15 of the 1980 Act defines a guarantee as any document, notice or other written statement, however described, supplied by a manufacturer or other supplier, other than a retailer, in connection with the supply of any goods and indicating that the manufacturer, or other supplier, will service, repair or otherwise deal with the goods following purchase.

37. Under s.16 of the 1980 Act, it is an offence for a manufacturer or supplier who provides a guarantee to fail to make it clearly legible or to fail to state clearly the name and address of the person supplying the guarantee (i.e. the guarantor), the duration of the guarantee from the date of purchase, the procedure for presenting a claim, what the manufacturer or other supplier precisely undertakes to do in relation to the goods and the charges, if any, to be met by the buyer.

38. S.18 of the 1980 Act provides that a guarantee is not an alternative to the implied rights given by the statute, but instead is an addition to them. A guarantee which purports to exclude or limit the buyer's statutory or contractual rights is void.

39. Under s.19 of the 1980 Act, the buyer of goods may sue a manufacturer (or importer, where the goods are imported) or other supplier who fails to observe the terms of the guarantee, as if they had sold the goods to the buyer and had committed a breach of warranty. The courts may enforce the observance of the terms of the guarantee or may award damages to the buyer. This right extends to all persons who acquire title to the goods within the duration of the guarantee.

• **Transfer of property (ownership) in the goods to the buyer**
40. The 1893 Act is not concerned with the contract for the sale of goods alone, but also deals with the property (ownership) problems associated with a sale. Property and possession must be distinguished because the property in goods sold may pass to the buyer although the seller retains possession of the goods. Similarly, although the buyer is in possession of the goods, the seller may still be the owner of them.

41. The importance of determining whether property in the goods remains with the seller or has been transferred to the buyer is outlined in 5 above and, because of its relevance, is repeated here.

(a) Unless otherwise agreed, the risk of accidental loss or damage passes with the property.

(b) Once the property has passed to the buyer, the seller can sue for the price, even if there has been no delivery, i.e. no transfer of possession.

(c) If the property has passed to the buyer, he may claim the goods if the seller becomes a bankrupt, or if the seller is a company it goes into liquidation.

(d) If the seller resells the goods after the property has passed to the buyer, no title is acquired by the second buyer unless he is protected by one of the exceptions to the *nemo dat quod non habet* rule (see 50 below).

42. The time when property is transferred from seller to buyer depends partly on whether the goods are specific, ascertained or unascertained.

(a) Specific goods are those identified and agreed upon at the time *when* a contract of sale is made. For example, if a seller shows a buyer a suite of furniture, and the buyer agrees to purchase that suite, that is a sale of specific goods.

(b) Unascertained goods are those defined by description only, and not identified until *after* the contract is made, for example, 2lb tomatoes.

(c) Ascertained goods are those identified and agreed upon *after* a contract of sale is made. For example, a contract to sell a greyhound pup from a litter not yet born is one for unascertained goods, but when the buyer chooses one upon the birth of the pups, the goods become ascertained.

43. Where there is a contract for the sale of unascertained goods, no property in the goods is transferred to the buyer unless and until the goods are ascertained (s.16).

44. If the contract is for the sale of specific or ascertained goods, property in the goods is transferred to the buyer at such time as it appears the parties intended it to be transferred. Their intention may be deduced from the conduct of the parties, the terms of the contract and the circumstances of the case (s.17).

45. Where the intention of the parties at the time of contracting is not clear, the following rules of s.18 shall be applied to decide the time at which property in the goods shall pass:

Rule 1
Where there is an unconditional contract for the sale of specific goods, which are in a deliverable state, property in the goods passes to the buyer when the contract is made, and it is immaterial whether the time of payment or delivery, or both, are postponed.

Case: Clarke v Reilly & Sons (1962)

The parties entered into a contract for the sale of a new car to the plaintiff, who agreed that he would trade in his old car and pay the balance of the purchase price in cash to the defendant. Pending delivery of the new car which he had purchased, the plaintiff was allowed to use the traded-in car. He was involved in an accident and seriously damaged the traded-in car. The seller attempted to repudiate the contract.

Held: Ownership of the traded-in car passed to the defendant as soon as the contract was made. The plaintiff was merely a bailee of the car and had taken reasonable care of it. The defendants were obliged to bear the loss.

Rule 2

Where there is a contract for the sale of specific goods and the seller is bound to do something to put the goods in a deliverable state, property in the goods does not pass to the buyer until the seller has done what is required of him and the buyer is notified to this effect.

Case: Underwood v Burgh Castle Brick and Cement Syndicate (1922)

The defendants contracted to purchase an engine, which at that time was embedded in a concrete floor. The engine was damaged whilst being detached from its base and loaded on to a rail wagon. The defendants refused to accept it and the plaintiff sued for the price.

Held: The engine had not been in a deliverable state when the contract was made. It was still in the plaintiff's ownership at the time of the damage, and so at their risk.

Rule 3

Where there is a contract for the sale of specific goods in a deliverable state, but the seller is bound to weigh, measure or test them for the purpose of determining the price, property in the goods passes to the buyer when the seller has done so and has notified the buyer to this effect.

This rule only applies when it is the seller who must weigh, measure or test the goods. If the buyer is to do the act, the property in the goods passes when the contract is made.

Rule 4

Where goods are delivered to a prospective buyer 'on approval' or on 'sale or return' terms, property in the goods passes to the buyer when:

(a) he signifies his approval or acceptance to the seller;

(b) he does any other act, such as pawning the goods, thereby adopting the transaction; or

(c) he retains the goods beyond the time agreed for their return without giving notice of rejection, or if no time was agreed, if he retains the goods beyond a reasonable time.

Case: Poole v Smith's Car Sales (1962)

The plaintiff gave his car to the defendants in August 1960 on a 'sale or return' basis. Having made several requests for the return of his car, the plaintiff finally recovered it in a badly damaged state in November 1960. The plaintiff sued for the price.

Held: Property in the car had passed to the defendants, since it had not been returned within a reasonable time. The defendants were obliged to pay the price agreed.

Rule 5

(a) Where there is a contract for the sale of unascertained goods, property in the goods passes to the buyer when goods of that description and in a deliverable state are unconditionally appropriated to the contract by one party, with the express or implied assent of the other.

Case: Pignataro v Gilroy (1919)

The plaintiff contracted to purchase 140 bags of rice from the defendant, who sent a delivery order for 125 bags at a warehouse to the plaintiff, and asked him to collect the remaining 15 bags from the defendant's own premises. The plaintiff took no action for a month, within which time the 15 bags were stolen through no fault of the defendant. The plaintiff sued to recover the price paid for the 15 bags.

Held: The defendant's appropriation of the goods for the contract, without the plaintiff's objection, constituted the transfer of ownership and risk to the plaintiff. The goods, therefore, belonged to the plaintiff when they were stolen.

(b) Where a seller delivers goods to a buyer, or to a carrier for transmission to the buyer, without reserving a right of disposal, he is deemed to have unconditionally appropriated goods to the contract.

Reservation of title to the goods by the seller

46. Where there is a contract for the sale of specific goods, or where goods are subsequently apportioned to the contract, the seller may, by the terms of the contract or appropriation, reserve the right of disposal of the goods until certain conditions are fulfilled (s.19).

47. The inclusion of a reservation of title clause in a contract provides a seller of goods, with a means of protecting his interest in goods which have not been paid for, or his interest in the proceeds of resales, in the event of a buyer becoming insolvent.

Case: Aluminium Industrie Vaassen B.V. v Romalpa Aluminium Ltd (1976)

The defendants purchased aluminium from the plaintiffs on terms that ownership of the material would only be transferred to the purchasers when they had paid to the suppliers all money owing to them. After having taken delivery of a consignment of aluminium, the defendants went into receivership. The plaintiffs, who had not received the purchase price, sought to enforce the above provision so as to secure payment before distribution of the defendants' assets.

Held: The aluminium, though in the possession of the defendants, did not belong to them. The plaintiffs were entitled to recover the remaining stock of aluminium and the money held by the receiver, representing the proceeds of sales of aluminium to the defendants' customers.

Case: Frigoscandia (Contracting) Ltd v Continental Irish Meat Ltd (1982)

The plaintiffs sold a refrigerating machine to the defendants, payments for which were to be paid on an instalment basis. The contract of sale was subject to a condition that property in the machine should not pass to the defendants until the final instalment had been paid. A receiver was appointed to the defendant company, and the plaintiffs sued for a return of the machine as there was still a sum outstanding in respect of the contract.

Held: The retention of title clause was effective in the circumstances, and the plaintiffs were entitled to retain the machine until all outstanding amounts had been paid.

48. However, in certain circumstances, a 'reservation of title' clause may not apply:

(a) unless it is registered as a charge (where the buyer is a company) or in a bill of sale (where the buyer is an individual); or
(b) if the goods are subjected to some process, whereby they become 'mixed' with other goods.

49. Therefore, in order to ensure that a straightforward reservation of title to goods still in the buyer's possession will remain effective, it is advisable that the supplier require that the goods in question be kept separate from the buyer's other stock.

Transfer of title by a non-owner

50. The common law maxim *nemo dat quod non habet* provides that a seller, or an agent acting for the seller, can give no better title to goods than the seller himself has.

51. This is reflected in s.21 of the 1893 Act, which provides that where goods are sold by a person who is not the owner, the buyer acquires no better title than the seller has, unless:

(a) the seller has the authority or consent of the owner; or
(b) the owner is precluded by his conduct from denying the seller's authority to sell.

52. However, there are a number of exceptions to this general rule, so as to protect an honest buyer from having nothing except an action against the seller. These exceptions fall under rules relating to:

(a) sale by mercantile agents;
(b) estoppel;
(c) sale under a common law or statutory power;
(d) sale in market overt;
(e) sale under a voidable title;
(f) disposition by seller who remains in possession after sale;
(g) disposition by buyer who obtains possession after agreement to sell;
(h) disposition under a hire-purchase agreement;
(i) sale under a court order.

(a) Sale by mercantile agents

If an ordinary agent sells goods without actual or apparent authority, there is usually no transfer of title to the buyer. But if a mercantile agent, i.e. an agent whose business is selling goods for others, has possession of goods (or documents of title to them) with the owner's consent, and sells them in the ordinary course of his business to a buyer who buys in good faith, and without notice that the agent has no authority to sell (or was exceeding his authority), the buyer then acquires title to the goods (s.21).

Case: Folkes v King (1923)

The plaintiff gave his car to a motor dealer for sale at not less than £575. The dealer sold the car to the defendant for £340, and the plaintiff sued to recover his car.

Held: The motor dealer was a mercantile agent for the plaintiff. In the circumstances, therefore, the plaintiff was bound by the sale.

(b) Estoppel

If the true owner of goods, by his conduct, leads a buyer to believe that the person who makes the sale owns the goods, the true owner is later estopped (prevented) from denying the seller's authority to sell (s.21).

Case: Central Newbury Car Auctions v Unity Finance (1957)

A third party was allowed by the plaintiffs to take possession of a car, and its registration book, pending completion of arrangements to buy it from a finance company on hire-purchase. The finance company refused the application for hire-purchase, but the third party had sold the car in the meantime to the defendants. The plaintiffs sued for recovery of the car.

Held: The plaintiffs were not estopped from denying that the third party to whom they had given possession of the car and registration book had authority to sell the car. Mere transfer of possession is not a representation that the transferee is the owner.

(c) Sale under a common law or statutory power

If a non-owner is entitled to dispose of the goods as if he were the true owner, at common law or under statute, a buyer will acquire good title to the goods. For example, at common law, a finder of goods, who makes a reasonable effort to find the true owner, is entitled to keep the goods and pass a good title to them. Under statute, various persons such as pawnbrokers, hotel proprietors, sheriffs, among others, have specific powers of sale of goods which come into their possession.

(d) Sale in market overt

A market overt is one established by statute, charter or long-standing custom. It takes place between sunrise and sunset, and concerns goods of a kind usually sold in the market.

If goods are sold in market overt according to the usage of the market, the buyer acquires a good title, provided he buys in good faith and without notice of any defects in the seller's title (s.22).

(e) Sale under a voidable title

If a seller of goods has a voidable title, but this title has not been avoided at the time of sale, a buyer acquires a good title to the goods, provided he buys in good faith and without notice of the seller's defect in title.

This applies only to contracts which are voidable, such as for fraud or misrepresentation, and not those which are void, such as for mistake (s.23).

Case: Anderson v Ryan (1967)

The owner of a Mini car agreed with a third party to exchange his car for a Sprite car. The Mini owner was completely unaware that the Sprite was, in fact, a stolen car. The third party sold the Mini to the defendant, who purchased it in good faith and for value. The defendant, in turn, sold it to the plaintiff, who subsequently had it repossessed by the Gardaí. The plaintiff sued for the cost of the car.

Held: The court dismissed the plaintiff's claim. The defendant had passed a good title to the plaintiff, because the third party had not avoided the defective title he had acquired on the exchange of the car.

(f) Disposition by a seller who remains in possession after sale

If a seller of goods, or a mercantile agent acting for him, continues in possession of the goods, or documents of title to them, and he sells the same goods to a person, who receives them in good faith and without notice of the previous sale, the transaction is as valid as if authorised by the true owner (s.24).

Case: O'Reilly v Fineman (1942)

The plaintiff purchased a suite of furniture from the defendant. However, that suite had already been sold to a third party, and when the mistake was discovered, the defendant refused to deliver the goods. As a result, the plaintiff sued for specific performance.

Held: An order for specific performance was not awarded, but damages for loss of bargain were, since there had been a breach of the implied condition as to title. However, had the plaintiff acquired possession of the goods, the first buyer would have been obliged to seek a remedy against the seller instead.

(g) Disposition by a buyer who obtains possession after agreement to sell

If a buyer, or a person who has agreed to buy, obtains possession of the goods (or documents of title), with the seller's consent, and resells or otherwise disposes of the goods to a person who receives them in good faith and without notice of the other seller's rights, title passes to that person, but only if the original buyer acts as a mercantile agent in the ordinary course of business (s.25).

Case: Newtons of Wembley v Williams (1965)

The plaintiffs sold a car to a third party, who paid for it by cheque. The third party was allowed to take possession of the car, on condition that title in the car should not pass before the cheque was cleared. The cheque was dishonoured, but in the meantime the car had been sold in a second-hand car market to the defendant. The plaintiffs sued for the recovery of the car.

Held: The defendant had acquired good title to the car, because the third party from whom he had bought it was a buyer in possession with the sellers' consent at the time of sale, and the transferor acted as a mercantile agent in the ordinary course of business.

(h) Disposition under a hire-purchase agreement
If a hirer of goods is a dealer in goods, and sells those of which he is hirer in the ordinary course of his business to a buyer who acts in good faith, and without notice that the hirer had no authority to sell, the sale shall be valid as if the hirer were expressly authorised by the true owner to make the sale.

(i) Sale under a court order
If goods are the subject of legal proceedings, rules of court authorise the court to order their sale, such as in the case of perishable goods.

• Performance of the sale of goods contract
53. It is the duty of the seller to deliver the goods and of the buyer to accept and pay for them in accordance with the terms of the contract for sale (s.27).

54. Unless otherwise agreed, delivery of the goods and payment of the price are concurrent terms, i.e. the seller must be ready and willing to give possession of the goods to the buyer in exchange for the price, and the buyer must be ready and willing to pay the price in exchange for possession of the goods (s.28).

Delivery

Method
55. Delivery is the voluntary transfer of possession from one party to another. There are five possible ways of effecting delivery:

(a) physical transfer of possession;

(b) physical transfer of the means of control (e.g. by giving the buyer the key of the warehouse);

(c) physical transfer of a document of title (e.g. a bill of lading);

(d) attornment (i.e. by arranging that a third party who holds the goods acknowledges to the buyer that he holds them on his behalf);

(e) alteration in the character of the seller's possession (e.g. if the seller agreed to hold the goods until the buyer wanted them).

Place

56. Except where there is a provision in the contract, the place of delivery is the seller's place of business, if he has one, and if not, his residence, provided that, if the contract is for the sale of specific goods, which to the knowledge of both parties when the contract is made, are in some other place, that place is the place of delivery (s.29).

Case: Board of Ordnance v Lewis (1855)

The defendant contracted to supply coal to several different locations specified by the plaintiffs. The defendant failed to comply with the agreement, and delivered different quantities than those specified to individual locations.

Held: The defendant was in breach of contract.

Time

57. In the absence of an agreed date of delivery, the seller is bound to make delivery within a reasonable time and at a reasonable hour (s.29).

Case: McAuley v Horgan (1925)

The defendant contracted to sell wool to the plaintiff, but no date was set for delivery. The wool ordered was never dispatched and the plaintiff sued for damages.

Held: The defendant was not entitled to avoid the contract on the grounds that no cheque was sent or money tendered by the plaintiff. The defendant had broken the contract and was liable for damages.

Costs

58. Unless otherwise agreed, the expenses of, and incidental to, putting the goods into a deliverable state must be borne by the seller (s.29).

Delivery of incorrect quantities

59. If the seller delivers *less* than the quantity that he contracted to sell, the buyer may reject them, or accept the lesser quantity and pay for them at the contract rate.

60. If the seller delivers *more* than the quantity that he contracted to sell, the buyer may reject the whole amount, accept the contract quantity and reject the excess, or accept the whole amount and pay for them at the contract rate.

Case: Wilkinson v McCann, Verdon & Co. (1901)

The defendants contracted to purchase flags worth £28 from the plaintiff. In fact, flags worth £65 were delivered to the defendants, who refused to take delivery of them. The plaintiff sued for the price of the flags.

Held: The defendants were justified in rejecting the whole amount.

61. If the seller delivers the contract quantity *mixed* with other goods which are not ordered, the buyer may either reject the whole amount or accept the goods contracted for and reject the rest. He cannot accept the incorrect goods (s.30).

Delivery by instalments
62. Unless otherwise agreed, a buyer is not bound to accept delivery by instalments.

Case: Norwell & Co. Ltd v Black (1931)

The defendants, a Dublin firm of furniture retailers, contracted to purchase a consignment of carpets and furniture from the defendants. On arrival of the goods, which did not sufficiently correspond with the order, the defendants refused to accept delivery on the grounds that the whole order had not been tendered together in one lot. They subsequently accepted goods which had formed part of the original consignment, but this was, in effect, a new contract. The plaintiff sued for breach of contract.

Held: The defendants had been entitled to refuse delivery by instalments.

63. Where a contract provides for delivery in stated instalments, which are to be separately paid for, the contract is severable. If one or more deliveries of instalments are defective, this may amount to a repudiation of the whole contract or merely give a right to claim compensation for the defective deliveries only. It depends on the ratio of defective to correct deliveries and the degree of probability that the defective deliveries will be repeated in future instalments (s.31).

Case: Tarling v O'Riordan (1878)

The defendant, a retail dealer, contracted to purchase clothes from the plaintiff in two instalments. The first instalment was received in perfect conformity with the order and was accepted. Part of the second instalment was not in accordance with the order, and the defendant rejected all the clothes of the second instalment.

Held: The defendant was entitled to reject the whole instalment.

Delivery through a carrier

64. Delivery of goods to a carrier, whether named by the buyer or not, for the purpose of transmission to the buyer, is prima facie deemed to be a delivery of the goods to the buyer.

65. However, if in fact the carrier is the agent of the seller, delivery of the goods to the carrier is not deemed to be a delivery to the buyer.

Case: Michel Freres Société Anonyme v Kilkenny Woollen Mills (1961)

The plaintiffs, a French manufacturing firm, contracted to sell yarn to the defendants. A delivery date, but not a place of delivery, was specified in the agreement. The plaintiffs consigned the yarn to a carrier before the delivery date, but it did not reach Ireland until after that date. The defendants refused to accept the yarn, and the plaintiffs sued for damages for breach of contract.

Held: The defendants were entitled to refuse to accept the yarn when it arrived in Ireland. Delivery of the goods to the courier was not delivery to the defendants in accordance with the contract.

66. The seller must make a reasonable arrangement with the carrier, having regard to the nature of the goods and the other circumstances of the case.

67. Unless otherwise agreed, where goods are sent by the seller by a route involving sea transport, under circumstances in which it is usual to insure, the buyer must have notice in time to insure them during their sea transit, and, if the seller fails to give such notice, the goods shall be deemed to be at his risk during the sea transit (s.32).

Acceptance

68. Where goods are delivered to a buyer, which he has not previously examined, he is not deemed to have accepted them until he has had a reasonable opportunity of examining them to see if they are in conformity with the contract (s.34).

69. The buyer is deemed to have accepted the goods when:

(a) he informs the seller that he accepts them; or

(b) he does any act in relation to them which is inconsistent with the ownership of the seller, e.g. resells them or converts raw materials into finished goods; or

(c) he retains the goods, after the lapse of a reasonable time, without informing the seller that he has rejected them (s.35).

70. Where a buyer rightfully rejects the goods, he does not have to see to their return, unless otherwise agreed, but need only inform the seller (s.36).

71. Where a buyer wrongfully refuses to take delivery of the goods within a reasonable time, he becomes liable to the seller for any loss caused, and for storage during the period the seller was forced to retain the goods for him.

Payment

72. Unless otherwise agreed, stipulations as to time of payment are not deemed to be of the essence of a contract of sale, i.e. a default of payment does not entitle the seller to repudiate the contract.

• Remedies for breach of a sale of goods contract

73. As with other contracts, the parties to a contract for the sale of goods are entitled to the usual common law and equitable remedies. The seller, however, has also statutory rights under the sale of goods legislation.

Buyer's remedies against the seller

74. Where a seller is in breach of a condition of a contract, a buyer may reject the goods and rescind the contract, unless he has lost his right to do so by accepting the goods, or part of them, under s.35. He may, in addition, sue for damages.

75. Where a buyer has paid the price, but the consideration for it has failed (e.g. if a seller has no title), he may sue for the return of the price (s.54).

76. Where a seller is in breach of a warranty of a contract, or if a buyer is obliged, or chooses, to treat a breach of condition as a breach of warranty, a buyer may sue for the loss or reduce the amount paid to the seller by an allowance for the breach of warranty.

77. Where a contract is for specific or ascertained goods, a buyer may sue for an order of specific performance. The court, however, would only be likely to order specific performance where damages would be inadequate, e.g. where the goods are unique in some special way.

78. Where a seller wrongfully neglects or refuses to deliver the goods, a buyer can claim damages for non-delivery. The measure of damages is the difference between the contract price and the market price on the date fixed for delivery, or if no date was fixed, at the time of refusal to deliver.

Seller's remedies against the buyer

79. A seller may sue a buyer for the contract *price* if:

(a) ownership of the goods has passed to the buyer, and he wrongfully refuses to pay according to the terms of the contract; or
(b) the contract price is payable on a certain day and the buyer wrongfully neglects or refuses to pay it, regardless of delivery of the goods.

80. A seller may sue a buyer for *damages* for non-acceptance if the buyer wrongfully neglects or refuses to accept and pay for the goods. Once again, the measure of damages is the difference between the contract price and the market price on the date fixed for acceptance, or if no date was fixed, at the time of refusal to accept.

Seller's remedies against the goods

81. Either, or both, of the seller's remedies against the buyer may be of little value to the seller if the buyer is insolvent. The sale of goods legislation, however, gives an 'unpaid seller' (i.e. one to whom the whole price has not been paid or tendered, or who has received conditional payment, e.g. by cheque or bill of exchange, which has been dishonoured), the following rights in respect of the goods:

(a) a lien on the goods, so long as they are in his possession;
(b) a right of stoppage in transit if the goods are in the hands of a carrier; or
(c) a right of resale.

(a) Lien

82. A lien is the right to retain possession of goods (but not to resell them) until the contract price has been paid. Even if some of the goods have been delivered to the buyer, the unpaid seller has a lien on the remainder, unless part delivery indicates his agreement to give up his lien altogether.

83. In order to exercise a lien, one of the following conditions must be satisfied:

(i) the goods must have been sold without any stipulation as to credit; or
(ii) the goods have been sold on credit but the credit period has expired; or
(iii) the buyer has become insolvent.

84. The unpaid seller loses his lien:

  (i) when he delivers the goods to a carrier for transmission to the buyer without reserving a right on their disposal; or

  (ii) when the buyer or his agent lawfully obtains possession of the goods; or

  (iii) when the seller waives his lien (s.43).

(b) Stoppage in transit

85. A seller has a right to stop goods in transit when a buyer becomes insolvent (i.e. he has ceased to pay his debts in the ordinary course of business or cannot pay his debts as they fall due), and to repossess the goods until he has received payment of the contract price.

86. The goods *cease* to be in transit, and the seller's right of stoppage in transit ends:

  (i) on delivery to the buyer or his agent (whether at the agreed destination or before); or

  (ii) if, on reaching the agreed destination, the carrier acknowledges to the buyer that he is holding the goods on the buyer's behalf; or

  (iii) if the carrier wrongfully refuses to deliver the goods to the buyer or his agent (ss.44–5).

(c) Resale

87. Generally, a right of lien or stoppage in transit does not give an un-paid seller any right to resell the goods. He may do so, however, in the following exceptional circumstances:

  (i) when the goods are of a perishable nature; or

  (ii) when the seller has expressly reserved a right of resale under the terms of the contract; or

  (iii) when the buyer, having been given notice of the unpaid seller's intention to resell the goods, does not pay for them within a reasonable time period.

88. If an unpaid seller resells the goods, the second buyer acquires a good title, even if the seller is not entitled to resell. The original buyer will not be able to recover the goods, although he may in that case sue the seller for damages.

• Supply of services

89. The 1980 Act introduced statutory implied terms into contracts for the supply of services, where the supplier is acting in the course of a business, as follows:

(a) that the supplier has the necessary skill to render the service;

(b) that he will supply the services with due skill, care and diligence;

(c) that, where materials are used, they will be sound and reasonably fit for the purpose for which they are required; and

(d) that, where goods are supplied under the contract of service, they will be of merchantable quality (s.39).

90. Any implied term of a contract for the supply of services may be negotiated or varied by an express term of the contract, *unless* the recipient of the service deals as a consumer, in which case it must be shown that such an express term is fair and reasonable and has been specifically brought to the consumer's attention.

IMPORTANT CASES

Numbers in brackets refer to paragraphs of this chapter

PROGRESS TEST

Numbers in brackets refer to paragraphs of this chapter

1. Distinguish between a 'sale' and an 'agreement to sell', and explain the importance of this distinction. (4, 5)
2. What is the implied condition as to the seller's right to pass good title to the goods? (17)
3. In what circumstances is it an implied condition that the goods correspond with description? (19–21)
4. When is there an implied condition that goods sold be of a merchantable quality? (22–3)
5. Explain the implied condition that the goods shall be fit for the disclosed purpose. (24–6)
6. What is a sale of goods by sample, and what is implied in such a sale? (27)
7. Can a seller of goods exclude the statutory conditions and warranties from a contract for the sale of goods? (30–35)
8. What protection does a guarantee afford a buyer of goods? (36–9)
9. Differentiate between (a) specific, (b) unascertained, and (c) ascertained goods. (42)
10. Briefly outline the statutory rules which determine when property (ownership) in goods passes to the buyer. (43–5)
11. Explain what is meant by a 'reservation of title' clause, and the steps which should be taken to ensure its effectiveness. (46–9)
12. Describe, briefly, five exceptions to the *nemo dat quod non habet* common law maxim. (52)
13. When is a seller deemed to have delivered goods? (55)
14. State the implied terms of contracts for the supply of services, as introduced by the 1980 Act. (89)

chapter 27

HIRE-PURCHASE AND LEASING

Topics covered in this chapter are:

- Nature of hire-purchase
- Statutory requirements
- Implied terms
- Termination of agreement
- Restrictions on the owner's rights
- Credit-sales
- Leasing

Summary of the chapter

Sale is only one method of acquiring or distributing goods. This chapter examines the alternative methods of obtaining ownership or use alone of goods, and the statutory protection afforded to customers who avail of such methods.

• Nature of hire-purchase

1. The possession and use of goods can be obtained without purchase by means of a hire-purchase or lease agreement, under which the owner of the goods allows another person to use them in return for rental payments.

2. A hire-purchase is a bailment (i.e. a delivery of possession) of goods under which the bailee *may* buy the goods, or under which the property in the goods will, or may, pass to the bailee.

3. The bailee has an option to buy the goods, but he is not bound to exercise that option. He does not 'agree to buy" the goods at the time of the contract. Therefore, if he sells the goods to another person before he has exercised his option to purchase, he does not pass ownership in the goods.

Case: Helby v Matthews (1895)

The plaintiff hired a piano to a third party, on the agreement that he should pay monthly instalments, he could terminate the agreement by delivering the piano to the plaintiff, and if he paid all the instalments punctually he would become the owner of the piano, but until such time, the piano would remain the property of the plaintiff. Before he had completed paying all of the instalments, the third party pledged the piano with the defendant, a pawnbroker, as security for a loan. The plaintiff sued for recovery of the piano.

Held: The plaintiff was entitled to recovery, because the third party had sold the piano before exercising his option to purchase by paying all of the instalments, and, therefore, could not pass good title to the defendant.

4. Irish hire-purchase law is governed by the Hire-Purchase Act, 1946, as amended by the Hire-Purchase (Amendment) Act, 1960 and the Sale of Goods and Supply of Services Act, 1980.

5. A hire-purchase agreement may be made between a dealer and a consumer, but more commonly a finance company provides the credit. In the latter situation, the consumer negotiates with the dealer for the goods and, if the consumer requires hire-purchase facilities, he will be asked to fill in an application form by the dealer. This is an application to a finance company who, when they have established the credit-worthiness of the consumer, purchase the goods from the dealer. The finance company then lets them on hire-purchase to the hirer, who has originally been the customer of the dealer.

6. At common law, the hirer's only recourse, in the case of defective goods, was against the finance company. The hirer had got the goods from the finance company as owners, and had no right of action against the dealer.

7. Under s.32 of the Sale of Goods and Supply of Services Act, 1980, where goods are let under a hire-purchase agreement to a hirer dealing as a consumer, the person by whom the negotiations were conducted prior to the hiring shall be deemed to be a party to the agreement, and that person and the owner shall be answerable to the hirer for any breach of the agreement.

• **Statutory requirements of hire-purchase agreements**
8. Hire-purchase agreements are subject to the usual rules relating to the formation of a contract. There must be agreement between the parties, an intention to create legal relations, consideration, etc. However, certain statutory requirements also apply.

Notification of cash price
9. S.3 of the 1946 Act requires the owner to notify the hirer of the cash price of the goods, before the agreement is made. The owner may do this:

(a) by informing the customer in writing; or
(b) by having a ticket or label, which clearly states the cash price, attached to the selected goods; or
(c) by having the cash price clearly stated in any catalogue, price list or advertisement from which the goods have been selected.

Note or memorandum of the agreement

10. A hire-purchase agreement must be in writing, signed by the hirer and by, or on behalf of, all other parties to the agreement. The note or memorandum must contain:

(a) a statement of the hire-purchase or total purchase price;

(b) the cash price;

(c) the amount of each instalment, the number of instalments and the dates of payment;

(d) a list of the goods to which the agreement applies;

(e) a notice, as set out in the Schedule to the 1946 Act, informing the hirer of his right to terminate the agreement and the restriction on the owner's right to recover the goods.

11. A copy of the note or memorandum must be delivered or sent to the hirer within fourteen days of making the agreement.

12. If no note or memorandum of the agreement is made and signed, or if there is a failure to include the specified details or to send a copy to the hirer, the agreement, whilst remaining a valid one, will be unenforceable. However, a court has the discretion to waive the requirements if it is satisfied that non-compliance has not prejudiced the hirer and that it would be just and equitable to grant relief (ss.3, 4).

Case: Mercantile Credit Co. of Ireland v Cahill (1964)

The plaintiffs gave a car on hire-purchase to the defendant. When the parties signed the hire-purchase agreement, the required particulars were not filled in, and the terms included in the copy of the agreement sent to the hirer differed materially from those originally agreed. The defendant refused to pay any instalments and the plaintiffs sued to recover the full amount due.

Held: The defendant was lawfully in possession of the car under an agreement that was unenforceable against him. It would not be just and equitable to dispense with the statutory requirements, and, therefore, no order was made for the return of the car and a claim for the full amount was dismissed.

Case: British Wagon Credit Corporation v Henebry (1963)

The defendant entered into a hire-purchase agreement with the plaintiffs for a tractor. He had signed a proposal form at the time of the agreement, but the required statutory details were not filled in at that time. The tractor proved defective, and the defendant refused to pay any further instalments.

Held: The defendant was lawfully in possession of the tractor under an agreement that was unenforceable against him.

Provision of additional information

13. At any time before the final payment has been made, the hirer who pays 5p by way of expenses is entitled, on a written request, to be supplied with a copy of any note or memorandum of the agreement *and* also a statement giving details of:

(a) sums paid by him;
(b) sums which have become due, but remain unpaid; and
(c) future instalments.

14. If the owner fails, without reasonable cause, to comply with this request within seven days, the agreement becomes unenforceable whilst the default continues.

15. If the default continues for one month, the owner is guilty of an offence, and is liable to a fine not exceeding £10 (s.7).

Whereabouts of hired goods

16. When a hirer is under a duty to keep the goods in his possession, or control, he must, on receipt of a written request, inform the owner as to the whereabouts of the goods at the time when the information is given.

17. If the hirer fails, without reasonable cause, to comply with this request within fourteen days, the hirer is guilty of an offence, and is liable to a fine not exceeding £10 (s.8).

• Implied terms

18. S.9 of the Hire-Purchase Act, 1946 implied conditions and warranties relating to the owner's title, the merchantable quality and fitness for purpose of the goods. These provisions have now been replaced by more extensive conditions and warranties in ss.26 to 29 of the Sale of Goods and Supply of Services Act, 1980.

Title

19. Under s.26, there is an implied condition that the owner has, or will have at the time when property in the goods is to be transferred, a right to sell the goods, unless the hire-purchase agreement states that the owner should transfer only such title as he or a third party may have.

20. There is also an implied warranty that the goods are free from any charge in favour of a third party which was not made known to the hirer either before, or at the time the hire-purchase agreement was made, and that the hirer shall enjoy quiet possession of the goods, except so far as it may be disturbed by any person entitled to the charge disclosed.

Description
21. Under s.27, there is an implied condition that where goods are to be let by description, then the goods shall correspond with that description.

22. There is also an implied condition that where goods are let by sample as well as by description, then it is not sufficient that the bulk of the goods shall correspond with the sample, if the goods do not correspond with the description.

Merchantable quality
23. Under s.28, there is an implied condition that where goods are let *in the course of a business*, the goods shall be of a reasonable standard, and suitable for the purpose or purposes for which goods of that kind are commonly let, and as durable as is reasonable to expect having regard to any description applied to them, the price (if relevant), and all other relevant circumstances.

24. Such a condition is *excluded* if:

(i) any defects are brought specifically to the hirer's attention before the agreement is made; or

(ii) the hirer examines the goods before the agreement is made, as regards defects which that examination ought to reveal.

Case: Butterly v United Dominions Trust (Commercial) Ltd (1963)

The plaintiff took delivery of a motor car on hire-purchase from the defendants, and soon became aware of several defects. The car broke down completely after a short while. The plaintiff sued for breach of condition.

Held: The motor car was not of merchantable quality or fit for the purpose for which it was required. The plaintiff was entitled to rescind the contract, and to have his deposit and instalments returned.

Fitness for purpose
25. Under s.28(3), there is an implied condition that where goods are let *in the course of a business,* and the hirer expressly, or by implication, makes known to the owner any particular purpose for which the goods are being hired, then the goods supplied under the agreement shall be reasonably fit for that purpose, whether or not that is a purpose for which such goods are commonly supplied.

26. There is no such implied condition if:

(i) the hirer did not rely on the owner's skill and judgment; or

(ii) it would have been unreasonable for the hirer to rely on the owner's skill and judgment.

Sale by sample
27. Under s.29, there are implied conditions that:

(a) the bulk shall correspond with the sample in quality;

(b) the hirer shall have a reasonable opportunity of comparing the bulk with the sample; and

(c) the goods shall be free from any defect rendering them unmerchantable, which would not be apparent from a reasonable examination of the sample.

Exclusion of implied terms
28. Under s.31, any term in a hire-purchase agreement which excludes all, or any of the provisions of s.26, concerning the owner's title to the goods, is void.

29. Any term in a hire-purchase agreement which excludes all, or any of the provisions of ss.27, 28 and 29 is void where the hirer deals as a consumer, and in any other case will be unenforceable unless such exclusion is shown to be fair and reasonable.

• Termination of agreement

30. A hire-purchase agreement may be terminated before the last instalment falls due, either because the hirer decides not to continue with it, or because he defaults under the agreement.

31. A hirer is entitled to terminate the agreement, except in the case of the hiring of industrial plant or machinery, for use in an industrial process, with a cash price in excess of £200. Termination is done by the hirer so notifying in writing the owner or the person authorised to receive payments under the agreement.

32. When a hirer terminates the agreement, he may become liable to pay all outstanding sums, and any such further sum, which will bring his total payments up to *one-half* of the hire-purchase price (which may include installation charges), or such lesser sum as specified in the agreement.

33. If the hirer has not taken reasonable care of the goods whilst in his possession, he will be liable (in addition to the sums payable above) to pay compensation to the owner.

34. The hirer must, of course, allow the owner to retake possession of the goods. If, on termination of the hire-purchase agreement, the hirer wrongfully retains possession of the goods, the court may, in an action for repossession, order the hirer to deliver the goods to the owner, without giving the hirer the option to retain them by paying the value of the goods, unless it is satisfied that this would not be just and equitable.

35. Any provision in a hire-purchase agreement which excludes or restricts the hirer's right to terminate an agreement, or which imposes any liability on him, in addition to that outlined in the 1946 Act for terminating the agreement, is void.

36. Similarly, any provision in a hire-purchase agreement which imposes a greater liability on a guarantor than that allowed by statute is void.

• Restrictions on the owner's rights

Entry to premises (s.6)
37. Any term in a hire-purchase agreement which authorises an owner of goods to enter any premises, for the purpose of recovering goods let under that agreement, is void.

38. This restriction does not apply to a hire-purchase agreement for a motor vehicle. A term may be included which authorises an owner of a hired motor vehicle, or his agent, to enter premises, other than a dwelling house, in order to recover the motor vehicle.

39. The owner of the goods can, of course, enter the premises and recover the goods with the hirer's consent.

Recovery of goods (s.12)
40. Where *one-third* or more of the hire-purchase price has been paid or tendered by the hirer or the guarantor, the owner cannot enforce any right to recover possession of the goods other than by a court action (except for a limited right in relation to motor vehicles).

41. If the owner seizes the goods without a court order:

(a) the hire-purchase agreement is terminated;
(b) the hirer or guarantor can recover all sums already paid; and
(c) the hirer or guarantor is released from all liability.

Case: McDonald v Bowmaker (Ireland) Ltd (1949)

The plaintiff hirer, having paid in excess of one-third of the hire-purchase price on a lorry, fell into arrears with his payments. The defendants terminated the hire-purchase agreement, and demanded return of the lorry. They accompanied this with a threat of legal proceedings. The plaintiff returned the lorry voluntarily and sued for a return of the instalments paid.

Held: The plaintiff was not entitled to recover the amount already paid in instalments under the hire-purchase agreement. He had chosen to waive the provisions enacted for his protection by returning the lorry voluntarily to the defendants.

Recovery of motor vehicles (s.16, 1960 Act)

42. If one-third of the hire-purchase price of a motor vehicle has been paid, and it is abandoned, or left unattended, in circumstances which have resulted, or are imminently likely to result, in damage or undue depreciation, the owner may still enforce a right to recover, provided he has commenced an action to recover possession of the vehicle.

43. The owner of the motor vehicle is obliged to make an application to the court within fourteen days of taking possession, or otherwise the hirer shall be released of all liability and be entitled to recover all sums already paid under the agreement.

44. Moreover, if the court finds that the owner was not entitled to enforce his right to repossess the motor vehicle, it may award the hirer such damages against the owner as it considers proper.

The owner's remedies

45. Upon breach of a condition of a hire-purchase agreement by the hirer, the owner of the goods is entitled to rescind the contract, and has also got the following options:

(a) he may repossess the goods, where less than one-third of the purchase price has been paid, provided he does not enter premises without authority;
(b) he may claim return of the goods or their value, as well as damages for failure to take reasonable care of the goods;
(c) he may claim damages where the hirer fails to return the goods or has transferred them to another party; or
(d) he may claim arrears of instalment payments instead of rescinding the contract.

The court's discretion (s.13)

46. After one-third of the hire-purchase price has been paid, the court, in dealing with an action by an owner to recover possession of goods from a hirer, may:

(a) order the hirer to deliver the goods to the owners;

(b) order the hirer to deliver the goods, but with a postponement to allow the hirer, or any guarantor, to pay the unpaid balance of the price in such a manner, and subject to such conditions as the court thinks just; or

(c) apportion the goods, if possible, between the owner and hirer, subject to such terms as to further payments, if any, as the court thinks is justified.

47. The court may, on an application by the owner for judgment, apportion the goods into parts, where they are divisible. It is then the duty of the owner to furnish evidence of the value of the parts into which the goods may be divided. Otherwise, the court may give the hirer the option to retain the entire goods on payment of the balance due under the agreement, where this is relatively small.

Transfer of ownership

48. A hirer under a hire-purchase agreement is merely a bailee of the goods, and has no property in these goods until he exercises his option to purchase them. Therefore, a third party, who acquires the goods from the hirer will not usually get a good title to them, under the *nemo dat quod non habet* rule that nobody can acquire a better title to the goods than that which the transferor had.

49. Such a sale will be valid, however, if:

(a) it is a sale in market overt; or

(b) the hirer is a dealer in the type of goods hired, and he sells the goods in the ordinary course of business, provided the third party buys in good faith and without notice of the hirer's lack of authority to tranfer property in the goods.

• Credit-sales

50. The Hire-Purchase Act, 1946 deals not alone with hire-purchase agreements, but also with credit-sale agreements. A credit-sale agreement, for the purposes of the Act, is one for the sale of goods, under which the purchase price is payable by five or more instalments (s.1).

51. The difference between the two types of agreements is that in the case of a credit-sale agreement, property in the goods passes as soon as the contract is made, whereas in the case of a hire-purchase agreement, the property *may* pass at some future date.

52. Credit-sale agreements are subject to the same formalities prescribed for hire-purchase agreements under hire-purchase legislation. However, since credit-sales are *sales* of goods, the terms implied in a sale of goods contract apply.

53. The buyer of goods under a credit-sale agreement becomes the owner when the contract is made. The goods, therefore, unlike as in the case of a hire-purchase agreement, cannot be recovered by the seller unless there is a reservation of title clause. He can only sue the buyer for the balance outstanding.

• Leasing

54. The use of goods may also be acquired without purchase by means of a leasing agreement, under which the owner of goods allows a third party to use them in return for rental payments. Such agreements, there-fore, are merely bailments of goods for reward, and no property in the goods passes, or is ever intended to pass, to the third party acquiring use of the goods.

55. Leasing agreements vary from short-term leases to long-term financial and operating leases.

56. In a *financial* lease, the lessor or owner is *not* responsible for repair and maintenance of the goods. The rental payments usually cover the initial capital cost of the goods leased, and the profit of the lending institution. Therefore, the goods are frequently relet to the lessee at a nominal rent, once the primary lease period is completed, or sold to the lessee at a negotiated price.

57. In an *operating* lease, the lessor or owner *is* responsible for repair and maintenance of the goods. The leasing period will usually be less than that of the expected life of the goods, so rental payments will not normally cover the initial capital cost of the goods leased. The goods therefore, are usually sold off by the owners on completion of the lease.

58. The Sale of Goods and Supply of Services Act, 1980 protects a person acquiring goods by lease to virtually the same extent as it protects the buyer of goods. Leasing agreements are also subject to the statutorily implied terms as regards title, description, merchantable quality, fitness for purpose and, where applicable, terms as regards spare parts and after-sale service.

59. Any term in a leasing contract which excludes all, or any, of these implied terms, is void where the lessee deals as a consumer, and in any other case will be unenforceable, unless such exclusion is shown to be fair and reasonable.

IMPORTANT CASES

Numbers in brackets refer to paragraphs in this chapter

IMPORTANT STATUTES

Hire Purchase Act, 1946
Hire Purchase (Amendment) Act, 1960
Sale of Goods and Supply of Services Act, 1980

PROGRESS TEST

Numbers in brackets refer to paragraphs in this chapter

1. Define a hire-purchase. (2, 3)
2. In the case of defective goods, what recourse is available to the hirer? (6, 7)
3. How may the owner notify the hirer of the cash price of the goods? (9)
4. List the requirements relating to a note or memorandum of the hire-purchase agreement. (10, 11)
5. Briefly outline the implied conditions and warranties applicable to hire-purchase contracts. (18–27)
6. What will a hirer's liability be upon termination of a hire-purchase agreement by him before the last instalment falls due? (32, 33)
7. What restrictions exist on the owner's right to recover goods? (40–44)
8. Identify those remedies available to an owner upon breach of a condition of a hire-purchase contract by a hirer. (45–7)
9. Distinguish between credit-sale and hire-purchase agreements. (51–3)
10. Explain the difference between (a) a financial lease, and (b) an operating lease. (56, 57)

chapter 28

INSURANCE

Topics covered in this chapter are:

- The insurance contract
- Principles of insurance
- Types of insurance contract

Summary of the chapter

Insurance exists to offset the loss suffered by an individual, or business concern, on the happening of some unforeseen event. This chapter examines the conditions under which the insured party may be so covered upon such an occurrence.

• The insurance contract

1. An insurance contract is one whereby the insurer, in return for repayments called premiums, agrees to pay a sum of money to the injured on the happening of a specified event, or agrees to indemnify the insured against any loss caused by the risk insured against.

2. Therefore, three elements are essential to an insurance contract:

(a) *consideration* must pass to the insurer. This usually takes the form of periodic payments, called premiums;

(b) there must be some degree of *uncertainty* as to whether the event insured against will happen, or if it is bound to happen, as to when it will happen; and

(c) the event, if or when it happens, must be *adverse* to the interest of the insured.

Formation of an insurance contract

3. An insurance contract is formed in the same way as other contracts, i.e. by agreement, consideration and an intention to create legal relations.

4. The person seeking insurance usually completes a proposal form, which generally requires particulars of the proposer, details of the cover sought and any other information considered necessary to enable the insurer to assess the risk involved.

5. The completed proposal form is then sent directly to, or through an agent of, the insurance company. If it is *rejected,* that is the end of the matter and no contract will come into effect.

6. If the proposal is accepted, the insurer will issue a policy conforming with the proposal. Normally, however, the proposal will be met with a statement that the policy will not become operative until the first premium is paid. Thus, either party is free to withdraw from their commitment between the time that the proposal form is submitted and the first premium is paid.

7. Pending a decision to accept or refuse a proposal, an insurance company may provide the proposer with temporary cover. This may be done verbally, but is usually done by the issuing of a cover note. This is a short-term contract which is operative for a specified period, unless in the meantime the proposal is rejected. It is distinct from the insurance policy.

8. The person seeking insurance may go to an insurance broker or agent of the insurance company. If the role of the broker extends to filling up the proposal, he is an agent of the insurance company. However, if the role of the broker does *not* extend to filling up the proposal, and he nonetheless does so, he becomes the agent of the proposer. In such a case, were the company to avoid the contract, the insured might have recourse against the broker.

Case: Connors v London & Provincial Assurance Co. (1913)

The plaintiff signed his name on a proposal form, and a broker for the defendants, with full knowledge of the facts, carelessly completed the proposal form. The broker's authority, however, was confined by the defendants to the submission of proposal forms. When the defendants discovered the true facts, they sought to avoid the policy. The plaintiff initiated an action to prevent them from doing so.

Held: The broker's authority was confined to the submission of the proposal form. The defendants, therefore, were not bound by any statement or representation of the broker.

• Principles of insurance

Utmost good faith (uberrimae fidei)
9. All insurance contracts are *uberrimae fidei* (of utmost good faith). Unless a full disclosure is made to the insurer of all material facts which are known, or ought to have been known, to the insured at the time of making the contract, then the contract is voidable at the option of the insurer.

10. A fact is material if it would influence the judgment of a prudent insurer in deciding whether to accept such risk and, if so, what premiums and conditions to impose.

Case: Chariot Inns Ltd v Assicurazioni Generali SPA (1981)

The plaintiff, when seeking fire insurance for its licensed premises, had to answer a series of questions contained in a proposal form. The answer given to the question, 'Material Damage: Give claims experience for loss over the last five years', was 'None'. The plaintiff had in fact been paid two years earlier on a claim for material damage suffered to property belonging to it, which had been stored in the premises of an associate company. An insurance policy was issued to the plaintiff. The licensed premises was subsequently damaged by fire. The defendants sought to avoid the contract of insurance because of the non-disclosure of the previous fire.

Held: The defendants were entitled to avoid the contract. Non-disclosure of the previous fire was material to the risk which the defendants had been asked to incur.

11. If an insurance policy is voidable due to fraudulent misrepresentation, the insurer may avoid the insurance contract, whether or not damage has resulted from the breach, without having to return any premiums paid.

Case: Griffin v Royal Liver Friendly Society (1942)

The plaintiff, when seeking a life assurance policy, filled in a proposal form containing the following question: 'Is the proposed in good health and nature of last illness?'. He answered 'None', while he had in fact been suffering from tubercular illness for some years. The defendants sought to avoid the policy, on discovering the true facts, and the plaintiff initiated an action to prevent them from doing so.

Held: the defendants were entitled to avoid the policy.

12. If the policy is voidable due to innocent misrepresentation, the premiums can be recovered by the insured, unless the policy itself provides that if it is found to be void, then any premiums paid cannot be recovered.

13. A duty of disclosure is not at an end when a proposal form is completed, but continues up to the moment the proposal is accepted, or later, depending on the circumstances.

Case: Harney v Century Insurance Co. Ltd (1983)

The plaintiff, when seeking a health insurance policy, completed a proposal form containing the following statement: 'The office must be notified of any changes in the health and circumstances of the life to be insured prior to the assumption of risk.' He signed the form on 23 May. He then attended his doctor on 9 August with a head-cold, received antibiotics and continued working. The insurance policy was issued after this date, with a clause stating that the 'date risk assumed' was 31 August. The plaintiff's condition subsequently deteriorated, and when he claimed disability benefit under the policy, the defendants sought to avoid the policy on the grounds that they had not been informed of material facts affecting the risk, prior to the date of its assumption.

Held: Non-disclosure of the head-cold was not material to the risk. Consequently, the defendants were not entitled to avoid the insurance policy.

14. The *contra proferentem* rule may be applied to insurance contracts in order to ease the duty of disclosure in special circumstances. Where a term of an insurance contract is so ambiguous as to admit to two different constructions, the court will choose the meaning unfavourable to the party who drew up the contract to the benefit of the other party.

Case: In re Sweeney and Kennedy's Arbitration (1950)

A motor insurance policy contained a condition that drivers covered by the policy were not under twenty-one years of age, or had less than twelve months' driving experience. When the policy had been issued, that was factually correct, but subsequent to this, the insured employed his son in his business. The son was involved in an accident while driving one of the company's motor vehicles, before having reached twenty-one years of age. The insurer attempted to avoid the contract.

Held: The insurer had used ambiguous expressions, which had to be construed *contra proferentem*. The policy, therefore, was correct in so far as it related to the facts which existed when the policy was issued, and the court held the insurer liable to indemnify the insured for the loss suffered.

Insurable interest

15. An insurance contract is void unless the insured person has an insurable interest in the subject matter of the insurance, or the life assured. He must benefit by its continued existence or be prejudiced (i.e. suffer) by its destruction or loss.

Case: O'Leary v Irish National Insurance Co. Ltd (1958)

The plaintiff sought car insurance from the defendants. He filled out a proposal form which contained a question as to the owner of the car. He stated that he was the owner of the car—which was in fact untrue. After the plaintiff was involved in an accident, the defendants repudiated the policy and the plaintiff sued to enforce it.

Held: No valid contract of insurance had ever existed, since the plaintiff had no insurable interest in the car.

16. Any policy in which the insurer has no insurable interest is a wager, and void under the Gaming and Lotteries Act, 1956.

17. Under the Life Assurance Act, 1774 (applied to this country by the Life Assurance Act, 1886), insurance cannot be taken out by a person on the life of another unless he has an interest in the life of that other.

18. A person has an insurable interest in his own life, as has one spouse in the other's life. However, an insurable interest is not assumed in the relationship of parent and child, brothers and sisters or more distant relatives. It *may* exist, however, in certain circumstances, such as when the child is supporting the parent, or vice versa.

19. Where a person has a pecuniary or legally enforceable interest in the life of another, he is deemed to have an insurable interest. A creditor has an interest in his debtor's life, an employer has an interest in his employee's life, etc.

20. Such an insurable interest need only exist at the date on which the policy is made. For example, a creditor who has taken out life assurance up to the amount of the debt on the life of the debtor, may claim on that policy at its maturity date, even if the debt has been honoured in full before that date.

21. The insurable interest in *property* is the loss which the insured would suffer on the occurrence of the risk. For example, an owner, a tenant, a mortgagee and a prospective purchaser may all have an insurable interest in the same piece of real property.

22. The insurable interest in fire and other types of property insurance, such as theft, must exist *both* at the date on which the policy is made and at the date of loss.

Indemnity
23. An indemnity is an undertaking to give protection against damage or loss. Insurance contracts, other than insurance of the person, are contracts of indemnity, i.e. the insurer undertakes to make good (indemnify) the insured's actual loss, so far as it does not exceed the sum insured. It follows, therefore, that the insured is not allowed to profit from his policy, and a number of rules have been established to enforce this principle.

Amount recoverable

24. An insurance contract will usually provide that the insurer will pay the sum insured, or the amount of the actual loss suffered, whichever is the lesser. For example, if a person insures his house for £30,000 and it is burnt down, if £20,000 will restore it, then he may claim £20,000 and no more. If it will cost £40,000 to restore it, then he may claim £30,000.

25. The measure of indemnity is:

(a) in the event of total loss, not the cost price, but the market value of the property at the time and place of the loss; or
(b) in the event of partial loss, the cost of repairs.

Case: St Alban's Investment Co. v Sun Alliance & London Insurance Co. Ltd (1983)

The plaintiffs insured a premises against fire with the defendant insurers. When the premises was destroyed by fire, the plaintiffs entered a claim for the cost of rebuilding the damaged premises.

Held: The plaintiffs were entitled to the market value of the premises at the time of its destruction, and not the cost of rebuilding.

26. If the property is not insured for its full market value, the insurers are still liable for a partial loss up to the full limit of the sum insured. It is common, therefore, for the insurers to include a 'subject to average' clause, whereby if the amount insured is less than the value of the property, the insurers are only liable for that proportion of the actual loss which the sum insured bears to the value of the property. For example, if property with a market value of £10,000 is only insured for £5,000 under a policy containing a 'subject to average' clause, and damage is caused which totals £2,000, the insurer will only be liable for £1,000.

27. One exception to the rule that an insured cannot recover more than his actual loss arises under a valued policy. With such a policy, the measure of indemnity is agreed at the time when the policy is issued. The insured can recover the agreed value if the loss is total, even though it may exceed the insured's actual loss. If the loss, however, is partial, the insured can recover such proportion of the agreed value as is represented by the depreciation in the actual value.

Subrogation

28. Subrogation entitles an insurer, who has paid an indemnity to an insured, to all the rights of the insured against any third party liable in respect of the loss. This ensures that the policy holder obtains no more than a full indemnity.

29. The insurers bring the action in the name of the insured, who is compelled, under the terms of the policy, to lend his name to the proceedings in return for a promise that he will not be liable for costs. Once the insurer has been indemnified, any surplus belongs completely to the insured.

30. An insured, who renounces or compromises any right of action he has against a third party, without the consent of the insurer, must repay to the insurer the benefit of which he has thereby deprived them.

Contribution

31. The risk may be provided against with more than one insurer. This is called 'double-insurance'. However, where two or more insurance contracts cover the same interest in a common subject matter in respect of the same risk, the law does not allow the insured to recover under each and so make a profit on his loss.

32. An insured may recover the total loss which is covered from one of the insurers. In such an event, however, the insurer who pays him acquires a right to 'contribution', i.e. a right to claim a rateable proportion of the amount paid out from the other insurer(s).

33. The insurance contract may contain a 'rateable proportion' condition, which obliges the insured to claim against all the joint insurers for a pro-rata payment on any loss arising.

34. Finally, some insurance policies may contain a clause which excludes all liability if another policy exists which covers the same risks.

• Types of insurance contract

Life assurance

35. This is a contract by which the insured person agrees to pay a lump sum or annual payments to the insurer, over a specified period, in return for an undertaking by the insurer to pay a definite sum:

(a) on the insured's death;
(b) on the insured's death, if it occurs within a specified time; or
(c) on the insured reaching a specified age, or on his death if sooner.

36. The insurable interest necessary in such contracts is outlined in paragraphs 17 and 18, and will not be repeated here. Students are advised to reread these paragraphs carefully at this time.

37. A life assurance policy may be assigned. An assignment is the transfer of the right to receive the policy money from the person originally entitled to a third party, called the assignee. In practice, this is often done to secure a loan.

38. A legal assignment is effected by an endorsement on the policy itself, or by a separate document evidenced in writing. The assignee must give notice in writing to the insurer in order to protect his interest in the policy. The assignee, thereafter, has a right to sue the insurers in his own name, if necessary, for the policy money.

39. An equitable assignment may be effected by a verbal or written agreement, or by mere delivery. No special form is required, once it is clear that the insured has intended to assign the policy. An insurer will require a joint discharge from both the assignor and assignee of an equitable assignment upon making payment under the policy.

Fire insurance
40. This is a contract which indemnifies the insured in the event of injury or loss caused by fire to specified property during a definite period of time.

41. An insurable interest must exist for the insured, not only when the contract is made, but also when the loss occurs.

42. If damage is caused by the wilful act of the insured, such as deliberately setting fire to the insured property, then he cannot recover on the loss. If, however, the damage is merely caused by his negligence, this will not defeat his claim.

Motor vehicle insurance
43. Under the Road Traffic Act, 1961, a motorist must insure against any liability he may incur as a result of causing the death or injury of a third party by negligent use of the vehicle in a public place.

44. If the user of a motor vehicle is not insured against liability for causing injury to third parties, both the owner and user are guilty of a criminal offence.

Theft insurance
45. The principles applicable to life and fire insurance also apply to theft.

Accident insurance
46. Personal injury to a policy holder is frequently covered by life assurance policies. If a person does not have a life assurance policy, he may still insure himself against personal injury in the form of a personal injury policy. He may also insure against liability arising from injuries to third parties by way of a public liability policy.

IMPORTANT CASES

Numbers in brackets refer to paragraphs of this chapter

PROGRESS TEST

Numbers in brackets refer to paragraphs of this chapter

1. Describe the three essential elements of an insurance contract. (2)
2. Differentiate between a 'proposal form' and a 'cover note'. (4, 7)
3. What is meant by *uberrimae fidei*, in relation to an insurance contract? (9–14)
4. Under what circumstances is an insurable interest in the subject matter of the policy assured by statute? (18, 19)
5. Explain what is meant by the principle of indemnity. (23)
6. How do the rules relating to (a) subrogation, and (b) contribution, enable the enforcement of the principle of indemnity? (28–34)
7. Briefly outline the difference between life assurance and fire assurance. (35–42)

EXAMINATION QUESTIONS

Section 4: Commercial Law

1. (a) Distinguish between a holder in due course and a holder for value.
   (b) What is the effect of the following crossing on a cheque 'not negotiable—Account payee only'?

   I.C.S.A. (December 1990)

2. (a) What is a bill of exchange? Explain the endorsements which can appear on a bill of exchange.

(b) Ian was the secretary of the Save 'n' Spend Holiday Club. He made out a crossed cheque for the signature of the club's treasurer payable to Jack, a member of the club. The treasurer signed the cheque and gave it to Ian to pass on the Jack. Ian then forged Jack's endorsement on the cheque and negotiated it for value to Keith, who acted in good faith. The cheque was debited to the club's bank account.

What action, if any, may the club take against Keith and their bankers?

A.C.C.A. (June 1990)

3. You are required to explain the meaning of each of the following terms:

(a) agency by ratification;
(b) negotiable instruments;
(c) breach of warranty of authority;
(d) retention of title (Rompala) clause.

C.I.M.A. (November 1987)

4. Explain briefly the terms implied by statute in a contract for the sale of goods.

I.A.T.I. (Summer 1990)

5. What are the differences in a contract for the sale of goods between specific and unascertained goods? Why is the distinction of importance?

A.C.C.A. (June 1990)

EUROPEAN
—————— COMMUNITY LAW ——————

chapter 29

EUROPEAN COMMUNITY LAW

Topics covered in this chapter are:

- Origins of the European Community
- Institutions of the Community
- Sources of Community law
- The Single European Act

Summary of the chapter

This chapter examines the legal and institutional structures of the EC and their implications for law in Ireland.

• Origins of the European Community

1. The idea of a closely knit association of European States did not find political expression to any great degree until after the Second World War. Only after Europe had yet again been devastated by war was the futility of constant national rivalry truly appreciated. Subsequent moves towards co-operation sprang from two main factors:

(a) Europe's realisation of her own weakness—the USA and Soviet Union now had far greater military, political and economic power than any of the individual European States could achieve, thereby displacing Europe from her position at the centre of the world stage.
(b) The need to prevent renewed military conflict—the two world wars, both of which had seen Europe as the main battlefield and principal sufferer, gave rise to this becoming the guiding principle of all political action.

2. On 18 April 1951, six countries (France, Germany, Italy, Belgium, the Netherlands and Luxembourg) signed a Treaty in Paris which brought the European Coal and Steel Community (ECSC) into existence. The Treaty, which entered into force on 23 July 1952, has the objective of pooling the coal and steel production of the Member States under a joint High Authority, within an organisation open to any other country in Europe that wishes to join. It is responsible for ensuring the most rational distribution of coal and steel with the maximum of efficiency.

3. Further attempts at economic integration led to the Six signing Treaties in Rome on 25 March 1957, which established the European Atomic Energy Community (Euratom) and the European Economic Community (EEC), and which entered into force on 1 January 1958. These had an objective of creating a union of European States, bound together by common economic goals, namely, the harmonious development of economic activities, continuous economic expansion and a faster rise in the standard of living. Together, the three Communities are commonly referred to as the European Community (EC).

4. Ireland, Britain and Denmark joined all three communities by signing treaties on accession on 22 January 1972, which came into force on 1 January 1973. In order for Ireland to do so, it was necessary to amend the Constitution to allow laws of the Community made externally, and not by organs established under the Constitution, to be part of our domestic law. A political referendum, on 10 May 1972, adopted the necessary constitutional amendment.

5. On 1 January 1981, Greece became the tenth member of the Community, while on 1 January 1986, Spain and Portugal duly became the eleventh and twelfth members of the Community, after the signing of accession treaties and their ratification by the parliaments of the Member States and the applicant countries.

6. The latest enlargement by no means marks the end of the Community's expansion. Turkey and Austria have already formally applied for membership, while Malta and Cyprus have indicated that they intend to do so too. At the time of writing, the rapidly changing face of central European political structures offers potential for an even larger Community but, for the moment, the completion of the single European market by 1992 among the twelve Member States is the primary concern.

• Institutions of the Community

The Commission
7. This is the executive body, or civil service, of the Community. It consists of seventeen Commissioners appointed by the mutual agreement of the Member States. It is provided by the Treaties that each Member State must have a national on the Commission, and the present practice is for the five larger countries, i.e. Germany, France, Italy, Spain and Britain, to appoint two each.

8. Throughout their four-year term of office, which is infinitely renewable, Commissioners must remain independent of the governments of the Member States and of the Council of Ministers. The Council cannot remove any Commissioner from office. The European Parliament, however, can pass a motion of censure compelling the Commission as a body to resign, in which case it would continue to handle everyday business until the Commission's replacement.

9. Each Commissioner has a personal staff, called a cabinet, which works directly with him and which helps him prepare his contribution to the work of the Commission, and his contacts with the services, with the other institutions, with the Member States and with the general public. In addition, the Commission has a staff of about 14,500. They comprise a Secretariat-General, a Legal Service, a Statistical Office, twenty-two Directorates-General and a small number of specialised services.

10. Each Commissioner has special responsibility for one or more portfolios or broad areas of Community activity, such as agriculture, energy, transport, external relations, etc. Despite this autonomy, however, the Commission is bound to act with collective responsibility. It must adopt the various measures incumbent on it under the Treaties as a body. The Commission, headed by a President and currently with six Vice-presidents, meets at least one day each week for this purpose.

11. When particularly sensitive matters are being discussed, the Commission sits alone, the only official present being the Secretary-General. In other cases, the officials responsible may be called in. Although its decisions can be taken by majority, many are in fact unanimous. Where a vote is taken, the minority abides by the majority decision, which becomes the position of the full Commission.

12. The Commission has been assigned a wide range of duties under the Community Treaties. It is required to:

(a) act as guardian of the Treaties;
(b) serve as the executive arm of the Communities; and
(c) initiate Community policy and defend the Community interest in the Council of Ministers.

13. The Commission has to see to it that the provisions of the Treaties and the decisions of the Community institutions are implemented properly. It investigates a presumed infringement either on its own initiative or on the strength of complaints from governments, companies or private individuals. Once an infringement has been established, the Commission requests the Member State in question to submit its comments within a specified time period, generally two months. If the disputed practice is allowed by the Member State to continue, and it is unable to satisfy the Commission, then the Commission will issue a reasoned opinion, which the Member State must comply with before a specified deadline. If it does not do so, the Commission may refer the case to the European Court of Justice, whose judgment is binding on both parties.

14. The Commission has been conferred with wide executive powers by the Treaties and the Council of Ministers. It has particularly extensive legislative powers to issue decisions and regulations implementing certain Treaty provisions or Council of Ministers' acts. It applies Treaty rules to specific cases (involving governments or companies), administers safeguard clauses in the Treaties, and administers appropriations for the Community's public expenditure and the four major Community funds.

15. The Commission initiates Community policy by submitting proposals to the Council of Ministers for enactment. When drafting its proposal, the Commission takes the often widely varying interests of the individual Member States into account in order to establish where the general interest lies. Once a proposal is lodged, a dialogue takes place between the ministers in the Council, who put their national points of view, and the Commission, which seeks to uphold the interest of the Community as a whole and find European solutions to common problems. Because of its non-partisan position, the Commission acts as a mediator between the Member States through the negotiations within the Council of Ministers in order to find an acceptable compromise without sacrificing the Community interest.

16. The Commission also represents the Community in dealing with non-Member States and other international organisations.

The Council of Ministers

17. The Council consists of representatives of the governments of the twelve Member States. Although the 'main' representative for each is its Foreign Minister, membership of the Council varies with the subject down for discussion. Meetings are thus often attended by the ministers responsible for the subject area in question (e.g. agriculture, finance, transport, science, etc.). Presidency of the Council rotates in alphabetical order every six months.

18. While the Council of Ministers represents the sovereignty of the Member States, and considers and protects national interests, it is also obliged to take the Community interest into account. It is required to take decisions necessary for the attainment of the goals laid down in the Treaties. Some of its responsibilities include:

(a) ensuring freedom of movement;
(b) ensuring freedom to provide services and the right of establishment;

(c) defining common policies; and
(d) establishing the Community budget.

19. The Council of Ministers is formally the legislative body for the Community, since no major proposals can be implemented without its consent. The Commission drafts proposals concerning Community policy and development for the Council of Ministers to discuss.

20. Where the Council of Ministers acts on a proposal from the Commission, unanimity is required to amend that proposal. The majority rule only applies if the proposal is accepted *in toto*, without amendment. When decisions are taken in the Council of Ministers by majority vote, France, Germany, Italy and Britain have 10 votes each, Spain has 8, Belgium, Greece, the Netherlands and Portugal have 5 each, Denmark and Ireland have 3 each and Luxembourg has 2 votes. Therefore, while the Council of Ministers can adopt the Commission's proposal as it stands by a majority vote, it can depart from the proposal if there is unanimity, or it may fail to come to a decision at all. In practice, however, majority voting has been hardly used since the 'Luxembourg compromise' 1966, which effectively gave each Member State a right, on the grounds of an essential national interest being at stake, to veto any major decision by insisting on unanimity.

21. The Single European Act, signed in Luxembourg in February 1986, has substantially extended the Council of Ministers' scope for taking majority decisions, particularly as regards the internal market. Although the unanimity requirement has not been completely eliminated, the Act reflects a general acknowledgment that majority voting should be used more often than in the past. A large number of Council of Ministers' decisions are now taken on a majority basis.

The European Council
22. In December 1974, the Heads of State or Government of the Community countries decided to meet regularly within a 'European Council' with their Foreign Ministers, the President and one of the Vice-presidents of the Commission, with a view to defining new objectives and giving a fresh stimulus to European integration. This was formally incorporated into the Community's institutional framework by the Single European Act.

23. Meetings of the European Council are free of institutional formalities. It is simply a meeting of politicians, with neither civil servants nor experts present. In recent years, such meetings have provided political impetus in areas such as economic and monetary union, direct elections to the European Parliament, reform of agricultural policy, social policy measures and the accession of new members.

24. The European Council has experienced difficulties in the implementation of conclusions reached. To limit intervention by the European Council in the general running of the Community, therefore, it was agreed in 1986 to restrict meetings to two a year, except in exceptional circumstances. None the less, the importance of the European Council in the workings of the Community has steadily increased—a trend which is likely to continue as the authority of the Heads of State or Government grows stronger.

The European Parliament (the Assembly of the European Communities)

25. On 7 and 10 June 1979, direct elections to the European Parliament were first introduced, with each Member State using its own national electoral system. These are held every five years, the most recent being in June 1989.

26. The European Parliament has 518 members, the proportion of representation being dependent upon the population size of the Member States. The composition on 13 June 1988 was as follows:

Belgium	24	Ireland	15
Denmark	16	Italy	81
Germany	81	Luxembourg	6
Greece	24	Netherlands	25
Spain	60	Portugal	24
France	81	United Kingdom	81

27. Parliament is presided over by a President, assisted by fourteen Vice-presidents. Elected members organise themselves into groups based on political, social and economic philosophies, regardless of nationality. The largest of these are the Socialist Group, the Group of the European People's Party and the European Democratic Party.

28. The European Parliament operates by way of eighteen standing committees. Each committee specialises in some particular aspect of Community activity, such as agriculture, energy, monetary affairs, etc. The appropriate Member of the Commission or his representative appears before the committees to give an account of the decisions taken by the Commission, the proposals presented to the Council of Ministers and the position adopted by the Commission *vis-à-vis* the Council of Ministers. Committee work, therefore, takes up most of a Member of European Parliament's (MEP) time. Eight plenary sessions of one week's duration, involving the entire European Parliament, are also held each year.

29. The European Parliament has no real legislative powers. Its stated objective since direct elections is that the power to enact legislation should be shared between the European Parliament and the Council of Ministers. For the present, however, its role is mainly of a consultative and a supervisory nature.

30. The consultative function of the European Parliament involves exercise of the advisory powers conferred on it by the Treaties. Parliament may deliver opinions on Commission proposals before the Council of Ministers makes a decision. Since its opinions are not binding, however, its influence on the Council of Ministers' decisions is relatively slight.

31. The supervisory function of the European Parliament is confined to the Commission, which is obliged to defend and justify its position in public debates before the European Parliament. It must also present an annual general report on the activities of the Communities for discussion. Parliament thus keeps constant watch on the Commission's doings, making sure that it represents the Community interest, ready at any time to call it to order if it gives the impression of yielding to the lobbying of governments. Ultimately, therefore, the Commission is responsible to the European Parliament and it can even be forced to resign by a motion of censure carried by a two-thirds majority.

32. The European Parliament also has widespread budgetary powers. In certain cases it may not alone reallocate, but also increase, expenditure up to specified limits. It has the right to reject a budget as a whole, which it did with the 1980 and 1985 budgets. This has allowed the European Parliament to impose its point of view on the Council of Ministers on a number of occasions.

33. While the Single European Act failed to produce any increase in the legislative powers of the European Parliament, it did confer on it the power of assent in relation to the accession of further member states or the association with non-member countries. Moreover, it also introduced a co-operation procedure applicable to qualified majority decisions having an influence on the completion of the internal market. Although the Parliament has been critical of this new procedure, it should help in some small way towards strengthening the European Parliament's influence on the Community decision-making process.

The Court of Justice

Now 15

34. The Court of Justice, based in Luxembourg, consists of 13 judges, and is assisted by 6 advocates-general. Judges are appointed by common accord of the governments of the Member States, and hold office for a once-renewable term of six years. Every three years, 6 or 7 judges and 3 advocates-general are replaced alternatively, thereby ensuring continuity of the Court's decisions.

35. Although there is no specific nationality requirement, each Member State has one judge in the Court of Justice at present. The thirteenth judge has tended to be chosen from the nationals of the large Member States.

36. Judges are chosen from persons whose independence is beyond doubt, and who are qualified to hold the highest judicial offices in their respective Member States. They select one of their number to be President for a renewable term of three years. The President directs the work of the Court of Justice.

37. Advocates-general are appointed on the same terms as judges, and have to satisfy the same criteria with respect to independence and training. Until recently, they were all nationals of the larger Community countries. Lately, however, there have been appointments of nationals of the smaller Member States.

38. An advocate-general does not participate in the Court of Justice's deliberations. Instead, at a separate hearing some weeks after lawyers have addressed the Court, he comments on the various aspects of the case in an unbiased manner, weighs up the provisions of Community law, compares the case in point with previous rulings, highlights its possible implications for future development within the Community and ultimately proposes an appropriate legal solution to the dispute.

39. The general tasks of the Court of Justice consist of the interpretation, application and development of Community law. Thus, the Court of Justice has jurisdiction in:

(a) actions brought by the Commission or by Member States for an infringement of the Treaties by a Member State;
(b) actions brought by Member States, corporate bodies or private individuals, against the Commission and the Council of Ministers, or by one of the latter Community institutions against the other on the grounds of lack of competence, infringement of the Treaties, violation of a procedural requirement or abuse of power;
(c) preliminary rulings on the interpretation of the Treaties, or on the validity of any of the Community's institutions.

40. The Court of Justice reaches its judgment by majority vote. However, no dissenting opinion is made public. Those judges participating in the deliberation sign the single judgment, which is then pronounced at a public hearing. The Court of Justice's decision is binding on the national courts of Member States. There is no right of appeal against such decisions. If a Member State does not comply with the ruling, new proceedings may be brought for a declaration by the Court that the obligations arising from its first decision have not been complied with. While the Treaties do not provide any sanctions where a Member State fails to give effect to a judgment, the experience has been that Member States have complied, sooner or later, with the Court of Justice's judgment.

41. The Single European Act, signed on 17 February 1986, has allowed the Council of Ministers, acting unanimously at the request of the Court of Justice and after consulting the Commission and European Parliament, to attach to the Court of Justice a Court of First Instance.

42. The composition of this Court of First Instance is determined by the Council of Ministers. Like the judges of the Court of Justice, they must satisfy specified criteria with respect to independence and training. They too are appointed by common accord of the governments of the Member States, and hold office for a renewable term of six years. Membership is partially renewed every three years, thereby ensuring continuity of the Court's decisions.

43. Not all classes of actions may be heard by this Court of First Instance. Actions brought by officials of the European Communities, actions for damages and competition cases may be dealt with by such a court. Decisions on such actions, however, may be appealed to the Court of Justice on points of law.

44. The aforementioned institutions have responsibility for achieving the aims of the European Community. Other Community organs include the Court of Auditors and the Economic and Social Committee.

The Court of Auditors
45. The Court of Auditors consists of twelve members, appointed unanimously by the Council of Ministers, after consultation with the European Parliament. It has been in operation since October 1977.

46. The functions of the Court of Auditors include:

(a) auditing the accounts of the European Community and of the Community bodies;

(b) examining whether revenue and expenditure have been properly and lawfully received and incurred;

(c) checking that financial management has been sound; and

(d) reporting back to the Community institutions.

The Economic and Social Committee

47. The Economic and Social Committee consists of 189 members, representing the various sectors of economic and social life of the Community. It assists the Council of Ministers and the Commission, and must be consulted before decisions are taken on a large number of subjects. It is also free to submit opinions on its own initiative. This process ensures that the various interest groups are actively involved in the development of the Community.

• Sources of Community law

Treaties

48. The 'primary legislation' of the European Community has been created directly by the Member States. It consists of the Treaties establishing the European Communities themselves, including the annexes, schedules and protocols attached to the Treaties, and the subsequent additions and amendments thereto.

49. These written sources of Community law include:

(a) Treaty establishing the European Coal and Steel Community (ECSC) of 18 April 1951 (otherwise known as the 'Treaty of Paris');

(b) Treaty establishing the European Atomic Energy Community (Euratom) of 25 March 1957 (otherwise known as the 'first Treaty of Rome');

(c) Treaty establishing the European Economic Community (EEC) of 25 March 1957 (otherwise known as the 'second Treaty of Rome');

(d) Treaty establishing a single Council and a single Commission of the European Communities (Merger Treaty) of 8 April 1965;

(e) Treaty concerning the accession of Ireland, Denmark and Britain to the EEC and Euratom of 22 January 1972.

50. The Treaties set out broad objectives to be achieved by the institutions of the Community. The specific details are left to the Council of Ministers and the Commission, who have limited law-making powers which they may exercise in accordance with the provisions of the treaties.

51. The primary law of the Community takes precedence over national law. A legal consequence of this precedence is the fact that any provision of national law which conflicts with the Community law is invalid. In theory, however, Community law and national constitutional law are separate. In some Member States (e.g. the Netherlands), the precedence of Community law has been provided for in the national constitution. Friction between Community law and Irish constitutional law resulted from the Supreme Court's refusal in 1987 to permit the Government to proceed with ratification of the Single European Act without the specific permission of the population by referendum. This delayed the entry into force of the Act by six months and served as a warning that Ireland's membership of the European Community and ratification of the Single European Act do not rule out the possibility that a referendum will be required again for further developments.

Community legislation

52. The legal acts which the Council of Ministers and the Commission have at their disposal when carrying out the tasks conferred on them by the Treaties are enumerated and described under Article 189 of the EEC Treaty, 1957. This 'secondary law' of the Community consists of:

(a) Regulations. These are used mainly to secure uniformity of law throughout the Community (e.g. Regulation No. 17 on restrictive practices of 6 February 1962 and Regulation No. 1612/68 on freedom of movement of 15 October 1968). They have general application, are binding in their entirety and are directly applicable in all Member States without the need for further legislation. They confer rights and impose obligations on those to whom they are addressed.

(b) Directives. These also have general application, but do not have immediate binding force. They are addressed to Member States and lay down the result to be achieved, but leave the choice of the form of the measures and methods used in the implementation of the Directives to the individual national authorities.

Once the Council of Ministers adopts a Draft Directive which has been placed before it by the Commission, then the Member States have until a specified date to incorporate the provisions of the Directive into their own national laws. For example, the Eighth Directive, harmonising the qualifications for auditors, as well as dealing with their education and training, was adopted in April 1984. Member States had until 1988 to implement it, and until 1990 before its provisions needed to be applied.

(c) Decisions. These are the usual means whereby the Community institutions deal with individual cases, and in the competition field, for example, have had a far-reaching impact on the behaviour of undertakings. They may be addressed by the Council of Ministers or Commission to a Member State, or to one or more individuals in the Member States. Their content may be expressed either in concrete or abstract terms. Decisions are immediately binding in their entirety upon those to whom they are addressed.

(d) Recommendations and opinions. These are not legally binding and give rise to no legal obligation on the part of the addressees, who are for the most part Member States. Recommendations are usually made on the initiative of the Community institution issuing them, suggesting that the addressee take a specific course of action without legally obliging him to do so. Opinions, on the other hand, are delivered as a result of an initiative of one or more persons, and contain a general assessment of certain facts or prepare the ground for subsequent legal proceedings. Because of their lack of binding force, the importance of recommendations and opinions is primarily political and psychological.

• The Single European Act (SEA)

53. The Single European Act, which was signed on 17 February 1986 and came into effect on 1 July 1987, contains the first major amendment to the Treaty of Rome since its adoption in 1957. The adoption of the Single European Act has provided the required political impetus and legal framework to halt the economic fragmentation of the Community and to complete, within a given timeframe, the aims of the original Treaties. The SEA has formally enshrined the commitment to freedom of movement of capital, goods and persons within the Community.

54. The Single European Act contains provisions covering the Community institutions, the internal market, economic and monetary co-operation, social policy, research and technological developments, foreign policy co-operation and the environment. These provisions take the form of amendments and additions to the original Treaties.

55. The decision-making process on matters concerning the establishment and functioning of an internal market prior to 1 January 1993 has possibly been the most important feature of the Single European Act. The original requirement for decisions to be taken by unanimity had made any decision-making a complex and slow process. Its replacement by qualified majority voting as regards the aforementioned matters has stimulated quicker decision-making by all the institutions involved.

56. The role of the European Parliament is also modified by the Single European Act. Closer liaison between both the Council of Ministers and the Commission with the European Parliament is demanded through the first and second reading of proposals as they pass from the stage of Commission initiative to Council of Ministers' adoption. This provides the European Parliament with a greater input to the Community legislative process than was the case heretofore.

57. The co-operation procedure inherent in the Single European Act, however, remains dependent on the political will of the institutions involved. Many decisions on completing the internal market have already been adopted, and this indicates that the process is indeed well under way.

PROGRESS TEST

Numbers in brackets refer to paragraphs of this chapter

1. What treaty established the EEC, and what were its immediate and long-term aims? (3)
2. Describe the composition of the Commission. (7, 9)
3. List the functions of (i) the Commission, (ii) the Council of Ministers, (iii) the European Parliament, and (iv) the Court of Justice. (12, 18, 30, 31, 32, 39)
4. What are the primary sources of Community Law? (48, 49)
5. Distinguish between (i) Regulations, (ii) Directives, and (iii) Decisions in Community law. (52)
6. Identify the main objectives of the Single European Act. (54, 55)

EXAMINATION QUESTIONS

Section 5: European Community Law

1. Outline the powers and functions of the Commission of the European Community.

I.A.T.I. (Autumn 1990)

2. Write a note on the Court of Justice of the European Community, with particular reference to its jurisdiction to give preliminary rulings on request from National Courts.

I.A.T.I. (Summer 1990)

EMPLOYMENT
LAW

EMPLOYMENT LAW

Summary of the chapter

A contract of employment forms the basis for a relationship between an employer and an employee. This chapter examines how this contract is, like other contracts, governed by the ordinary principles of common law but, unlike other contracts, is modified by statute and is a dynamic agreement, the terms of which may be regularly altered by the consensus of the parties involved.

• Contract of employment

1. An employment has been held to exist when a person is working under a 'contract of service'. The person is employed to provide his labour or skill in whatever way his employer dictates in return for wages. The work is done subject to the employer's detailed control. The relationship between the employer and employee is regulated by a contract of employment or 'service'.

2. A contract of employment is governed by the ordinary principles of contract law. It is, however, a dynamic agreement which may be modifie‹ by statute.

Formation of the contract

3. A contract of employment may be created verbally, in writing, or may be implied by the conduct of the parties. Generally, no formality is required, except that a contract for the employment of a seaman or a contract of apprenticeship in specified industries must be in writing.

4. Under the Irish Statute of Frauds, 1695, a contract of employment which is not to be performed within one year is unenforceable unless it is evidenced by writing.

• Terms of the contract

5. As with other types of contracts, the terms of the contract of employment may be expressed or implied.

6. The express terms are those which are agreed verbally or in writing between the employee and the employer (or his agent). These may include details of pay, hours of work, holidays, sick leave, etc.

7. Not all of the terms of the contract of employment will be expressly agreed between the parties. A term may be implied in fact, because it lends business efficacy to the contract. It may be implied by custom and practice in the trade, industry or locality, provided those customs are well known and are reasonable.

• Common law duties of the employee

8. Employees have been held to have the following implied duties towards their employers:

(a) *To give personal service.* The employee must attend and be available to do the work he has contracted to do, during agreed working hours. The employee must not, without the permission of the employer, delegate the performance of duties to another.

(b) *To obey lawful orders.* The employee must obey all lawful orders given by the employer, provided these are within the terms of the contract, and do not place the employee in personal danger.

(c) *To exercise reasonable care and skill.* The employee must exercise due care and skill in the performance of his work. Where he claims to have the skill and experience to perform the work undertaken, he must also carry out his tasks diligently and efficiently.

(d) *To act in good faith.* The employee must act honestly and in the interests of the employer, when dealing with the employer's property or in exercising any trust placed in him. He must not accept bribes or make secret profits. He must disclose all inventions made using the facilities of the employer.

(e) *To maintain secrecy.* The employee must not disclose confidential information obtained by him in the course of, and as a result of, his employment. Neither must he exploit his employer's trade secrets or customer contacts. However, the employee may disclose information if it is such that it is in the public interest to do so, or if it is disclosed to someone who has a proper interest to receive it.

(f) *To indemnify his employer.* The employee may be liable to compensate his employer for any loss suffered by him as a result of the wrongful act of his employee. However, this rarely happens unless there is evidence of collusion or wilful misconduct on the employee's part.

• Common law duties of the employer

9. In the absence of any specific provisions in the contract of employment, the employer has the following implied duties towards his employee:

(a) *To provide work (in some cases)*

In general, there is no duty on an employer to provide work for his employee to do, so long as he continues to pay him his agreed wages. There are, however, some exceptions:

- (i) if employment is essential to provide a reputation for future employment, e.g. acting or journalism;
- (ii) if remuneration depends upon the amount of work performed, e.g. if he is employed on a commission basis or to do piece work;
- (iii) if an employee is employed to perform a particular task, or to fill a particular post, the employer is in breach of contract if he abolishes the post or removes the employee from it.

(b) *To pay wages or remuneration*

The employer has a duty to pay the employee the agreed remuneration or what is reasonable in the circumstances.

Case: McEvoy v Moore (1902)

The plaintiff was instructed to go to the defendant's premises with a view to being employed as a stableman. The period of employment and associated remuneration were not discussed. The plaintiff subsequently sued for payment of wages.

Held: The plaintiff was entitled to remuneration at the normal rate for work of that type.

(c) *To provide for the safety of the employees*

The employer owes a special duty of care towards his employees. This duty may arise in tort, or it may be implied in the contract of employment. The employer has a duty:

- (i) to employ competent employees who are not a danger to their fellow employees;
- (ii) to provide, and maintain, a safe place of work for the benefit of the employees;
- (iii) to provide, and maintain, proper equipment so as not to subject the employee to unnecessary risk; and
- (iv) to devise a system of working which is reasonably safe for his employees.

(d) *To indemnify his employees*

The employer must indemnify his employee in respect of all losses, liabilities and expenses incurred whilst acting on the employer's behalf, except where:

> (i) the employee knew that the act was unlawful; or
> (ii) the employee knew that the employer had no right to give the order.

• Statutory regulation of the terms of the contract

Minimum Notice and Terms of Employment Act, 1973

10. The Act gives employees the right to have information about the terms of their employment set out in writing *and* lays down minimum periods of notice to be given by employers and employees when terminating a contract of employment.

11. The provisions of this Act apply to most employers and to employees normally working eighteen hours a week or more for the same employer. There is no income limit. The provisions *do not* apply to:

(a) workers employed for less than eighteen hours a week by the same employer;
(b) close relatives of the employer;
(c) established civil servants;
(d) members of the permanent Defence Forces or Garda Síochána; or
(e) seamen.

12. An employer is required to supply a new employee, within one month of his taking up employment, with a written statement of the following terms of his employment:

(a) date on which he commenced employment;
(b) details of his pay, including overtime, commission and bonuses, and the method of calculating them;
(c) whether pay is to be weekly, monthly or otherwise;
(d) details of hours of work and overtime;
(e) holiday entitlements;
(f) sick pay entitlements and pension schemes, if any;
(g) period of notice of termination to be given; and
(h) expiry date of contract, if employment is for a fixed period of time.

13. The statement may refer the employee to an easily accessible document which contains the information (such as an employment agreement registered with the Labour Court, or an Employment Regulation Order of the Labour Court), rather than specifying the details.

14. Existing employees may request similar information, which must be provided by the employer within one month of that request.

15. An employee is entitled to receive a minimum period of notice before the employer can exercise a right of dismissal, once he has been in 'continuous service' with the same employer for at least thirteen weeks, and normally works at least eighteen hours a week.

16. An employee's service is generally regarded as 'continuous' unless he is either dismissed or voluntarily leaves his job. It is not usually affected by lay-offs, strikes or lock-outs, or by dismissal followed by immediate reemployment.

17. The required period of statutory notice increases according to the length of service of the employee in accordance with the following scale:

Length of Service	*Prescribed Period of Notice*
13 weeks – 2 years	1 week
2 years – 5 years	2 weeks
5 years – 10 years	4 weeks
10 years – 15 years	6 weeks
15 years +	8 weeks

18. An employer is entitled to at least one week's notice from an employee who has been in employment for thirteen weeks or more.

19. A clause in a contract providing for shorter periods of notice than the minimum stipulated in the Act is void. However, the Act does not preclude an employer or employee from waiving his right to notice or accepting payment in lieu of notice.

Truck Acts, 1831–96
20. The Truck Acts safeguard employees engaged in manual work against abuses in relation to the payment of wages, by providing protection against payment in kind, against interference with the employee's freedom to dispose of his wages as he thinks fit, and against unreasonable or unfair deductions from wages.

21. Manual workers must be paid in legal tender, which consists of bank notes and coins, or by bearer cheque drawn on a bank which is within fifteen miles of the place of employment and which is licensed to issue bank notes. The Currency Act, 1927 removed the bank's powers to issue bank notes, and had the accidental effect of making payment by cheque illegal.

22. Payment of wages must not be made in licensed premises, except in the case of employees employed in such places.

23. Statutory deductions may be made from remuneration in respect of income tax, social welfare contributions and court orders for the payment of maintenance or debts. Deductions may only be made and paid to other third parties with the employee's consent.

Payment of Wages Act, 1979

24. The main purpose of this Act is to amend the Truck Acts, 1831–96, so as to allow employees engaged in manual work, who are covered by those Acts, to be paid their wages otherwise than in cash, where both those employees and their employers agree.

25. Employees may be paid wages, otherwise than in cash, by:

(a) cheque;
(b) banker's draft;
(c) postal or money orders;
(d) credit transfer; or
(e) any other such method as specified in regulations made by the Minister for Labour

26. Payment of wages otherwise than in cash must have the mutual agreement of employer and employee(s). Non-cash payment may be effected if:

(a) both the employer and employee(s), or the person whom they authorise in writing to act on their behalf, sign a document for that purpose; or
(b) there is a written agreement to that effect between the employer and trade union(s) involved.

27. Where deductions are made from remuneration, all employees are entitled to receive an itemised pay statement from their employer.

28. Every pay statement must contain the following information:

(a) the gross amount of the salary or wages payable;
(b) the nature of the deduction(s); and
(c) the amount of the deductions.

29. Employers are required to take such reasonable steps as are necessary, not only to ensure that the statements are treated as confidential until they become the property of the employees, but also to ensure that the information which is contained in the statements is treated as confidential by those who are privy to it.

Holiday (Employees) Act, 1973

30. This Act lays down a minimum, legally enforceable entitlement, for employees working the required number of hours, to three weeks' annual holidays (with pro rata entitlements for periods of employment of less than a year) and to public holidays.

31. Employees who are *not* covered by the Act include:

(a) outworkers;
(b) seafarers;
(c) lighthouse and lightship employees;
(d) fishermen;
(e) non-industrial State employees and established civil servants; and
(f) employees living with an employer who is a relative.

32. To qualify for annual leave, an employee must have worked for the employer at least 120 hours (110 hours if under eighteen years) in a calendar month. Alternatively, an employee who, during a 'leave year' (i.e. 1 April to 31 March), works for the one employer for at least 1,400 hours (1,300 hours if under eighteen years), is likewise entitled to three weeks' annual holidays.

33. If an employee is ill while on annual leave, and provides a medical certificate to that effect, that period covered by the medical certificate will not be counted as part of his annual leave.

34. The time at which annual leave may be taken is determined by the employer, so long as he consults the employee or trade union at least one month beforehand, and that the annual leave is taken either during the current leave year or within six months after its end.

35. The pay for annual leave must be at the normal weekly rate and must be given in advance.

36. If an employee ceases employment with annual leave due to him, the employer must compensate him for holidays at the rate of one quarter of his normal weekly remuneration for each calendar month during which he worked at least 120 hours (110 hours if under eighteen years of age).

37. The Act provides entitlement to eight public holidays:

(a) 1 January (New Year's Day), if falling on a weekday or, if not, the next day;

(b) 17 March (St Patrick's Day), if falling on a weekday or, if not, the next day;

(c) Easter Monday;

(d) the first Monday in June;

(e) the first Monday in August;

(f) the last Monday in October;

(g) 25 December (Christmas Day), if falling on a weekday or, if not, the next Tuesday;

(h) 26 December (St Stephen's Day), if falling on a weekday or, if not, the next day.

38. In respect of each public holiday, an employee is entitled to a paid day off on the holiday, or a paid day off within a month, or an extra day's annual leave, or an extra day's pay—as the employer may decide.

39. The employer may substitute a Church holiday for a public holiday (except Christmas or St Patrick's Day), provided that he gives the employee notice of the substitution at least fourteen days beforehand. The following Church holidays may be substituted:

(a) 6 January (the Epiphany), except when it falls on a Sunday;

(b) Ascension Thursday;

(c) Corpus Christi;

(d) 15 August (the Assumption), except when it falls on a Sunday;

(e) 1 November (All Saints' Day), except when it falls on a Sunday;

(f) 8 December (the Immaculate Conception), except when it falls on a Sunday.

Office Premises Act, 1958

40. This Act, as amended by the Safety in Industry Act, 1980, contains provisions which identify the minimum standards of accommodation and amenities which must be provided for office workers.

41. It applies to all offices in which more than five persons are employed on clerical work, other than those occupied by the Defence Forces, or those used at irregular intervals only and for short periods.

42. Persons employed on clerical work in shops do not come within the scope of the Act, but are covered by similar provisions in the Shops (Conditions of Employment) Acts, 1938 and 1942, which apply to wholesale and retail premises, and to hotels.

43. Every office must be kept clean; dirt and waste must be removed daily, and floors washed, or cleaned by some other effective method, at least once a week.

44. Offices must not be so overcrowded as to cause risk of injury to the health of the workers. A minimum of 50 sq. ft of floor space must be allowed for each worker.

45. A reasonable temperature must be provided and maintained in every room, but no heating system which allows injurious or offensive fumes to escape into any room may be used.

46. Each room must be adequately ventilated by the circulation of fresh air, but harmful draughts must be prevented.

47. Suitable and sufficient lighting, whether natural or artificial, must be provided in every part of the office which is in use.

48. Sufficient and suitable sanitary conveniences must be provided, maintained and kept clean. Separate conveniences are required for male and female staffs (except where only members of the same family are employed). Adequate and suitable facilities for washing must be conveniently accessible and kept clean.

49. All floors, steps, lifts, passages and gangways must be of sound construction and properly maintained. Substantial handrails must be provided on every staircase; an open side should be guarded by a lower rail or other effective means.

50. Exits for use in case of fire must be conspicuously marked, and workers must be made familiar with fire-escape arrangements.

Anti-Discrimination (Pay) Act, 1974
51. This Act entitles men and women to receive equal treatment in regard to pay, by establishing the right of a woman to equal pay for like work and by providing the means for the enforcement of that right. This Act applies to men as well as women.

52. A woman has the right to be paid the same rate of remuneration as a man who is employed on 'like work' by the same employer or associated employer (i.e. in a work-place or work-places located in the same city, town or locality). Not only must such a woman be paid the same rates of basic pay, but also the same overtime rates, bonuses, holiday and sick pay, etc.

53. A man and a woman are to be regarded as being employed on like work where:

(a) both perform the same work under the same or similar conditions, or where each is in every respect interchangeable with the other in relation to the work; or

(b) the work performed by one is of a similar nature to that performed by the other, and any differences between the work performed or the conditions under which it is performed by each occur only infrequently, or are of small importance in relation to the work as a whole; or

(c) the work performed by one is equal in value to that performed by the other in terms of the demands it makes in relation to such matters as skill, physical or mental effort, responsibility and working conditions.

54. The Equality Officers of the Labour Court investigate disputes about equal pay entitlements and issue recommendations. An employee or an employer, a trade union or an employer organisation, or the Employment Equality Agency may refer the matter to an Equality Officer for investigation and recommendation.

55. Either an employee or an employer may appeal to the Labour Court against the recommendation of the Equality Officer, or for a determination that the recommendation has not been implemented.

Employment Equality Act, 1977

56. This Act makes it unlawful to discriminate on grounds of sex or marital status:

(a) in the recruitment of employees;
(b) in conditions of employment;
(c) in training;
(d) in work experience; or
(e) in opportunities for promotion.

57. The Act covers all employees except:

(a) those in employments which are specifically excluded, such as those in the Garda Síochána, Defence Forces and prison service; or
(b) where the sex of the employee or prospective employee is an occupational qualification for the job, such as in acting.

58. Unlawful discrimination may be direct or indirect. Direct discrimination on grounds of *sex* arises where a person treats a woman, on grounds of her sex, less favourably than he treats or would treat a man. Indirect discrimination on grounds of sex arises where a woman is required to comply with a requirement, which is not essential for the job, e.g. a minimum height requirement.

59. Direct discrimination on the grounds of *marital status* arises where a person is treated less favourably than another person of the same sex, but of a different marital status, e.g. a marriage bar in employment. Indirect discrimination on grounds of marital status arises where a married woman is required to comply with a specific requirement, which is not essential for the job, and the proportion of single women able to comply with the requirement is greater, or vice versa.

60. It is unlawful for an employer to discriminate on grounds of sex or marital status:

(a) in the arrangements he makes for recruitment, e.g. the criteria used for selection, interview procedures, the instructions he gives to an employment agency;
(b) in the terms on which he offers the job; and
(c) by refusing or deliberately omitting to offer a person the job.

61. Moreover, an employer must not discriminate:

(a) in the provision of training, on or off the job;
(b) in regrading or the classification of jobs;
(c) in work counselling;
(d) in the provision of work experience;
(e) in the opportunities he gives the employees for promotion;
(f) in dismissals, disciplinary measures, or in any other disadvantages to which employees may be subjected, e.g. lay-offs, redundancies, etc.;
(g) by having discriminatory rules or instructions.

62. An allegation of unlawful discrimination may be referred to the Labour Court, which will decide whether to seek a settlement of the case by conciliation, or to refer the case to an Equality Officer for investigation and recommendation.

63. Either an employer or an employee may appeal to the Labour Court against a recommendation of an Equality Officer, within forty-two days from the date of issue. The Labour Court will hear the appeal, and:

(a) state that unlawful discrimination did, or did not, occur;
(b) recommend a specific course of action; or
(c) award compensation (not exceeding 104 weeks' remuneration) to the complainant.

64. The Act also provided for the establishment of the Employment Equality Agency (EEA), and its functions are:

(a) to work towards the elimination of discrimination in relation to employment;
(b) to promote equality of opportunity in employment between men and women generally; and

(c) to keep under review the working of the Anti-Discrimination (Pay) Act, 1974 and the Employment Equality Act, 1977, and make recommendations for any amendment of these Acts which are necessary.

65. The EEA also has the function at its discretion, and where there are special considerations, to assist individuals in their pursuit of a remedy in cases of unlawful discrimination.

Protection of Young Persons (Employment) Act, 1977
66. The Act extends the scope of the legislative protection given to young workers under the age of eighteen. It contains provisions as to:

(a) the minimum age for entry into employment;
(b) limits to the working hours of young people;
(c) rest intervals; and
(d) prohibition of night work.

67. An employer may not employ anyone under 18 years of age, without first requiring the production of a birth certificate. Furthermore, an employer must obtain written permission from the parent or guardian before employing a person aged 14 to 15 years.

68. The employment of children under 15 is generally prohibited. However, a child over 14 may be permitted to do light, non-industrial work during school holidays, provided that it doesn't interfere with his or her schooling and is not harmful to health or normal development.

69. The limitation on hours of work of young persons aged between 15 and 16 years is a maximum of 8 hours in any day and 40 hours in any week.

70. The limitation on hours of work of young persons aged between 16 and 18 is a maximum of 9 hours in any day, 45 hours in any week, 172 hours in any 4 weeks and 2,000 hours in any year.

71. Employees who work on more than 5 days a week and whose work on Sunday exceeds 3 hours, must be given at least 24 consecutive hours rest once in every 7 days.

72. A spell of work shall not continue for more than 4 hours in the case of a person between 14 and 15 years of age, and for more than 5 hours in the case of a person between 15 and 18 years of age, without a rest interval of at least 30 minutes.

73. Persons between the ages of 14 and 15 must not be employed for a period of 14 consecutive hours at night, including the interval between 8 p.m. and 8 a.m.

74. Persons between the ages of 15 and 18 must not be employed for a period of 12 consecutive hours at night, including the interval between 10 p.m. and 6 a.m., except for industrial workers who must not be employed between 8 p.m. and 8 a.m.

75. The Act also requires employers to keep a record of the following particulars of each employee under age 18 whom he employs:

(a) full name;
(b) date of birth;
(c) time of commencement of work each day;
(d) time of termination of work each day;
(e) rate of wages or salary paid for normal working hours per day, week, month or year, as the case may be;
(f) total wages or salary paid to each such employee.

Maternity Protection of Employees Act, 1981

76. The Act provides maternity protection for employees in employment which is insurable for the purpose of the Social Welfare code, and who ordinarily work for 18 hours or more per week for the one employer.

77. An expectant female employee is entitled to take 14 consecutive weeks' maternity leave. Of the 14 weeks, an employee must take at least 4 weeks before the end of the week in which her baby is due, and 4 weeks after that week. The remaining 6 weeks may be taken before or after the birth as she wishes.

78. To exercise her right to take maternity leave, an employee must:

(a) notify her employer in writing, at least 4 weeks before she intends to go on maternity leave, of her intention to take the leave; and
(b) give her employer, or produce for his inspection, a medical certificate, confirming her pregnancy and indicating the expected week of her confinement.

79. A claim may be made for pay-related maternity allowance during maternity leave by employees who satisfy the contribution conditions. It is payable for a basic period of 14 weeks, with a possibility of extension of this period in certain cases of late birth. The amount payable is 70 per cent based on a weekly average of gross yearly earnings in the relevant income tax year. It is tax free and, in addition, the employee may benefit from a tax refund or tax credit. There is a minimum payment.

80. An employee may take up to 4 consecutive weeks' additional maternity leave immediately after her maternity leave, even where that has been extended for a late birth. The employer is not obliged to pay an employee during additional maternity leave. Neither is maternity allowance payable. An employee who chooses to take additional maternity leave must ensure that her employer is notified in writing not later than 4 weeks before the end of her maternity leave.

81. The Act does not oblige an employee who has taken maternity leave to return to work afterwards. But if she does wish to return, she must give prior notice to her employer in writing of her intention to return to work, not later than 4 weeks before the date on which she expects to return.

82. Where the employer cannot comply with this right of the employee, he must offer suitable alternative employment to the employee. The Employment Appeals Tribunal will determine any disputes arising from this arrangement.

• Termination of the contract of employment
83. Under common law, a contract of employment may be terminated by:

(a) agreement with notice;
(b) death of the employer or employee;
(c) frustration;
(d) insolvency; or
(e) breach.

Termination by agreement with notice
84. The ending of a contract of employment is most often achieved without any breach of its terms. A contract can be terminated at common law by either party giving the notice required by the terms of the contract, or by giving reasonable notice where none is specified in the contract. What is regarded as reasonable notice will depend on a number of factors, such as the nature of the work, the method of payment and the custom of the trade. Alternatively, an employer may pay wages in lieu of notice—subject to the protection given to employees under the Unfair Dismissals Act, 1977.

Case: McDonnell v Minister for Education (1940)

The plaintiff, a lecturer, was employed by the defendant. She was given three months' notice of termination of her contract of employment upon her marriage. She took an action against the defendant for wrongful dismissal.

Held: As no notice was specified in the contract of employment, six months was a reasonable period in the circumstances.

85. If an employee is an office holder, i.e. a person occupying a relatively permanent position created by statute, charter, articles of association, or statutory regulation, termination by notice is not sufficient. Such an employee is entitled to be notified of the grounds of his dismissal and to be given an opportunity of defending himself.

Termination by death of the employer or employee
86. Death of either the employer or the employee will end the contract, unless there is an express or implied term to the contrary. This will not apply if one 'person' is a company, which will have perpetual existence. Any liabilities arising under the contract of employment are not extinguished upon the death of either party. For example, any outstanding remuneration must be paid to the estate of the employee.

Termination by frustration
87. If either party is incapable of performing his part of the contract due to circumstances *beyond his control*, it will be terminated by frustration. Illness may be a frustrating event if it renders future performance impossible or fundamentally different from that envisaged by the parties when they entered into the contract. A period of imprisonment may also frustrate a contract of employment.

Termination by insolvency
88. Insolvency or bankruptcy of either party will not automatically terminate the contract of employment, unless it is an essential element of the relationship. In practice, however, an employer who becomes insolvent will not be in a position to pay remuneration to his employee(s). An employee may submit a claim in bankruptcy for remuneration outstanding, and, in the absence of proper notice, a claim for wrongful dismissal. He may also lodge a claim for redundancy payments.

89. An order for compulsory winding-up (liquidation) of a company terminates the contracts of employment of all the employees. However, a voluntary winding-up will not automatically terminate employees' contracts if the liquidator chooses to carry on the business—unless it is obvious that the company will be unable to fulfil its obligations, under the contracts.

Termination by breach

90. A contract of employment may be ended by breach if the employee resigns without sufficient reason and without notice, or goes on strike or fails to perform the contract and to observe its conditions.

91. It may also be ended by breach if the employer dismisses the employee without notice when he has not sufficient justification to do so, or if the employer repudiates some essential term of the contract, e.g. a complete change of duties.

92. These common law rules have been supplemented by statute:

The Unfair Dismissals Act, 1977

93. The Act protects employees from being unfairly dismissed from their jobs by laying down criteria by which dismissals are to be judged unfair, and by providing an adjudication system and redress for an employee whose dismissal has been found to be unjustified.

94. Many workers are excluded from the protection of the Act. The most important of these are:

(a) employees with less than one year's continuous service, but this does not apply when the dismissal results from pregnancy or trade union activities—dismissal for such reasons is indefensible;
(b) employees who have reached normal retiring age;
(c) close relatives of the employer, employed and living at his residence or farm;
(d) members of the Defence Forces or Gardaí;
(e) Fás trainees or apprentices;
(f) State employees (except specified industrial grades);
(g) officers of a Local Authority, Health Board, VEC or County Committee of Agriculture;
(h) persons working under fixed-term contracts (in some cases);
(i) persons who, under their contract, ordinarily work outside the State;
(j) persons undergoing promotion or training for a year or less, and this is specified in a written contract of employment;
(k) persons undertaking training for the purpose of obtaining qualifications or registration as a nurse, pharmacist, health inspector, etc.; or
(l) persons working under illegal contracts of employment.

95. An employee is deemed to have been dismissed if:

(a) the employer terminates the contract of employment, with or without notice;

(b) the employee, because of the conduct of the employer, terminates the contract of employment, with or without notice (i.e. 'constructive dismissal'); or

(c) the contract is for a fixed term and is not renewed.

96. Any dismissal is presumed to be unfair unless and until the *employer* proves to the contrary. To justify a dismissal, an employer must show that it resulted from one or more of the following causes, or that there were other 'substantial grounds' for the dismissal:

(a) lack of skill, or physical or mental ability, or adequate health, or such formal professional or technical qualifications as are appropriate for the work the employee was employed to do;

(b) conduct of the employee of such a serious or continuing nature as to amount to serious misconduct. This will not include isolated acts or behaviour which has not warranted a warning by the employer;

(c) redundancy, in accordance with fair or agreed procedures; and

(d) the fact that continuation of employment would contravene another statutory restriction. For example, to continue to employ an under-age employee would be a contravention of the law.

97. Dismissals will be always automatically unfair, and can never be justified where it is shown that they have resulted wholly or mainly from any of the following:

(a) trade union membership or activities, either outside working hours or during working hours at times permitted by the employer;

(b) religous or political opinions;

(c) race or colour;

(d) participation in legal proceedings against the employer;

(e) unfair selection for redundancy, where there are no grounds for a redundancy, or where an employee is selected for redundancy contrary to a fair or agreed procedure;

(f) pregnancy, or the exercise by an employee of her rights under the Maternity Protection of Employees Act, 1981.

98. Claims of unfair dismissal must be made within six months of the date of dismissal. There is no procedure under the Act whereby this time-limit may be extended.

99. An employee can initiate the claim before a Rights Commissioner, who is a civil servant appointed by the Minister for Labour. The employee must send a copy of his application to his ex-employer. The Rights Commissioner hears the evidence in private and issues a recommendation. If the action is settled, no further claim on the same issue is allowed. If the recommendation is not acceptable, either party may appeal to the Employment Appeals Tribunal within six weeks.

100. The case may be referred to the Employment Appeals Tribunal in the first place, if the employer objects to it being heard by a Rights Commissioner or if the employee so wishes. The Employment Appeals Tribunal consists of three persons: a legally qualified Chairman, a representative of the ICTU and a representative of employers' organisations.

101. The Employment Appeals Tribunal will issue a determination on a case coming before it either by way of appeal or by original claim. This may in turn be appealed to the Circuit Court, and from there to the High Court.

102. If an employer does not comply with the terms specified in a determination within six weeks, the Minister for Labour may, at his own expense, take the case to the Circuit Court on behalf of the employee to enforce the redress to which he is entitled.

103. Apart from showing that the dismissal was for a fair reason, the employer is also obliged to establish that he acted reasonably in deciding to dismiss. The employer must:

(a) conduct an adequate investigation of the circumstances before deciding to dismiss, so that the dismissal is not based on incorrect or incomplete information;
(b) give the employee a chance to 'state his case' before being dismissed;
(c) give the employee at least one warning before being dismissed, which allows him sufficient time to improve, a reasonable work situation within which to do so and a fair process for monitoring his progress;
(d) relate the penalty proportionally to the offence; and
(e) follow agreed disciplinary procedures.

104. Where an employee has been held to have been unfairly dismissed, he is entitled to redress consisting of whichever of the following remedies the Rights Commissioner, the Employment Appeals Tribunal or the Circuit Court considers appropriate depending on the merits of the case:

(a) the reinstatement of the employee in the same position and on the same terms as before his dismissal. He will be entitled to all arrears of salary and there will be no break in his service;
(b) the re-engagement of the employee in the same position, or in a reasonably suitable alternative one, on such terms and conditions as the adjudicating body considers reasonable; or

(c) financial compensation, up to a maximum of 104 weeks' pay, in respect of such loss suffered by the employee as a result of the dismissal. The exact amount depends, among other things, on where the responsibility for the dismissal lies, the measures taken to reduce the financial loss or the extent to which negotiated procedures were followed.

Redundancy Payment Acts, 1967–79

105. Redundancy payment may be made where an employee is dismissed because the employer's requirement for employees has ceased or diminished. The Act provides for lump-sum payments to be made to redundant workers based on their ages, years of continuous service and gross weekly wages.

106. A redundancy fund is operated by the State, financed by contributions paid by employees and employers. The fund is used:

(a) to give rebates on lump-sum payments made by the employer;
(b) to pay a lump-sum directly to an employee where his employer refuses; or
(c) to pay outstanding sums due to employees in the event of an employer being unable to pay because of insolvency. An employer is entitled to a rebate of 60 per cent of any redundancy payment he has been legally obliged to make.

107. For a person to be entitled to redundancy payment he must:

(a) be over 18 years of age and under the old age pension age;
(b) be employed by the same employer for at least 20 hours per week; and
(c) be employed continuously by the same employer for at least 2 years by the date the employment was terminated due to redundancy.

The following events do not break continuity:

    (i)   change in job with the same employer;
   (ii)   change in ownership of the business;
  (iii)   engagement by an associated employer;
  (iv)   absence up to 18 months due to sickness or injury;
   (v)   absence of up to 13 weeks taken for purposes of pregnancy, or a lay-off, or holidays;
  (vi)   a lock-out or participation in a strike; or
 (vii)   any other causes authorised by the employer which do not last longer than 26 weeks.

108. Dismissal must be deemed to have been by reason of redundancy. There is no dismissal, and therefore no redundancy payment, where an employee leaves voluntarily or where the contract is frustrated. The dismissal is presumed to have been by reason of redundancy unless the employer can prove to the contrary. However, case law has shown that an employee will not have a justifiable claim for redundancy payment if:

(a) the contract of employment is renewed; or
(b) he unreasonably refuses a suitable offer of alternative employment.

109. The amount of the payment is related to the employee's length of continuous employment, age and wage. The calculation of redundancy pay is carried out as follows:

(a) one week's pay (up to a maximum of £211.54); plus
(b) half of the week's pay for every year of continuous employment between the age of 14 and 41; plus
(c) one week's pay for every year of continuous employment from the age of 41 onwards.

110. An employee may, if possible, negotiate a higher redundancy payment but, where applicable, he must get the statutory minimum.

IMPORTANT CASES

Numbers in brackets refer to paragraphs of this chapter

IMPORTANT STATUTES

Numbers in brackets refer to paragraphs of this chapter

PROGRESS TEST

Numbers in brackets refer to paragraphs of this chapter

1. When may formality be required in a contract of employment? (3)
2. Identify the common law duties of an employee to his employer. (8)
3. List some of the terms of employment which an employer is required to supply in writing to a new employee. (12)
4. Describe those circumstances whereby a man and a woman are to be regarded as being employed on like work. (53)
5. What are the functions of the Employment Equality Agency (EEA)? (64)
6. Identify those details which an employer is required to keep a record of, relating to each employee under age 18 whom he employs. (75)
7. How may an employee exercise her right to take maternity leave? (78)
8. Describe five methods by which a contract of employment may be terminated. (83)
9. What workers are excluded from the protection of the Unfair Dismissals Act, 1977? (94)
10. How may an employer justify a dismissal on 'substantial grounds'? (96)
11. What redress is available to an employee who has been held to have been unfairly dismissed? (104)
12. What are the prerequisites for an employee to be entitled to redundancy payment? (107)

EXAMINATION QUESTIONS

Section 6: Employment Law

1. Outline the implied duties of an employer towards his workers.
   C.I.M.A. (November 1984)

2. *P* Ltd employs 500 employees. In 1987 it advertised for a marketing adviser, and *Q* was recruited. When *Q* was appointed it was agreed between him and *P* Ltd that *Q* would be responsible for the payment

of his own income tax and national insurance contributions, that he could work the agreed hours of work each week whenever he chose, and that he could work for other employers as long as they were not competitors of *P* Ltd.

During 1989, *P* Ltd became dissatisfied with *Q*'s work and in March 1990 the decision was made to reduce the importance of *Q*'s work and to reduce the remuneration accordingly. In April 1990, *Q* resigned from *P* Ltd and now wishes to seek compensation for unfair dismissal. *P* Ltd claims that *Q* was never employed under a contract of service but under a contract of services.

Advise *Q*.

A.C.C.A. (June 1990)

3. Give a brief account of the main statutory provisions governing the law of unfair dismissal.

I.A.T.I. (Autumn 1990)

4. It is easy today to engage workers but difficult either to dismiss them or to provide them with other than a full week's work.

Discuss this statement.

C.I.M.A. (November 1987)

LAW OF PERSONS

Partnerships
Companies

chapter 31

PARTNERSHIPS

Points covered in this chapter:

- Definition
- Formation
- Relationship with third parties
- Relationship with each other

- Dissolution
- The Limited Partnerships Act, 1907

Summary of the chapter

Partnerships are most commonly used nowadays as a form of association by professional people, such as accountants and solicitors, since they must maintain individual professional accountability to their clients. This chapter examines how the relationship between such people and their clients is regulated.

• Definition

1. A partnership is defined as 'a relation which subsists between persons carrying on a business in common with a view to profit' (s.1, Partnership Act, 1890).

2. A 'business' includes 'every trade, occupation or profession' (s.45, Partnership Act, 1890).

3. It should be noted that it is not possible for complete strangers to carry on business in common, since there will be an absence of mutual obligation between the parties. Furthermore, if a business is carried on with the intention of making a profit, it is not necessary that a profit be made in order for a partnership to exist.

• Formation

4. No formalities are required for the formation of a partnership. The relationship may come into existence when the parties make an express contract, as where they execute formal 'articles of partnership', or when they make an implied contract, as where their conduct indicates an implied partnership agreement between the parties.

5. However, while a contract of partnership may be created orally or by implication, such informality is rare. Generally, the partners have a written agreement or deed drawn up, called the 'Articles of Partnership', which contains all the provisions of the partnership contract. A partnership agreement will usually provide for the following matters:

(a) the place and nature of the business;
(b) the name of the firm;
(c) the date of commencement and duration of the partnership;
(d) the capital of the firm and the proportion being contributed by each partner;
(e) the salary, if any, to be paid to each partner;
(f) the ratio in which profits and losses are to be divided;
(g) the method for keeping regular accounts and preparing an annual profit and loss account and balance sheet;
(h) the amount of drawings which each partner may take from the business;
(i) the death, retirement or bankruptcy of a partner;
(j) the dissolution of the partnership;
(k) the admission and expulsion of partners;
(l) the calculation of goodwill in the event of the death or retirement of a partner;
(m) the powers and duties of partners;
(n) the procedure to be used in solving disputes.

Case: Macken v The Revenue Commissioners (1962)

A painting contractor, his son and daughter agreed, in or around September 1953, that they should form a partnership effective from 1 January 1954. A partnership deed to this effect was signed on 30 April 1954. The defendants took an action so as to have the court declare that a partnership existed from 1 January 1954.

Held: No partnership existed until the deed was executed. All that had existed was an intention to form a future partnership effective from 1 January 1954.

6. A partnership requires a minimum of two members. The maximum membership is restricted by statute. The upper limit of partners in a limited partnership (i.e. one where *some* of the partners have limited liability) was fixed to twenty for an ordinary business and ten for a banking partnership by the Limited Partnerships Act, 1907. This restriction was extended to general partnerships (i.e. where *each* partner is liable for the debts of the partnership) by the Companies Act, 1963, but was amended by the Companies (Amendment) Act, 1983 to exclude persons practising as accountants or solicitors.

7. Persons acting in partnership are collectively known as the 'firm', and the name under which trading takes place is called the 'firm name'. Where a partnership is carried on under a name which does not consist of the true surnames of all the partners, the partnership name must be registered under the Registration of Business Names Act, 1963, and the true names of each of the partners have to be disclosed on every business letter, trade circular, trade catalogue or showcard issued by the firm.

• Relationship with third parties

8. Every partner is an agent of the firm and his other partners for the purpose of the business of the partnership; and the acts of every partner who does any act for carrying on in the usual way business of the kind carried on by the firm of which he is a member bind the firm and his partners, unless the partner so acting has in fact no authority to act for the firm in the particular matter, and the person with whom he is dealing either knows that he has no authority, or does not believe him to be a partner (s.5, Partnership Act, 1890).

9. Acts carried out by a partner within the scope of his apparent authority, even where no actual authority has been obtained, will bind the firm and his partners.

Case: Mercantile Credit Co. Ltd v Garrod (1962)

A partnership existed for the purpose of the letting of garages and the provision of a motor repair service. The deed of partnership expressly excluded the buying and selling of cars, but the defendant, a co-partner, sold a car to the plaintiffs. The plaintiffs sued the firm.

Held: The transaction was valid and binding on the firm, since the co-partner had acted in a manner which could be considered as commonly practised in a garage.

10. Partners have been held to have apparent authority:

(a) to purchase on account goods necessary for the business;
(b) to sell the firm's goods or personal chattels;
(c) to engage and discharge employees;
(d) to accept payment of debts owing to the firm;
(e) to sign cheques;
(f) to borrow money and pledge security; and
(g) to employ a solicitor to represent the firm in legal proceedings.

11. However, a partner will not have apparent authority:

(a) to execute a deed;
(b) to guarantee a loan;
(c) to accept property other than money in payment of a debt; or
(d) to submit a dispute to arbitration.

12. An act, or instrument, relating to the business of the firm and done, or executed, in the firm name, or in any other manner showing an intention to bind the firm, by any person so authorised, whether a partner or not, is binding on the firm and on all the partners (s.6, Partnership Act, 1890).

13. Where a partner pledges the credit of the firm for a purpose apparently unconnected with the ordinary business of the firm, the firm is not bound by such a pledge unless it has been specifically authorised by the other partners. The partner will be personally liable (s.7, Partnership Act, 1890).

14. The firm is not bound by the act of a partner whose power to bind the firm has been restricted, and who contracts in excess of his powers with a third party who has notice of this restricted authority (s.8, Partnership Act, 1890).

Personal liability of partners
15. Each partner is jointly liable for the whole of the firm's debts and obligations incurred while he is a partner (s.9, Partnership Act, 1890).

16. Therefore, if a creditor obtains a judgment against the firm, the judgment operates against each partner to the full extent of his wealth. However, if instead of proceeding against the firm the creditor proceeds against only some of the partners and obtains a judgment, the other partners are discharged from liability.

17. Where a partner is responsible for any wrongful act or omission done in the ordinary course of the firm's business or with the authority of the other partners, the firm is liable for any loss, damage or injury caused to a third party (s.10, Partnership Act, 1890).

Case: Hamlyn v Houston & Co. (1903)

A partner of the defendant firm bribed the plaintiff's clerk in order to obtain information.

Held: The partnership was liable in tort, since it was the business of the partnership to obtain such information by legitimate means.

18. Where a partner receives money or property while acting within the scope of his actual or apparent authority, the firm is liable in the event of its misapplication (s.11, Partnership Act, 1890).

Case: Cleather v Twisden (1884)

The plaintiffs, trustees of a will, deposited bonds with a partner of the defendant firm of solicitors. The partner converted the bonds and disappeared with the proceeds. The plaintiffs took an action against the remaining partner to recover the misappropriated amount.

Held: The defendant was not liable for the loss, since it was not within the ordinary scope of the business of solicitors to retain bonds for their clients.

19. Every person who represents himself by words spoken or written, or by conduct, or who knowingly allows himself to be represented as a partner in a particular firm, is liable to any third party who has, on the faith of such representation, given credit to the firm (s.14, Partnership Act, 1890).

20. However, the estate of a deceased partner will not be liable for partnership debts incurred after the date of death where the partner's name continues to be used, unless the deceased partner's personal representatives allow the name to be represented as still alive.

• Relationship with each other

21. The relations of partners to one another are generally provided for by the Articles of Partnership but, in the absence of such, the provisions of the Partnership Act, 1890 are used as the basis for solving any difficulties which subsequently arise.

22. The mutual rights and duties of partners may be varied with the consent of all the parties. This consent may be either express or implied from the conduct of the partners (s.19, Partnership Act, 1890).

Partnership property

23. Partnership property consists of all property, and rights and interests in property, originally brought into the partnership or subsequently acquired, for the purpose and in the course of the partnership. Partnership property must be held and applied exclusively for the purpose of the partnership and in accordance with the partnership agreement (s.21, Partnership Act, 1890).

24. A creditor can only issue an execution order against the partnership property if he obtains a judgment against the firm. A charging order, however, may be obtained against any partner's interest in the partnership property, and the court may appoint a receiver to collect all profits attributable to the partner's share of the business and to apply them to the money due. The other partners may at any time pay the creditor(s) and redeem the interest charged, or purchase the partner's share in the business if it is offered for sale (s.23, Partnership Act, 1890).

Rights and duties

25. In the absence of an agreement as to the rights and duties of the partners, or if the agreement made by them does not cover a particular difficulty that subsequently arises, the general rules governing these matters are contained in ss.24, 25, 28, 29 and 30 of the Partnership Act, 1890.

26. All the partners are entitled to share equally in the capital and profits of the business, and must contribute equally towards the losses, whether of capital or otherwise, sustained by the firm (s.24(1)).

27. The firm must indemnify every partner in respect of payments made and personal liabilities incurred by him in the ordinary and proper conduct of the partnership business, or in relation to anything necessarily done for the preservation of partnership business or property (s.24(2)).

28. Any partner who makes a payment or advance of capital beyond the amount which he has agreed to subscribe is entitled to interest at the rate of 5 per cent per annum from the date of the payment or advance (s.24(3)).

29. No partner is entitled to receive interest on the capital subscribed by him before the profits have been ascertained (s.24(4)).

30. Every partner has the right to take part in the management of the business (s.24(5)).

31. Partners are not entitled to remuneration for acting in the business (s.24(6)).

32. No new partners may be introduced without the unanimous consent of all the existing partners (s.24(7)).

33. Any differences arising in relation to ordinary matters connected with the partnership business may be decided by a majority of the partners, but unanimous consent is required in relation to a change in the nature of the partnership business (s.24(8)).

34. Every partner has the right to have access to and inspect and copy the partnership books, which are to be kept at the principal place of business of the partnership (s.24(9)).

35. A partner cannot be expelled from the partnership by a majority decision of the other partners unless there is an express power of expulsion conferred by the partnership agreement and this has been exercised in good faith and for a proper purpose (s.25).

36. Partners are bound to give true accounts and full information of all things relating to the partnership to any other partner or to his legal representative (s.28).

37. Every partner must account to the firm for any benefit obtained by him without the consent of the other partners from any transaction concerning the partnership or from the use of the firm's property, name or business connection. This duty extends to transactions undertaken after a partnership has been dissolved and before the affairs of the partnership have been completely wound up.

38. A partner who carries on a business of the same nature as, and competing with, the partnership business without the consent of the other partners must account for and hand over all profits made by him in that business to the partnership (s.30).

• Dissolution

39. Subject to any clause or clauses in the Articles of Partnership, the Partnership Act, 1890 provides a number of ways by which a partnership may be dissolved and terminated.

40. A partnership is dissolved:

(a) by passage of time, if the partnership was entered into for a fixed term;
(b) by termination of the venture or undertaking, if the partnership was entered into for a single venture or undertaking;
(c) by any partner giving notice to the other partners that he intends dissolving the partnership, if it was a partnership-at-will (i.e. for an undefined time);
(d) by the death or bankruptcy of any partner;
(e) by subsequent illegality, being the happening of any event which makes it unlawful for the business of the partnership to be carried on, or for the members of the firm to carry on in partnership;
(f) by order of the court (ss.32–5).

41. The court may issue a decree for the dissolution of the partnership in any of the following circumstances:

(a) if a partner has been shown to the satisfaction of the court to have become a lunatic or permanently insane;

(b) if a partner has become otherwise permanently incapable of carrying out his duties in accordance with the partnership agreement;

(c) if a partner has been found guilty of any conduct which is seriously damaging to the carrying on of the business of the firm;

(d) if a partner wilfully and persistently breaks the partnership agreement;

(e) if the business of the partnership can only be carried on at a loss; and

(f) if, in the opinion of the court, circumstances render it just and equitable that there should be a dissolution (s.35).

42. Any partner may notify the public of dissolution of the partnership and may require the other partners of the firm to concur for that purpose (s.37).

43. After the dissolution of a partnership, the authority of each partner to bind the firm continues, so far as may be necessary, to complete transactions begun but unfinished at the time of the dissolution, and to wind up the affairs of the partnership, but not otherwise. However, the other partners are in no way bound by the acts of a partner who has become bankrupt unless they hold him out as having authority for particular transactions (s.38).

44. Every partner is entitled, on the dissolution of a partnership, to have the partnership property applied in payment of the debts and liabilities of the firm. Any surplus after such payment may then be applied in payment of what may be due to the partners themselves. Any partner or his representative(s) may, on dissolution of the partnership, apply to the court to wind up the affairs of the company (s.39).

45. Where one partner has paid a premium to another on entering into a partnership for a fixed term, and the partnership is dissolved before the expiration of that term otherwise than by the death of a partner, an application may be made to the court for the repayment of all, or part, of that premium. The court will not order repayment, however, where the dissolution is wholly or chiefly due to the misconduct of that partner who paid the premium, or where the partnership has been dissolved by an agreement containing no provision in relation to a return of any part of the premium (s.40).

46. Where a partnership contract is rescinded due to fraud or misrepresentation of one of the partners, the partner who rescinded it is, without prejudice to any other right, entitled to:

(a) a lien on, or right of retention of the surplus of the partnership assets after satisfying the liabilities, for any sum of money paid by him for the purchase of a share in the partnership and for any capital contributed by him;

(b) stand in the place of creditors of the partnership for payments made by him towards partnership liabilities; and

(c) be indemnified by the guilty partner against all the debts and liabilities of the firm (s.41).

47. Where the surviving or continuing partners of the partnership carry on the business of the firm with its capital or assets without any final settlement of accounts with the outgoing partner, then in the absence of agreement to the contrary, the outgoing partner or his representatives are entitled to such share of the profits made since the dissolution as the court may find to be attributable to the use of his share of the partnership assets (s.42).

48. The amount due from surviving or continuing partners to an outgoing partner or his representatives is, subject to any agreement between the partners, a debt accruing at the date of the dissolution or death (s.43).

49. After a dissolution of partnership, the partnership property must be converted into money and applied, subject to any agreement, as follows:

(a) Losses are to be paid:

   (i) firstly out of profits, if any;

   (ii) next, out of capital; and

   (iii) finally, if necessary, by the partners individually in the ratio to which they were entitled to share profits.

(b) The assets of the firm, including sums, if any, contributed by the partners to make up losses, are to be applied:

   (i) to pay the debts and liabilities of the firm to non-partners;

   (ii) to pay each partner rateably the amount due to him from the firm for advances, as distinct from capital;

   (iii) to pay each partner rateably due to him from the firm for his capital contribution; and

   (iv) to pay the ultimate residue, if any, to the partners in the ratio to which they shared profits and losses.

• The Limited Partnerships Act, 1907

50. A limited partnership consists of one or more general partners with full liability for the firm's debts and obligations, and one or more limited partners whose liability is limited to their initial capital contribution, which must be left in the firm during its existence (s.4).

51. A limited partnership must be registered with the Registrar of Companies, and the register is open to scrutiny by the public (s.5).

52. The statement of registration, signed by all the partners, must contain the partnership name, the nature of business, the place of business, the full name of each of the partners, a statement that the partnership is limited, the name of each limited partner, the amount contributed by each partner, the term of the partnership and its date of commencement (s.8).

53. A limited partner cannot become involved in the management of the firm. However, if he does, he becomes fully liable for the debts and liabilities of the firm incurred at that time (s.6).

54. The death, lunacy or bankruptcy of a limited partner does not cause a dissolution of the partnership.

55. The limited partnership became virtually redundant with the passing of the Companies Act, 1907, which made it possible to form a private company consisting of only two members, and which also had benefits of a limited liability.

IMPORTANT CASES

Numbers in brackets refer to paragraphs of this chapter

IMPORTANT STATUTES

Partnership Act, 1890
Limited Partnerships Act, 1907

PROGRESS TEST

Numbers in brackets refer to paragraphs of this chapter

1. Define a partnership. (1)
2. What formalities are required for the formation of a partnership? (4, 5)
3. May a partner bind the firm by his acts without having the authority of his co-partners to do so? (8, 9)
4. To what extent is a partner liable for the debts and obligations of the firm? (15–20)
5. What is partnership property, and in what circumstances may a creditor issue an execution order against the same? (23–5)
6. Describe the rules governing the rights and duties of the partners, contained in the Partnership Act, 1890, in the absence of an agreement as to these matters. (26–39)
7. How may a partnership be dissolved? (41)
8. Under what circumstances may a court issue a decree for the dissolution of the partnership? (42)
9. What rights has a partner who rescinds a partnership contract due to fraud or misrepresentation? (47)
10. How, subject to any agreement, must partnership property be applied after a dissolution of partnership? (50)
11. Define a limited partnership, and describe the registration requirements of the same. (51–3)

chapter 3 2

COMPANIES

Points covered in this chapter:

- Origins of company law
- Formation of a company
- Memorandum of association
- Articles of association

- Share capital
- Management
- Liquidation
- Comparisons between partnerships and companies

Summary of the chapter:

A company is a separate legal entity which provides stability, limited liability and, above all, continuity of existence to its members. This chapter examines the rights and powers of such entities, as regulated by statute.

• Origins of company law

1. Up to 1963, there were a number of companies Acts on the statute book. The Companies Act, 1963 repealed and consolidated the Companies (Consolidation) Act, 1908, the Companies Act, 1913, the Companies (Particulars as to Directors) Act, 1917 and the Companies Act, 1959. The Companies Act, 1963, containing 399 sections and 13 schedules, is the largest Act to have been passed by the Dáil.

2. The Companies (Amendment) Act, 1983 enacted into Irish law the provisions of the EC Second Directive on Company Law. It had the effect of regulating the maintenance and alteration of capital, the formation of public companies and the reregistration of companies.

3. The Companies (Amendment) Act, 1986 complied with Ireland's obligations under the EC Fourth Directive on Company Law. It provides that companies are required to file financial statements in a specified format with their annual returns in the Companies Registration Office. The detail required is dependent on whether the company is defined as 'large', 'medium' or 'small', for the purpose of the Companies (Amendment) Act, 1986.

4. The Companies (Amendment) Act, 1990 provides for the introduction of an examiner, under the protection of the court, to give companies experiencing difficulties every opportunity to reorganise themselves so that they can survive.

5. The Companies Act, 1990 is by far the most thorough reform of company law since 1963. Its provisions are designed to curb abuse of limited liability, deal with the problem of insider dealing, give creditors greater redress in cases of malpractice by directors, and improve the management of companies.

• Formation of a company

6. The normal method of incorporation is by registration in accordance with the provisions of the Companies Acts, 1963 to 1990. A company may be registered as a private or public limited company.

7. A private company is a company with share capital and which:

(a) restricts the rights to transfer its shares;
(b) must have at least two members and not more than fifty, excluding employees and past employees;
(c) prohibits any invitation to the public to subscribe for any shares or debentures in the company (s.33, Companies Act, 1963).

8. A public company is any registered company which is not private. It can have from seven members upwards.

9. The following documents must be prepared and sent to the Registrar of Companies, whose office is at Dublin Castle, for the purposes of the registration of a *private* company:

(a) Memorandum of Association (s.17, Companies Act, 1963);
(b) Articles of Association (s.17, Companies Act, 1963);
(c) a statutory declaration by a solicitor or a person named in the articles of association as a director or secretary that all the requirements of the Companies Act, 1963 necessary for registration have been complied with (s.19, Companies Act, 1963);
(d) a letter of confirmation from the Minister for Industry and Commerce as to the availability of a proposed name for the company (s.21, Companies Act, 1963);
(e) a statement of capital duty, in accordance with the Finance Act, 1973;
(f) a statement of (i) the particulars of the first directors' names, addresses, nationalities and occupations; (ii) the details of the first secretary or secretaries; (iii) the situation of the registered office of the company (s.3, Companies Amendment Act, 1982); and
(g) a bank draft for the registration fee (s.369, Companies Act, 1963).

10. For the purpose of the registration of a *public limited* company, it is necessary to deliver to the registrar of companies, in addition to the above, a statutory declaration stating that:

(a) the nominal value of the companies allotted share capital is not less than £30,000;
(b) the amount paid up, at the time of the application, on the allotted share capital of the company (s.6, Companies Amendment Act, 1983);
(c) the amount, or estimated amount, of the preliminary expenses of the company of the persons to whom these expenses have been paid or are payable; and
(d) any amount or benefit paid or given or intended to be paid or given to any promoter of the company and the consideration for the payment or benefit.

11. When all of the documents and fees have been received by the registrar of companies and he has examined and approved of them, he registers the company and issues a certificate of incorporation which is conclusive proof of the existence of the company.

12. A company may be registered with either limited or unlimited liability.

13. A company may be *limited by guarantee*, whereby the members' liability is limited to the amount which each member has guaranteed in writing to contribute to the company in the event of the assets of the company being insufficient to discharge all the debts of the company when it is being wound up. A public limited company is prevented from being formed by s.7, Companies Amendment Act, 1983 if it is limited by guarantee. This type of company, therefore, is best suited for non-profit making and charitable organisations.

14. A company may be *limited by shares*, whereby the members' liability is limited to the nominal value of the shares held by them in the company. If the shares are not fully paid up, the individual member's liability to unpaid creditors is limited to the amount unpaid or outstanding on his shares in the event of the company going into liquidation.

15. Finally, a company may have *unlimited liability*, whereby the members are liable for all the debts of the company, even if this results in the debts having to be paid from their own private assets.

16. The most important consequence of registration is that a company is recognised by law as having an existence and reality which is separate from its members. Some of the consequences of this separate legal entity are that a company can make contracts, can sue and be sued, and can own property.

Case: Salomon v Salomon & Co. (1897)

The plaintiff, with his wife and five children, formed a limited company, and sold his business to the company as a going concern. The price was paid by the issue of 20,000 fully-paid £1 shares, and debentures to the value of £10,000 secured on the company's assets. The company ran into financial difficulties and, on liquidation, the assets only realised about £6,000, whereas it owed £7,000 to unsecured creditors and £10,000 to the plaintiff as holder of the secured debentures. The liquidator, on behalf of the unsecured creditors, claimed that Salomon, the virtual owner of the company, should not be paid on his secured debentures until the other creditors were paid first.

Held: The company was completely separate from the plaintiff, who was entitled to have his loan repaid to him. Since the shares were fully paid up, the debts of the company were its own affair and not those of the plaintiff, who was merely the company's agent.

17. It is only on rare occasions that the law will ignore the separate legal personality of the company, and will 'lift the veil of incorporation' to hold the members personally liable for the actions of the company. Some such situations, as when membership falls below the legal minimum, are outlined in the Companies Act, 1963. In other cases, the law will look at the realities if the company is being used to evade legal obligations or is acting solely as the agent of another company.

Case: Gilford Motor Co. v Horne (1933)

The defendant entered into a contract of employment which provided that he would not solicit his employer's customers upon the termination of his employment. After the termination of his employment, the defendant set up a company with his wife and son as directors and shareholders, which subsequently issued circulars to his former employer's clients. The plaintiffs sought an injunction to restrain the defendant and the company from soliciting their customers.

Held: The court would lift the veil of incorporation to see that the company was but a device by which the defendant sought to avoid his contractual obligations. The court granted the injunction, thereby preventing both the defendant and the company from distributing the circulars to the plaintiffs' customers.

• Memorandum of association
18. A memorandum of association must be delivered to the registrar of companies before incorporation can take place. The document contains

the rules and regulations that govern the company's dealings with the outside world. S.6, Companies Act, 1963 requires the memorandum to contain the following clauses:

(a) name clause;
(b) objects clause;
(c) limited liability clause;
(d) share capital clause;
(e) association clause.

(a) Name clause

The memorandum of association must contain the company's name, which in the case of a company limited by shares or by guarantee must be followed by the word 'limited' or 'Teoranta' (or the abbreviation 'Ltd' or 'Teo' respectively). Furthermore, in accordance with s.4, Companies (Amendment) Act, 1983, in the case of a public limited company the name must be followed by the words 'public limited company' or 'cuideachta phoiblí theoranta' (or the abbreviation 'plc' or 'cpt' respectively). A company is restricted in the name it chooses. The Minister for Industry and Commerce may consider a name to be undesirable and refuse its registration if:

(i) it is the name of an existing company;
(ii) it suggests or implies a connection with any government department, local authority or state agency;
(iii) it is regarded as being misleading;
(iv) it includes a registered trade mark, with production of the consent of its owner.

(b) Objects clause

The memorandum of association must specify the objects of the company, which limit the company's contractual capacity. A company may adopt any object it wishes provided such objects are legal, and it is usual for promoters to include a wide variety of objects. Where a company enters into a contract which is beyond the powers granted to it by virtue of the objects clause, the contract is said to be *ultra vires* (beyond its powers), and null and void. However, although the contract is *ultra vires*, the third party may be able to enforce it against the company by virtue of s.8, Companies Act, 1963 which provides that the company cannot defeat the third party's claim unless it can be shown that the third party was actually aware at the time of entering the contract that the act or thing was not within the powers of the company. This provision has since been joined by Regulation 6, European Communities (Company) Regulations, 1973, which provides that if a third party contracts with a company in good faith, he is entitled to enforce an *ultra vires* contract against the company. Under no circumstances, however, may a company ratify an act of its own, or its directors, which is *ultra vires*.

(c) Limited liability clause

The memorandum of association must state that the liability of the member is limited, if the company is to be limited by shares or by guarantee. No member will be required to pay a sum greater than the amount unpaid, if any, on the shares in the event of a winding-up of the company.

(d) Share capital clause

The memorandum of association must state the amount of the proposed share capital and its division into different classes of a fixed amount. No subscriber of the memorandum may take less than one share. The minimum authorised share capital of a public limited company, in accordance with s.5, Companies Amendment Act, 1983, must be at least £30,000.

(e) Association clause

The memorandum of association must contain the witnessed signatures of the subscribers, whereby they agree to be bound to the provisions of the memorandum, the number of shares which each subscriber wishes to take in the company.

• Articles of association

19. The articles of association of a company contain the rules and regulations governing the internal management of the company and the rights of the shareholders.

20. In this respect, the articles of association are also of importance to outsiders dealing with the company. The power of the director to bind the company depends on the authority conferred upon him, and any director acting beyond his authority does not bind the company, but is personally liable to the outsider.

21. A company may draft special articles for its own use or it may adopt all or any of the model sets of articles contained in Table A of the Companies Act, 1963.

22. Part I of Table A contains a model set of articles of association for a public company limited by shares, and Part II contains a model set of articles of association for a private company limited by shares.

23. The following are some of the more usual matters dealt with in articles of association:

(a) division of share capital, shareholders' rights, transfer and forfeiture of shares, alterations of capital;
(b) appointment, rotation and removal of directors, powers and duties of directors, appointment and removal of the secretary and the use of the company seal;
(c) declaration of dividends, transfers to reserves, preparation of accounts and holding of audits;
(d) winding-up of a company.

24. Unless a particular article in Table A is specifically excluded, it applies to a company. It is therefore advisable to identify by number those articles in Table A which the company wishes to exclude.

25. The articles of association must be printed, divided into paragraphs, numbered consecutively, bear a stamp as if they were contained in a deed and be signed by each subscriber of the memorandum in the presence of at least one witness, who must attest the signature.

26. Once registered with the registrar of companies, the memorandum and articles of association are binding on each member of the company just as if they had been respectively signed and sealed by each member, and create a contract which can be enforced by the company against the members, by the members as against each other, and by the members as against the company.

27. The articles of association may be amended, subject only to the provisions of its memorandum and the Companies Act, by the passing of a special resolution by the members in a general meeting.

• Share capital
28. The nominal, or authorised, share capital of a company is the amount fixed in the memorandum of association, which may be divided into different varieties of shares, and which, in turn, are purchased by the shareholders.

29. A company may confer different rights on different classes of shares. It is usual for the capital of a company to consist of two classes of shares, namely:

(a) ordinary shares;
(b) preference shares.

(a) *Ordinary* shares give holders full members' rights: voting rights at a general meeting, the right to receive a dividend declared by the board of directors, and the right to participate in the distribution of capital in the event of the winding-up of the company when all debts have been paid. However, although holders of ordinary shares may receive substantial dividends if profits are high, they do not receive a guaranteed return on their dividends, and may as a result receive no dividends if profits are low. (b) *Preference* shares normally carry no voting rights, but are entitled to a fixed percentage dividend each year with priority over that payable on the ordinary shares, and enjoy the same priority over ordinary shares in the distribution of capital in the event of the winding-up of the company. Preference shares may be cumulative, whereby the holder is entitled to arrears of dividends together with current dividends, or non-cumulative. Preference shares may also be redeemable, whereby the company may buy them back from the holders at some future time.

30. A company may also create debentures, which are written acknowledgments of loans given to the company by third parties. The position of a debenture holder is different to that of a member of the company. Debenture holders do not have any voting rights; they receive a fixed interest payment before any shareholders receive a dividend and, in the event of a winding-up of a company, they are entitled to a repayment of their loans before any of the members receive a refund of their share capital.

31. Companies are prohibited by the provisions of the Companies Acts, 1963–86 from buying their own shares or from assisting in the purchase of those shares. It may, however, acquire their own fully paid up shares otherwise than for valuable consideration, such as by way of a gift.

32. A company so authorised by its articles of association may, by resolution at a general meeting, alter the memorandum of association to increase its authorised share capital by the issue of new shares of such amount as it considers appropriate. Notification of such an alteration of share capital must be given to the registrar of companies within fifteen days.

33. A company may reduce its share capital, if so authorised by its articles of association or by special resolution, subject to confirmation by the court. Before confirming the reduction, the court must be satisfied that the company has provided for the debts of existing creditors or that consent has been received from them for the reduction of share capital. The court must also satisfy itself that the reduction of capital is not unfair or oppressive to the minority shareholders of the company. The burden of proof, to this extent, rests on the company itself.

• Management

34. The management of a company's business is performed by a body of persons elected by the shareholders known as the board of directors. Every company must have at least two directors, who collectively manage the company in accordance with the provisions of the company's articles of association.

35. The individual director has limited powers to act on his own on behalf of the company, and his powers are really derived from collective decisions taken by the board of directors as a body. The articles of association will usually provide that the board of directors has the power to recommend a dividend payment, to borrow money on behalf of the company, to allot shares and to appoint one of their number to the post of managing director for such period and on such terms as they see fit.

36. The managing director's rights and duties depend on the terms and conditions of his contract. Generally, however, the managing director is given the responsibility of ensuring that the objectives and policies formulated by the board of directors are implemented. A managing director may have his powers revoked, or his appointment terminated, by the board of directors if it so sees fits.

37. Every company must have a secretary, who may also be a director of the company. The secretary is responsible for seeing that the legal obligations of the company are complied with, such as ensuring that proper books and accounts are maintained and that the various statutory returns are made to the registrar of companies. He has the responsibility for taking and keeping the minutes of both board and company meetings. He also maintains the share register of the company, and is responsible for ensuring that interest and dividend payments are correctly made.

38. Every company must appoint an auditor, or auditors, at each annual general meeting, to hold office until the conclusion of the next annual general meeting of the company. The auditors have a duty to conduct an examination of the financial books and accounts of a company, and a scrutiny of the balance sheet and profit and loss account made up from these financial books and accounts. They must report to the members in general meeting whether in their opinion the accounts of the company have been prepared in accordance with the Companies Acts, 1963–90, and whether they give a true and fair view of the company's affairs. If they do not, the auditors must state why and, if possible, quantify the difference.

• Liquidation

39. A liquidation is the winding up of a company when:

(a) it has completed the business for which it was created;
(b) the members of the company decide to withdraw from business; or
(c) the company is unable to meet its obligations.

40. A *compulsory* liquidation may be ordered by the court upon petition by the company, any creditor, the Minister for Industry and Commerce or, in certain circumstances, by a past or present member of the company where:

(a) the company has passed a special resolution to be wound up by the court;
(b) the company does not begin business within a year from its incorporation or suspends its business at any other time for a whole year;
(c) the number of the company's members is reduced below two for a private company and below seven in the case of a public company;
(d) the company is unable to pay its debts; or
(e) the court is of the opinion that it is just and equitable that the company should be wound up.

41. In a compulsory liquidation, it is the High Court which appoints the liquidator to the company.

42. A *voluntary* liquidation may be initiated by the members of a company or its creditors. A company may be wound up voluntarily if:

(a) the period laid down by the articles for the duration of the company expires or an event takes place on the occurrence of which the articles state that the company is to be dissolved;
(b) the company resolves by special resolution that the company be wound up voluntarily; or
(c) the company, in general meeting, resolves by ordinary resolution that the company, by reason of its liabilities, cannot continue in business (s.251, Companies Act, 1963).

43. A *members' voluntary winding-up* is achieved by the directors making a statutory declaration to the effect that, having made a full enquiry into the company's affairs, they are of the opinion that the company will be able to pay its debts in full within a period not exceeding twelve months from the commencement of the winding-up. It is the members of the company who appoint the liquidator.

44. A *creditors' voluntary winding-up* may be made in the absence of a statutory declaration of solvency. The company must organise a creditors' meeting to be held not later than one day after the company meeting at which the voluntary winding-up is to be proposed. The directors must present a full statement of the company's affairs, together with a list of their claims, to this creditors' meeting. A liquidator may be appointed at both the company and creditors' meetings, but if they nominate different persons then the creditors' nominee will be liquidator.

45. The liquidator takes control of the company and, in accordance with the Companies Acts, 1963–90, he collects its assets, pays the liquidation expenses and the other debts and liabilities, and distributes the surplus, if any, amongst the members of the company according to their rights. When this is done, the company is dissolved.

46. An alternative to liquidation, however, is *receivership*. A receiver may be appointed by the court or under the terms of a deed of debenture if the company appears to be unable to pay its debts. His basic function is to collect and realise the assets which provide the security for the loan and to pay the debenture holders the amount due to them. Companies put into receivership do not necessarily finish up in liquidation, since the business continues after the cessation of the receiver's powers but, in practice, creditors are frequently induced into petitioning for a wind-up of the company upon the appointment of a receiver.

47. An examiner may be appointed, under the provisions of the Companies Act, 1990, within three days from the appointment of a receiver. The examiner facilitates the reorganisation of a company which is experiencing difficultly, thereby maintaining and securing existing employment, while simultaneously satisfying the requirements of the creditors.

The Companies Act, 1990

48. The Companies Act, 1990 was signed into law by the President on 22 December 1990. It did not come into effect automatically, however, so as to give regulatory bodies and other interested parties time to comply with its provisions. Instead, the Minister for Industry and Commerce must make separate Commencement Orders to bring the various provisions of the Act into operation.

49. The first Commencement Order, made by the Minister on 24 December 1990, brought Part V, and certain provisions of Parts I, IX and XIII into operation from 27 December 1990.

50. Part V of the Act deals with the problem of insider dealing. It generally prohibits a person, who is connected with a company and in possession of information not generally available but likely to have a material effect on the price of the shares concerned, from being involved in the purchase or sale of such shares. Primary responsibility for enforcement of Part V rest with the Stock Exchange. Persons convicted of insider dealing may face inprisonment or up to ten years and/or a fine of up to £200,000. Furthermore, they cannot deal in securities for twelve months from the date of conviction.

51. Part IX of the Act made a number of adjustments to the Companies (Amendment) Act, 1990 which provide for the introduction of an examiner to facilitate companies in difficulty. These adjustments were designed to make the earlier Act more effective.

52. Part XII of the Act provides for increases in the penalties for certain Companies Act infringements, such as the furnishing of false information. It also gives the Registrar of Companies the power to strike off companies who have not lodged returns for two years. Furthermore, Part XII gives the Minister for Industry and Commerce the power to prescribe that courts other than the High Court may deal with specified company law matters.

53. At the time of writing, no further orders have been made. However, the Minister proposes to make further Commencement Orders to bring into operation as soon as is practical the remaining provisions, including those relating to directors of bankrupt companies, the acquisition of information directly from companies without recourse to inspectors, the treatment of loans by companies to their directors, and the creation of a new type of investment company with variable capital.

• Comparisons between partnerships and companies

54. A partnership is formed by the express or implied agreement of the partners, with no formal written requirements. Its existence is a question of fact, to be decided by the court based on the intentions and conduct of the parties. A company is formed by registration under the provisions of the Companies Acts, 1963–90.

55. A partnership has no legal personality distinct from its members. Although a partnership may sue and be sued in the firm's name, it is also possible for each of the partners to be sued in their individual capacity. A company has a legal personality distinct from its members and officers, and it may make contracts, own property and sue and be sued in its own name.

56. A partnership must have at least two partners but, with the exceptions of solicitors, accountants or bankers, cannot have more than twenty partners. A private limited company must have at least two members and not more than fifty, while a public limited company must have at least seven members—with no upper limit.

57. Partners have, in general, unlimited liability with respect to debts incurred while being a member of the partnership. Under the Limited Partnerships Act, 1907, a limited partnership may be formed whereby it is possible for one or more of the partners to limit their liability, provided at least one partner continues with unlimited liability. The members of a company may have liability limited by shares or by guarantee.

58. Partners are entitled to take part in the management of the partnership, unless they are limited partners or the partnership agreement provides otherwise. Members of a company are not entitled to take part in the management of the company—unless they become directors.

59. Partners, with the exception of limited partners, have the implied authority to bind the partnership with their acts. A member of a company cannot bind a company by his acts if they are *ultra vires*, i.e. outside of the objects contained within the memorandum of association of the company.

60. Partners cannot transfer their share of the business without the consent of all the partners. Members of a public limited company may transfer their shares freely, while members of a private limited company must generally receive the consent of the directors of the company to transfer their shares.

61. Partnerships are dissolved by the death, bankruptcy or retirement of any partner. They may be dissolved with or without court action. Companies are not dissolved by the death, bankruptcy or retirement of any of their members or officers. Companies are dissolved, on application to the court, by a liquidator appointed by either the court, the creditors or the members of the company.

IMPORTANT CASES

Numbers in brackets refer to paragraphs of this chapter

IMPORTANT STATUTES

Companies Act, 1963
Companies (Amendment) Act, 1983
Companies (Amendment) Act, 1986
Companies (Amendment) Act, 1990
Companies Act, 1990

PROGRESS TEST

Numbers in brackets refer to paragraphs of this chapter

1. Define a private company. (7)
2. What documents must be submitted for the purposes of the registration of a company? (9, 10)
3. Describe how a company may (a) be limited by guarantee, (b) be limited by shares, and (c) have unlimited liability. (13–15)
4. Explain what is meant by 'lifting the veil of incorporation'. (17)
5. List the clauses which must be contained in a memorandum of association. (18)
6. State some of the more usual matters dealt with in articles of association. (23)
7. Differentiate between (a) ordinary shares, (b) preference shares, and (c) debentures. (29, 30)
8. Identify some of the powers vested in the directors of a company. (35)
9. What is the principal duty of the auditors to the members of a company? (38)
10. Under what circumstances may a compulsory liquidation be ordered? (40)
11. Explain the difference between a members' voluntary wind-up and a creditors' voluntary wind-up. (43, 44)
12. What is the function of a receiver? (46)
13. List five major differences between a partnership and a company. (54, 61)

EXAMINATION QUESTIONS

Section 7: Law of Persons

1. (a) *A*, *B* and *C* wish to set up business together, but they are unsure about whether to set up a private limited company or a partnership, as they know little about these different forms of business organisation.

    Explain the differences between a private limited company and a partnership.

   (b) *X*, *Y* and *Z* are in business as partners. The partnership agreement contains a provision which provides that *Z* is unable to make any contract on behalf of the firm worth more than £5,000.

    Some years after the partnership commenced *Z* entered into a contract for the purchase of goods for the partnership worth £7,000.

    To what extent is the partnership bound by the contract entered into by *Z*?

    A.C.C.A. (June 1990)

2. Compare and contrast a partnership formed under the Partnership Act, 1890 with a company formed under the Companies Acts, 1963 and 1990.

    I.C.S.A. (December 1990)

3. (a) List and explain the circumstances under which a partnership can be dissolved.

   (b) In what order are the assets of a partnership to be applied on dissolution?

    I.A.T.I. (Admission, Autumn 1989)

Q: How its developed

CAU.
Misrep.
Sale of goods

TELL HER
TO RING YOU
AT HOSPITAL!
SO O Can talK to Rosie